COMPARATIVE GOVERNMENT

COMPARATIVE GOVERNMENT

A READER

Edited by J. Blondel

ANCHOR BOOKS
DOUBLEDAY & COMPANY, INC.
GARDEN CITY, NEW YORK
1969

PREFACE

The idea for this Reader grew out of the increasing recognition that, after several decades of teaching comparative government on the basis of the successive study of foreign governments, political science was at last moving towards a systematic analysis of problems, an identification of major variables and a discovery of the conditions favouring particular forms of government rather than others. Yet, although the truly comparative literature has become vast, it is still scattered; only the most general theory has been presented in book form: middle-range theory is discussed in countless articles and books, some of which are even already difficult to find.

Obviously, any selection entails very difficult decisions. Even though we were guided by the principle that only studies devoted to *general* problems would be inserted, we were confronted with such a large number of possible alternatives that the choice had to be made, not in order to do justice to all those who have advanced our understanding of general comparative government, but in order to survey, as far as possible, the whole of the ground. We hope that the bibliography at the end of the volume will therefore be considered jointly with the extracts which are published in this Reader, which should be taken as an introduction to the subject, merely showing the direction according to which problems are being analysed.

This selection is entirely mine, and so are the comments in the Introductory section of the book. But I wish to thank particularly my colleague Dr L. Johnston for the advice which he gave me, and Mr I. A. D. Maclean, of Macmillan & Co., for the opportunity he offered me to undertake this work; I am most indebted to my students at the University of Essex, with whom I have discussed problems of systematic comparative government in the last three years; but most of all I am grateful to Miss K. George, for the very skilful and patient fashion in which she assembled the many documents which the preparation of a Reader entails.

Colchester,
January 1968

J. B.

CONTENTS

INTRODUCTION

The study of comparative government is one of the oldest, most difficult and most important which have attracted the attention of mankind. It can be traced back at least to the fourth century B.C., when Aristotle made the first recorded attempt at describing in some detail the characteristics of the tyrannies, oligarchies and democracies which prevailed in the various parts of the world he knew. Since Aristotle, numerous political scientists have endeavoured to classify political systems: the most celebrated effort was perhaps that of the French eighteenth-century lawyer, Montesquieu, whose work, the *Spirit of Laws* (1748), was to have profound consequences for the structure of American, French and other Western governments. Yet, despite many studies, the fundamental question still remains, for a large part, unanswered: why do some regimes prevail in certain parts of the world and not in others, which experience different forms of government? There are at present liberal democracies and dictatorships, each with their several sub-categories, such as, among the latter, various types of monarchical rule, single-party rule, military rule. Some countries are stable, others change, more or less frequently, the regime under which they live. What explanation can be given for these patterns?

The search for such an explanation is not only academically important, however, since we are not mere observers looking in a dispassionate fashion at interesting differences in human behaviour. The fact of tyranny or dictatorship affects, directly or indirectly, the citizens of any country. Thus in Ancient Greece, in absolutist Europe and in the contemporary world, the desire to understand the rise of old-fashioned dictatorships or of modern totalitarian rule has been accompanied by the wish to provide means of avoiding for the future and of limiting in the present the spread of tyranny. These efforts have often been unsuccessful, though it is perhaps too easy to forget the impact of the work done on the conditions and structures of constitutional government and liberal democracy. But new problems have been raised with the aspirations of new generations, the appearance of 'new nations' and the impact of economic development: the same general question has thus come to be posed in a different and more complex fashion.

Whether for practical or purely academic reasons, the study of comparative government has grown in recent years and become a major branch of study, with scholars working on detailed problems and theorists attempting grand syntheses. As a result, it may not be over-optimistic to believe that, in this or the next decade, major advances will occur, despite the increased complexity of the institutions and processes of government. Much more attention has been given to the necessity of constructing a *model* designed to encompass all the regimes which exist in the contemporary world; some preliminary work on a *general theory* has thus become possible; but most of the efforts have been devoted to *partial theories,* dealing with specific aspects of political life and trying to discover regularities and patterns behind the apparent accidents. It is to the examination of this general model and to the presentation of a number of partial theories that this book is devoted.

The study of comparative government is, and must be, the study of government on a comparative basis. Yet the field of 'comparative government' includes more books, whether texts or monographs, on specific governments or detailed aspects of the life of a particular country, than texts or monographs of a comparative character. What may seem in the first instance to be a paradox is in fact the reflexion of the special difficulties which beset the student of government as soon as he tries to work on a comparative basis. Although we shall concentrate, in the course of this reader, on works of a genuinely comparative character and deliberately avoid drawing from the large pool of individual country studies, it is important to state at the outset what special reasons lead many political scientists to have greater confidence in studies of a single system. We shall therefore devote the first section of this introduction to the examination of the difficulties of the comparative analysis of government. This will give a better perspective to the discussion, in the following section, of the conditions which a comparative model needs to satisfy in order to cover the whole range of patterns of government; this will also make more realistic, in the third section, the assessment of the present state of partial theories designed to account for individual parts of the governmental process. We should not be surprised to find limitations in both the general model and the partial theories: being measured against the complexity of the political processes which these have to 'explain', their practical usefulness and their theoretical validity may become better appreciated.

I

Institutions and processes of government have become more complex in the twentieth century: general descriptions of comparative government comparable to that of Aristotle would occupy many volumes. But the major problems which confront the student of government arise more from the special nature of political life than from the complexity of the processes. First, information-gathering is often difficult, in many respects patchy and sometimes lumbered with theoretical drawbacks. Second, the variables which have to be taken into account are not only numerous: they are sometimes difficult to use in a truly comparative fashion. Third, the interconnexion between law and practice, norm and behaviour creates in some cases almost insuperable problems of analysis.

DIFFICULTIES ENCOUNTERED IN COLLECTING INFORMATION

The difficulties encountered in gathering data about *individual* governments have often been discussed, though modern techniques of collection and analysis have proved helpful in this field. But some points make the study of *comparative* government even more difficult in so far as the level of analysis is likely to be that of the common denominator between the countries concerned. First, access to data is sometimes simply forbidden. Some countries are open, others are not; certain fields can be studied, others cannot. The student of government needs a high level of public information everywhere as well as a general climate favouring open access to information: he is likely to find such a climate in certain countries and in certain areas only. One reason why studies of Western countries are more advanced than those of totalitarian countries is simply that more knowledge can be readily obtained, both from secondary sources (such as newspapers) and from the actors themselves, in the West.

Clearly, the situation must not be seen wholly in black and white terms. Complete concealment is as rare as total openness. Even the most totalitarian of countries is not wholly closed to investigation: some facts necessarily come out, while others can be found through the analysis (often painstaking and time-consuming, though) of a number of 'clues'. Totalitarian countries need to publish certain facts in order to achieve their aims. For instance, it is difficult for them to conceal who belongs to the government and what was the past career of ministers. A careful study over time of the members of the government will be revealing in many ways: it will tell whether the government is 'stable' or 'unstable', what kinds of men lead the country, and indeed probably what factions exist within the ruling group. Conversely, no country is entirely open. In Western democracies, the number of fields in which access to information is limited or even practically nonexistent is relatively large. It may not be in the 'public interest' to disclose certain matters concerned with defence, foreign affairs or even home security; it may be 'embarrassing' to leak too many facts about Cabinet decisions, party discussions, even interest group negotiations. Moreover, a kind of informal 'censorship' operates, since political scientists often depend on the goodwill of the politicians for their information and therefore have to exercise some restraint before publishing their findings in order to maintain this goodwill. A comparative study of the amount of information which political scientists (or journalists) can obtain in various sectors of government might indeed be revealing: if countries were placed at different points of the 'closed-open' continuum, one would probably find large differences both among totalitarian states and among liberal democracies.

Second, data are difficult to gather because they are sometimes difficult to measure. Many political decisions seem to defy accurate measurement and consequently are scarcely amenable to precise comparative treatment. Suppose that an attempt is made to compare the role of legislatures in a number of countries with a view to finding precisely what degree of influence these still retain in the most important decisions. It is often said that executives have increased their power in the twentieth century: this proposition is difficult to test without a complex recourse to history and it might appear more practical simply to try to compare the relative position of legislatures in the world today. A number of problems immediately come to be raised. The 'influence' on 'policy decisions' can only be made comparable if we adopt a precise operational definition of these concepts. As no such definition is readily available, it would seem reasonable to concentrate on the relative role of legislatures in the one field in which they are all involved, namely legislation, and to forget the indirect influence, however great, which legislatures may have on non-legislative types of governmental policies (though this may sometimes be large and includes almost the whole field of foreign affairs). But even the role of legislatures in relation to legislation is difficult to assess: one can measure the number of amendments passed by a Chamber and consider whether the government had accepted or rejected these amendments; but the relative importance of these amendments varies; and it is not always easy to say whether the government accepted 'spontaneously', 'gracefully' or otherwise, the amendments which it did not directly oppose. Yet the analysis of legislation is possibly a field where comparative studies of governmental processes can be done most fruitfully. Other aspects of the subject are fraught with greater problems of definition and operationalisation: the more countries one tries to analyse, the more the indicators are likely to be vague and imprecise.

Third, information is difficult to gather because many events seem to be 'unique' and a comparative analysis appears consequently inappropriate. Yet, and somewhat unfortunately, the more one moves towards the 'centres of power' the more the decision-making processes appear to be 'unique'. There are millions of voters, hundreds of legislators, but only one British Prime Minister, German Chancellor or American President. Cross-national studies of chief executives are therefore somewhat frustrating for the political scientist who appears to have to concentrate on 'unique' situations, 'unique' personalities, 'unique' institutions, rather than on patterns of decisions. If he refuses to consider the uniqueness of these situations, the political scientist runs the risk of not being able to catch the richness of the whole position of the leaders of the countries concerned; but if he wants to take into account the full richness of the 'real' life, his work might simply become a succession of monographs on various holders of supreme offices and not a comparative study of chief executives.

The gathering of data of a comparative character is thus in

several ways a major problem for political scientists: questions of methodology are intertwined with the sheer difficulty of extracting information from unwilling governments or an uninformative press. Because government is about the most important decisions affecting communities, it is unrealistic to expect that the situation will ever be significantly altered; because there will always be only a few leaders at the top, the element of 'uniqueness' will always be a problem with which students of comparative government will have to contend. These are the structural constraints of the discipline; they have to be accepted, though they should not be given so much emphasis as to generate despondency among researchers.

DIFFICULTIES ARISING FROM THE RANGE AND CHARACTER OF THE BACKGROUND VARIABLES

In examining the kind of difficulties encountered by political scientists in gathering information, we raised indirectly the question of the variables with which the study should be concerned. Political life includes the activities of millions of voters or thousands of demonstrators as well as those of small numbers of leaders in the privacy of their offices. Its specific pattern is shaped by a wide range of factors, from economic conditions to the climate, from geographical characteristics to historical accidents. The complexity of these variables is evident even if one considers politics in an individual country; but some order must be introduced if comparative analysis is to make significant progress.

Admittedly, some students of governments have at times been tempted to reduce these variables to a much smaller number. Marxist or neo-marxist explanations of society have emphasised economic factors and, among these, ownership of capital, as the major variable. Theories based on climate or geography (seafaring countries v. land-based polities) have sometimes been put forward as accounting for the major differences between types of governments. But none of these single-variable theories has satisfactorily 'explained' more than a fraction of the differences which exist among political systems. As a result, the emphasis has changed in modern comparative government. Rather than to search vainly for a factor accounting for all the variations between governments, political scientists have now more realistically turned to another approach: they are attempting to measure the relative weight of all the variables and to describe as precisely as possible the extent to which a particular variable accounts for the characteristics of a political system.

Although there is now agreement about the necessity of a multi-variate analysis, the problems of method remain. At one extreme, some variables are relatively easy to measure with precision. It has been possible to give numbers to some socio-economic indicators and to relate them to aspects of political life. It has been possible for instance to measure the extent to which the rise of socialist parties in Western Europe was associated with the growth of an urban working class, the extent to which liberal democracy is associated with a high standard of living and the extent to which military rule is likely to take place in developing countries. But other factors are much less amenable to such a quantitative treatment. Certain 'unique' events appear to have had vast consequences. The French Revolution occurred in a particular country at a given moment in time: it did spread to many parts of Western Europe, admittedly, but, having had its origin in France, it had its deepest impact on the politics of that country. A century and a half of battles for and against revolutionary ideas can be traced to the 'unique' phenomenon of the outbreak of the Revolution in 1789. Historical developments such as these constitute as many direct lines linking events in a given polity at a given moment, not to other polities, but to the prior development of that polity. They tend to give to a country its original 'political culture'. But they are also difficult to measure adequately. Great historical events should therefore be placed at one end of a continuum on which broad socio-economic indicators such as per capita income or the occupational distribution of the population occupy the other end, while other factors, such as class, include a combination of 'measurable' and less 'measurable' elements and reflect traits of a specific culture as well as the general characteristics of all societies.

The opposition between unique historical events and general socio-economic characteristics is thus often blurred in practice. Pure socio-economic factors are mixed with pure cultural national traits. As a result, students of comparative government have endeavoured to take into account all the variables; this led them to be 'descriptive' towards the 'cultural' end of the continuum and 'quantitative' towards the other end. It became difficult for them truly to ascribe 'weights' to these variables: how can a precise assessment be made of the extent to which the presence of a large Communist party in France is due to economic factors such as income, to social variables such as status or to cultural characteristics such as the alleged 'anti-government' or 'anarchistic' attitudes fostered by the Revolution? The opposition between schools of thought among students of comparative government can be traced to a large extent to the difficulty of combining variables of this kind. Many political scientists have also naturally preferred to concentrate on one country in order to 'understand' it better.

Recent efforts are likely to bridge the gap between socio-economic explanations and cultural explanations, however. Through the development of survey techniques and their use in the measurement of attitudes, political scientists have begun to analyse the similarities and differences between political cultures. Instead of having simply to describe the unique characteristics of the development of a given polity, they can now isolate a number of general political or civic attitudes towards the polity and see whether citizens of various countries share these attitudes and, if so, to what extent and in what proportions. The results constitute general indicators of the cultural characteristics of the nations concerned. These indicators may not entirely reflect the 'weight' of history, but they constitute a very noticeable advance on the previous situation in which the impact of historical 'accidents' in various countries could not be assessed comparatively. It becomes possible to compare the detailed characteristics of the Anglo-Saxon 'culture' with those of the French or German 'culture'. Many hitherto 'unique' aspects of different societies can be introduced in the comparative model.[1]

There is a danger, however, which has not been as yet successfully met. The indicators of culture which are being devised through the study of citizens' attitudes tend to be 'culture-bound': they are the products of the cultural back-

---

[1] This type of study has only recently begun and it has not as yet a profound impact on substantive findings in comparative government, though writings on the political socialisation processes of individual countries have become numerous. The major cross-national study was published in 1963 by G. A. Almond and S. Verba, under the title *The Civic Culture*, Princeton U.P. The whole of this area of the study of government is likely to develop significantly in the near future.

ground of the political scientists who devise them. While socio-economic indicators appear to be 'objective', the questions which have to be asked in order to elicit cultural differences are devised by political scientists who are exposed to their own political culture. It may become possible to rank, and thus to compare countries according to some cultural indicators, but these indicators may simply show to what extent a given polity differs from the ideal cultural model which, consciously or not, the political scientist has in mind when he is preparing his questionnaire: the 'true' and specific culture of the countries concerned may not really be found.

This difficulty is serious: as we shall see, it does to some extent account for the limitations of various models used in comparative government. It is often alleged by critics, for instance, that Western models of comparative government tend to be based on implicit assumptions about freedom and democracy which lead to misunderstandings about the character of non-Western polities. It is probable that this difficulty will not be wholly overcome, at least as long as most of the work done in political science is the product of efforts of Western political scientists. But undeniably efforts have been made to introduce history and to take into account 'unique' developments in the contemporary models of comparative government. To that extent, the dilemma between a general, but somewhat one-sided comparative analysis and a study in depth of individual governments may perhaps be minimised, if not wholly avoided.

DIFFICULTIES ARISING FROM THE ROLE OF NORMS, INSTITUTIONS AND BEHAVIOUR IN GOVERNMENT

The study of comparative government aims at explaining why certain types of governments *do* exist under certain conditions. But one of the reasons why certain types of governments exist is because men have discussed forms of government and have decided in advance that certain forms of government *should* exist. We do know that these deliberate decisions are not without 'causes': they result from the interplay of the variables which we have just considered. But these decisions introduce an element of *value* or of *norm* in governmental systems. Standpoints are taken both about what government should do and about how it should do it. The question thus arises as to whether the practice conforms with the theory or as to whether the blueprint (the norm) corresponds to the reality (or behaviour).

For a long time the question was raised in the rather narrow terms of the contrast between constitutional rule and political practice. Norms, in politics, seemed embodied in constitutions: these were the documents through which the idea of good government was turned into reality. Nobody denied that there was a relationship between constitutions and their 'behavioural' antecedents. Choices made by constitution-makers were based both on value judgements about preferred systems of government and on the experience of previous governments and constitutions. But future behaviour was to be governed, one hoped in large part, by the decisions taken by the drafters of the basic law.

The presence of constitutions thus raised in one way, though in a somewhat narrow fashion, the question of the levels of analysis at which comparative government had to take place. It seemed that there were to be two different, though interlinked, such levels. One was to be concerned with governmental norms, the other with political behaviour. Neither could be said to be 'unimportant', neither could be wholly dismissed as the product of the other. If one wanted to 'predict' what would happen in a given polity in certain circumstances, one had to examine both what the norm said and what past behaviour made probable. Such a division was naturally to account for a major cleavage among students of comparative government. Some tended to spend more time on constitutional analysis, others on behavioural patterns. The real efforts — but also the most difficult enterprise — consisted in linking the two.

Yet the real difficulty confronting students of comparative government was not met as long as the problem was seen only in terms of the opposition between constitutional requirements and behavioural patterns. If all that had to be done consisted in examining what kinds of practices had led to the development of constitutions and what kinds of constitutional arrangements produced certain types of practices, the analysis would be empirically difficult, but, in theory at least, easily manageable. It would simply require an examination of the factors leading to the development of these constitutional arrangements and, conversely, of the subsequent consequences of the introduction of the constitution. Admittedly, an allowance had to be made for a constant feedback between constitution and practice: this would seriously complicate the analysis of the dynamics of constitutional development, but the same model could be kept, as long as constitution and practice were the only elements in consideration.

But the question of the relationship between norms and behaviour is more general and also more complex. It is more general in that constitutions are only a special case of a whole variety of attempts made by men to modify government. Constitution-makers of the eighteenth and nineteenth centuries wanted to legislate for the future in the direction of liberal government: they tried both to direct society and to leave it as free as possible to develop along its natural path. Hence the ambiguity of liberal constitutions: they stand half-way between the imposition of rules from outside and the total acceptance of the 'natural' development of society. But, if we look at political systems generally, we have to consider at one extreme the part played by norms imposed in an authoritarian fashion and, at the other, the effect of totally uninhibited patterns of behaviour.

Whether there is a constitution or not, certain natural practices tend to occur. These gradually become 'solidified'; they become customs, while others become less important and purely formal. The English Constitution is always cited as a prime instance of this type of development: the Monarch lost, by custom, his power to veto laws; the Prime Minister (whose office was a customary development) acquired, by custom, the right to dissolve Parliament. But such developments are not specific to Britain: they may be more pronounced in Britain, not perhaps because the English Constitution is 'unwritten', but simply because it is old. They take place elsewhere by a similar process. They may develop despite, against, or within the constitution as, in the United States, the practice by which the members of the presidential electoral college came to be bound to vote for the candidate under whose ticket they had been elected – a custom which had not been envisaged by the framers of the Constitution.

These 'natural' practices are the product of 'solidified' behaviour; but they become so 'natural' that they impose themselves on future generations. They become 'norms', not only in the positive sense that they are statistically expected to happen, but in the sense that members of the polity believe that they should be obeyed. There may be differences between 'natural norms': all may not be equally recognised as norms by all members of the polity. But in all countries many political arrangements exist which have ceased to be 'mere' practices in the ordinary sense of the word: by imposing themselves on future generations, alongside constitutional or other norms, they deserve to be classified as truly 'natural norms'.

These natural norms constitute one of the polar types with which students of comparative government have to contend. At the other extreme, some rules are forced on a society, however reluctant that society may be to agree to them. This is the origin of dictatorial or totalitarian government. If rulers want to preserve an order which is no longer 'acceptable' or if, on the contrary, they want to redraw completely the structure of society against bitter opposition, they will try to impose norms, deliberately, upon the system. Rules and norms of this kind can thus be said to be 'made'. They have to be forcefully imposed when the resistance which is provided by the natural norms is, itself, strong and forceful.

Different kinds of norms can be found in different societies — and political systems could be compared in terms of the extent to which deliberately or dictatorially imposed norms interplay with natural norms: constitutional norms would stand somewhere in the middle, as they are characterised by a limited degree of imposition coupled with a relatively large amount of leeway left to natural norms. But the relationship between norms and behaviour is complex because norms do not come to be always *directly* imposed on the political society. They do not necessarily appear in the form of 'commands' which members of the polity have to obey. They are also embodied in the polity in a much more concrete fashion. They give rise to 'structures', to 'institutions', which constitute as many concrete materialisations of the command of the rule and provide polities with procedures and permanent arrangements which implement the rule. Structures and institutions can, like norms, be imposed by men or emerge naturally from the development of the polity. Dictatorial regimes developed hierarchical structures; constitutional regimes invented legislatures, limited executives and courts; and customary 'natural' processes produced groups, factions and parties. Such structures have a normative role in that they organise the way in which members of the polity have to behave: the 'real' behaviour takes place within the context of these structures.

Comparative government has thus to contend with norms,

with institutions and with behaviour. But the relationship between these three elements is not simple: norms and institutions are not associated in a direct and uniform fashion. Some
structures may be produced by certain types of norms but be
used in a different normative context. Dictatorships use legislatures and parties to their own ends; hierarchies exist outside authoritarian rule; and the practices of legislatures have
often been modified by custom. Once created, a structure can
be modified or replaced; but there are considerable advantages
in keeping structures nominally alive rather than replacing
them: as we shall see, it may be difficult or dangerous for a
regime to attempt in too many fields a full-scale reorganisation.
Institutions become independent from the norms which
created them: they come to have, in themselves, a symbolic
value.

Two types of social processes play an important part in
this context. First, institutions can be and often are 'imported'.
Imitation takes place because members of a polity believe
that a structure which has been successful elsewhere will
contribute to a significant change in the behaviour or development of their own polity. The history of constitutional government in the nineteenth century is in large part a history of
imitation. British and American governmental *practices* seemed
valuable: it was felt reasonable to change the practices elsewhere by importing British or American institutional *structures*. In the second half of the twentieth century imitation
extended even beyond the boundaries of political processes,
as it seemed possible to force the pace of economic development through the implantation of certain political structures.
Many countries imitated the political practices of the Soviet
Union for this reason. The one-party system thus had a strange
history. First created in the Soviet Union because parties had
developed in the West as symbols of democracy, it has since
been exported to many developing states, and particularly to
African countries, as a recipe for the mobilisation of human
resources towards economic development.

Second, the imposition of a form of government, by deliberate action, leads to profound tensions which have to be met
by using a large number of political 'resources'. The greater
the number of deliberately imposed new arrangements proposed for a society, the more difficult it becomes to implement all of these arrangements at once; implementation thus
comes to depend on the extent to which the rulers are able to

prevent old practices from reappearing. One of the resources which can be used is *repression:* but repression is an unsatisfactory long term device. Thus leaders try to impose a new system by using their own *authority;* failing this, they tend to use existing structures and maintain them, even if these are to become 'empty', 'unreal' or 'formal'. If men are accustomed to certain structures, the continued use of these structures will help to develop the *legitimacy* of the new system, either because the old structures are not abolished and change seems to be limited (thus parliaments are kept in being in totalitarian States) or because these structures are used to impose new norms on the society (thus parties and representative groups, such as trade unions, are made to mobilise the energies of members of the polity towards an overall national goal).

We can now return to the problem raised for the study of comparative government by the existence of various types of norms. If the only norms which existed were the constitutional norms, the study of patterns of government would have to include comparisons at two levels, that of constitutional analysis and that of behavioural analysis, with the practical difficulties arising from the existence of links between constitution and practice. But if we are to include other types of norms, from natural and customary to deliberately imposed, and if we are to remember that such norms can derive from imitation as well as from the internal development of a particular country, a new problem arises: each structure has a different meaning and a different concrete life; this depends on whether a given structure appeared 'naturally' or was deliberately created, whether it was an indigenous product or was 'imported'. Since, as we noted, totalitarian systems often keep traditional structures (such as parliament, parties or groups) in being, we must avoid giving to these structures the same significance in all the systems. For example, we may want to compare two countries from the point of view of the influence of workers on governmental policies. In one of these countries unions may have had a long history of development and may have grown from a small percentage of the urban working class to large establishments in the course of a long and difficult struggle; in the other country the government may have decided to 'create' labour unions and to make it compulsory for workers to belong to these unions in order to have a job. Comparisons between the power, role and importance of unions will be interesting, but they will not reveal much about the role of workers in influencing governmental policies in the second country. Yet the existence of the compulsory unions in the second country will make it difficult to pass realistic judgements of a comparative character about the influence of workers on government in general.

The study of comparative government is thus fraught with special difficulties. There are difficulties arising from the nature of the data and from the desire for secrecy which governments often display. There are difficulties arising from the nature of the variables which have to be used in the study of government: the pull of comparative government is towards the use of 'general' or 'cross-national' variables; but the 'unique' character of each policy has, in some form, to be measured, if comparisons are realistically to account for the presence of a particular type of government. But difficulties also arise from the fact that men operate the governmental system and consciously try to manipulate it. They may want to manipulate it more or less; they may be aware of their own limitations or may be bold in their desires to make profound alterations; they may change institutions in the governmental field because they feel that these changes will lead to changes in the economic field as well. Governmental systems are thus modified in many different ways, at many different levels, by the actions of leaders; for perhaps limited periods only, men may seem to be in a position to impose almost any system on their polity. Models and theories must take into account all of these factors. It is not surprising that the models should be difficult to build and that a general theory should have taken a long time to develop.

II

Such a list of difficulties does not tend to suggest that the study of comparative government is impossible, but it explains why the development of a general theory has proved an arduous task. What political scientists had to do was to find a yardstick against which governmental systems could be individually measured, and thereby compared. But this yardstick had to meet two general conditions. It had to be fairly precise, as otherwise comparisons would be so vague as not to be very helpful for the understanding of the workings of political systems. It had to be independent from norms, as otherwise it would only be meaningful for those polities which were operating under these norms.

For a long time, these two requirements seemed mutually exclusive: no truly comparative analysis of government was undertaken outside the boundaries of constitutional systems. Constitutions provided political scientists with a detailed set of arrangements and a common framework applicable to all those polities which obeyed constitutional rules. Theorists had gradually refined the requirements of executives, legislatures and judiciaries; similar refinements had come to be applied to electoral systems. In the earlier part of the twentieth century, most countries seemed to be gradually moving towards constitutional rules: it could be suggested that only primitive societies would remain in the 'pre-constitutional' stage. The study of non-constitutional government could thus be left to anthropologists and the systematic study of comparative government did not require the consideration of such systems more than the study of modern economics required the study of barter economies.

But the development of 'natural' structures such as parties and the appearance of totalitarian States showed the narrow boundaries of a constitutional framework, although the study of comparative government seemed unable for a while to cater for systems and structures which developed outside constitutional arrangements. When writing in the 1950s, R. C. Macridis noted that the study of comparative government had become parochial and descriptive, rather than systematic and universal.[2] An increasingly large number of detailed studies of Western institutions, Communist systems and developing societies were being undertaken, but no general framework could integrate these systems and therefore account for the wide differences in patterns of government.

Considerable progress has been made since the mid-1950s, however, essentially as a result of the work of D. Easton, G. A. Almond and D. Apter. In an article published in 1957 and entitled *An Approach to the Analysis of Political Systems*,[3] D. Easton suggested that a solution to the problem of comparing governments could be found by examining political life in terms of a system receiving certain inputs from the so-

---

[2] *The Study of Comparative Government*, Random House, 1955. See below, extract 1, pp. 3–9.

[3] *World Politics*, April 1957, pp. 383–408.

ciety and converting them into outputs affecting that society. It could be noted that *all* governments processed inputs and transformed them into outputs: general comparisons could therefore be made; they would amount to a detailed examination of the content of both sides of the operation. But Easton's original presentation was broad and could not be directly applied. Indeed, even in his more recent works (such as *A Systems Analysis of Political Life,* which appeared in 1965,[4] Easton remains on a general plane and a concrete implementation of his model cannot be envisaged. But a new direction had been given to comparative analyses: political scientists were encouraged to examine the content and characteristics of the demands and supports which constituted the inputs and to look at the outputs in terms of the processes of decision-making which can be found in all governments.[5] Constitutional structures were no longer the only yardstick. If inputs and outputs could be defined with more precision, a new yardstick of a greater general validity would have been found.

STRUCTURAL-FUNCTIONALISM AND THE WORK OF G. A. ALMOND

Greater precision was to be brought to the model by G. A. Almond and J. S. Coleman, whose book on the *Politics of Developing Areas*[6] (1960) did constitute a landmark for the development of a general model of comparative government. The approach of Almond and Coleman (which was restated and somewhat refined in *Comparative Politics,* by G. A. Almond and G. B. Powell, which appeared in 1966),[7] was partly based on the theoretical sociological analyses of Talcott Parsons and on decision-making analyses due to H. Lasswell. Taking Easton's analysis as a starting point, Almond looked for the *functions* which could be included among the inputs and the outputs of all political systems. Having looked at the *conversion* process which takes place within the political system, he showed that six such functions could be isolated. First, on the input side, demands are (1) formulated (or articulated) and (2) combined (or aggregated). Second, on the output side, rules are (3) formulated (rule-making),

---

[4] John Wiley and Sons.
[5] See below, extract 2, pp. 10–14.
[6] Princeton U.P.
[7] Little, Brown & Co.

(4) applied (rule-application) and (5) adjudicated in individual cases (rule-adjudication). Third, these various activities are (6) communicated within the system and outside. Almond also showed that, apart from converting inputs into outputs, the system had also to be defined in terms of its ability to maintain and adapt itself (through a process of political socialisation) and in terms of the character of its achievements (capability). A precise yardstick had thus been found, which seemed to satisfy, at least to a large extent, the requirements which were mentioned earlier in this section.[8]

To use functions leads to some difficulties: similar difficulties had been experienced in biology when the notion came to be used. The term function suggests a form of teleological approach which, conceptually, is not wholly appropriate. First, it makes it difficult to distinguish between what might be labelled the deliberate aims of the participants and what takes place because the system simply *seemed* to achieve certain aims. Second, complete objectivity cannot be obtained, because the decision to label a particular type of action a 'function' rests, in the last analysis, on the interpretation which the observer places on certain types of developments: although many political scientists have agreed with the functional approach which Almond developed, it is not possible to demonstrate that these functions are the only functions of the system. Third, even if some form of consensus can be obtained among large numbers of political scientists on the functions performed by the political system, the danger remains that the approach might be somewhat culture-bound and that the functions attributed to the system might be too closely modelled on Western political systems.

All three types of criticisms do obtain, at least to a degree, even though Almond's modified presentation minimises some of the drawbacks of the original framework. But two points may be made. First, functionalism is not only the one existing tool for genuine comparative analysis: it is also a fairly realistic interpretation of the nature of political life. The image of functions may be too anthropomorphic: yet political systems operate as if they fulfilled functions. Second, the yardstick does not need to have an objective existence: it can be created or invented, as the aim is not to measure *one* system, but to compare systems with each other. The real requirement is that

---

[8] See below, extract 3, pp. 15–20.

functionalism should not be biased in favour of one *type* of system: if it were shown to be culture-bound and not to allow for a genuine understanding of all systems, the model would lose its validity. But there is no reason to suppose that all functional models are necessarily culture-bound, though Almond's particular model may be more Western-orientated than should perhaps be warranted. Nothing intrinsic in functionalism suggests that it would be impossible to make adjustments which would improve the framework and limit biases in favour of Western systems.

Almond's analysis is generally known as 'structural-functionalism'. While the yardstick by which systems are measured consists of the functions which are performed by the political system, the units which are being compared are the various structures which compose individual political systems. The model therefore suggests that students of comparative government should attempt in the future to see which structures or institutions fulfil the functions which are ascribed to all political systems. We saw, for instance, that one of the functions of all political systems is 'aggregation', which is defined as the way in which 'demands are combined in the form of alternative courses of action'. In this 'combination', various types of structures can play a part: political parties are perhaps the structures which, in Western democracies, usually attempt to combine and process demands; but, even in the West, various types of interest groups, trade unions and employers' organisations for instance, can also achieve the same aims, either alone or in conjunction with parties. Where parties are non-existent or weak, traditional kinship groups or churches, on the one hand, and the bureaucracy or other governmental structures, on the other, can help to combine demands, although, in the West, the 'function' of the bureaucracy tends to consist in the application of the rules made by legislatures and governments.

With Almond's method, it becomes possible to relate various types of structures to a particular function. Moreover, while the list of these functions is fixed (although Almond slightly modified his framework on this point since the original formulation which appeared in the *Politics of the Developing Areas*), the list of structures can be indefinitely expanded and depends on the characteristics of individual polities. To that extent, the model provides considerable flexibility for the study of comparative government. Almond himself does not attempt to limit the patterns of structure-function relationships, though he notes that, in the West, each particular function tends to be fulfilled by a particular type of structure.

Another potentially powerful development arising out of Almond's model lies in what Almond labelled the 'probabilistic theory of the polity'.[9] Though this is not likely to lead immediately to an empirical application, the method of analysis suggests a direction for research. Once the functions of the political system are defined operationally and the structures categorised with precision, it will become possible to write an 'equation' of each political system which will reveal *how much* of each function is fulfilled by a particular structure. We shall almost certainly find that each function is fulfilled by a large number of structures, and we shall find that polities can be distinguished not only by the kind of structures which are at play, but by the proportion in which these structures are at play. Political parties are likely to fulfil the aggregation function in many countries: but the extent to which aggregation is also fulfilled by interest groups, legislatures, governments, bureaucracies is likely to vary considerably. Polities would thus ultimately no longer be defined simply by a description of the various structures which characterise them (as these could not be defined truly comparatively), but by the specific structure-function relationships which characterise each of them.

This is a distant goal, but it must be attained if a general theory of political systems is to be attempted. Only when polities will become comparable in this — or a similar — probabilistic fashion will it be possible to consider the precise weight of the variables which account for patterns of governments. Differences between systems will no longer be described in such broad types as to limit our understanding of the movements between one type and another. Thus it will become possible to envisage the analysis of patterns of governments on a 'non-parochial' basis. Despite the drawbacks to which we are coming, the analysis of comparative government has gained, as a result of structural-functionalism, a general dimension which it did not have in the past and from which it is not likely to retreat in the future.

---

[9] *Politics of Developing Areas,* pp. 58 ff.

THE LIMITATIONS OF THE MODEL: THE NOTION OF STRUCTURE

Almond's general model is defined as structural-functionalism because, as we saw, the detailed variables with which the model is concerned are defined as structural: they cover groups, parties, legislatures, executives and any other institution by which political systems happen to be characterised. In this lies probably a danger for Almond's model, though, as we shall see, modifications might help to meet most of the difficulty. We noted in the previous section that comparative government has to be concerned with norms, structures and behavioural patterns and that the relationship between these three elements was complex and not uniform. Yet when considering structures Almond seems to postulate a simple relationship. His model is not concerned with norms and assumes that behavioural patterns are directly reflected through the structural arrangements: structures become 'indicators' of behaviour.

These assumptions are clearly not valid and they affect the power of the model in different ways. First, by not giving the 'norms' of the system any place in his model, Almond is forced to treat in the same fashion systems in which the prevailing norms are 'natural' and systems in which the prevailing norms are 'deliberately imposed' on the polity. In effect, he tends to treat all systems as if they were characterised by an overwhelming preponderance of 'natural norms': this stand-point is unavoidable as only 'natural' norms can emerge from the undisturbed evolution of societies; 'deliberately imposed' norms do not 'reflect' society; they are introduced in order to change patterns of behaviour. This characteristic of the model does not lead to major distortions for 'constitutional' systems, since, as we noted, constitutional government makes only limited attempts at modifying prevailing norms and since the ethos of constitutional government consists precisely in freeing society from the constraints which might prevent patterns of behaviour from manifesting themselves: consequently, constitutional government allows 'natural' norms to develop from the repetition of these behavioural patterns. But the model is much less powerful for totalitarian countries, in which the deliberate character of the norms is much more pervasive and the overall ethos much less permissive.

Second, by not taking norms into account, Almond cannot

consider the extent to which structures are related to norms
in different types of societies. It is therefore not possible to
examine whether the same structure can be used in order to
achieve different types of norms. Almond does see different
roles for the same types of structures in different societies:
but these different roles are necessarily considered only within
the context of 'natural' norms (and, with the limitations mentioned earlier, 'constitutional' norms). It is therefore assumed
that a structure such as a political party is the product of the
'solidification' of 'behavioural patterns' in any society: there
is no place in the model for political parties which are the
products of 'deliberately imposed' norms and which would attempt to ensure a penetration of these norms into the society.
The same remark could be made about groups or any other
structure which might have been created, not through a process
of 'solidification of behaviour', but through a deliberate action designed to 'counteract' behaviour.

Third, and as a result, Almond's analysis has only a limited
value in relation to behavioural patterns in certain types of
societies. As long as it can be assumed that structures constitute 'solidified patterns of behaviour', it may be realistic to
consider that structures are reliable indicators of behaviour,
albeit past behaviour. But where structures are imposed on
the political system as a result of certain types of norms, the
consideration of structures may be very confusing and may
indeed not lead to the measurement of behavioural patterns.

These drawbacks are serious: they lead, as we shall see
presently, to profound limitations in two important respects.
They could be overcome, however, in one of at least two
ways. First, it might be possible to consider norms and behavioural patterns separately and thereby not take structures
as the only variable characteristic of political systems. But
such a modification would create major methodological and
almost insuperable operational difficulties. Second, and more
realistically, it might perhaps be possible to take into account
the complex role of structures by assessing, in relation to each
polity, the extent to which a given structure has a 'natural'
or 'deliberate' origin. However deliberately imposed a system
is, and however profoundly it attempts to modify natural
patterns of behaviour through the imposition of structures,
natural norms do tend to develop either alongside or even
within these deliberately imposed structures. By being aware
that structures can thus play an 'ambiguous' role and by at-

tempting to measure the extent to which a given structure does constitute either the 'solidification' of a pattern of behaviour or an instrument of deliberate penetration of an 'imposed' norm, it might still be possible to restrict the analysis to the consideration of structures (in most cases, though as we shall see, not always), and yet give the model a truly general character which is still in part lacking.

COMPLETE FULFILMENT OF FUNCTIONS

The drawbacks of the model in its present form have at least two types of serious consequences. The first is concerned with the extent to which functions are fulfilled in a polity. Almond's analysis appears to postulate that any system tends to fulfil *completely* the whole of each of the six functions which are attributed to political systems. Political systems aggregate demands; these demands, as we saw, can be fulfilled by political parties, by groups, by bureaucracies or by any other structure: what distinguishes polities is, as we also noted, the relative distribution of the various structures which fulfil these demands. But nowhere is it suggested that there might be polities in which the aggregation of demands might not take place, or might take place only to a limited extent.

Admittedly, Almond notes that political systems can be differentiated by their 'capability', which is defined as 'the way in which (the political system) performs as a unit in its environment'. More specifically, one of the aspects of capability is described as 'responsiveness', which varies in degree and which corresponds to the extent to which the political system meets demands formulated by the mass of the population or simply by some section of it.

> In a bureaucratic empire the governmental activities may be at the whim of the king or emperor or of his immediate staff, with little concern to demands and pressures — if they exist — from other sources. The political elites would then constitute almost the sole source of political inputs. We would commonly characterise such a system as having a low responsive capability, although the specific sources of elite inputs would still be a matter for interest and study.[10]

The dimension of 'capability' which has been introduced

---

[10] Almond and Powell, op. cit., p. 201.

by Almond in this modified analysis probably attempts to meet the difficulty arising out of the apparent equal efficiency of all functions and of all systems in the original presentation. But 'capability' still does not make it possible to distinguish regimes by the extent to which individual functions are or are not fulfilled.

In fact, the introduction of 'capability' probably confuses the issue more than it helps to solve it. 'Capability' is connected with the whole of the system and not with any of its component functions; it is also connected with the relationship between the system and the outside world, for instance with the extent to which the system is 'capable' of taking into account the demands of large sections of the population rather than of small segments. It is not concerned with the way in which, once demands have been formulated and, in Almond's terminology, 'articulated', they become 'aggregated' and are ready to be turned into policies. Either Almond postulates that in all systems any demand which has been 'articulated' will become 'aggregated' — and indeed he should postulate that these demands are aggregated *directly after* having been articulated — or there must be a means of measuring whether, to what extent, and after which processes these demands become aggregated. Thus it is necessary to consider the efficiency of the political system within each of the functions, and not merely its general capability in relation to the rest of the social system. By introducing capability as a general, and almost blanket efficiency characteristic, Almond provides us with a vague formula which will scarcely help to differentiate political systems, while the distinction between function and structure should enable us to examine the performance of each part of the political system.

An obvious development of Almond's analysis would therefore be the introduction, in the case of each function, of a variable designed to measure the extent to which the function is performed by the particular system. The 'units' of performance would have to be relative, however, as there is no way of measuring in the abstract whether a system does perform entirely, in part, or not at all, one or several of the functions which political systems perform. Moreover, the functions of the system are connected: the 'articulation of demands' leads to the 'aggregation of these demands' which, in turn, provides the basis for the 'rule-making' processes which take place within the system. One way of measuring the extent to which demands are aggregated 'efficiently' would be to compare the amount of 'aggregation' which takes place in a given system at a certain moment in time to the amount of articulation which had taken place at the previous time point. Such an analysis would require considering 'patterns of behaviour' and would therefore need to go beyond the sole examination of 'structures' to be truly realistic.

Generally, therefore, Almond's analysis is probabilistic in one respect only, that of the specific relationship between each structure and each function. But the logic of the model surely is that there should also be a probabilistic relationship between each function and all the structures which help to fulfil that function. The search for indicators by which to measure precisely the extent of fulfilment of a particular function is likely to be a long one: but so is the search for indicators giving a probabilistic account of the overall structural-functional relationship in a polity. Indicators are likely to be easier to find in the case of some functions or when certain types of structures are involved: but the model must describe political arrangements irrespective of the ease with which, at present, empirical findings can be obtained.

STRUCTURAL-FUNCTIONALISM AND TOTALITARIANISM

Almond's model was constructed in order to enable political scientists to compare the political systems of complex developed societies with those of developing countries in which structures were often less differentiated, in which constitutional arrangements were either non-existent or not implemented and in which most of the 'demands' were made through traditional groupings rather than through modern associations and interest groups. But the model became general and, even in its first formulation, it aimed at being applicable to modern totalitarian systems as well as to liberal-democratic countries. Yet little space was devoted to dictatorships: it seemed to be assumed that, in these regimes as in other political systems, inputs and outputs could be 'filled' with the same structures as elsewhere. By 1966, when the model became overtly aimed at accounting for political life in any political system, greater care was taken to introduce totalitarian systems in the analysis. But despite some improvements — and, here too, despite the role played by the concept of 'capability', which we have already encountered — Almond's general model still does not allow for full comparisons between dictatorships and other systems.

We examined earlier some of the theoretical reasons why the model is likely to be biased in favour of 'natural' structures and against 'deliberately imposed' structures. Yet, even in its present formulation, the model is not only unsatisfactory in that the problem raised by the deliberately imposed character of structures in totalitarian systems is not fully discussed; it is also unsatisfactory in that it does not consider fully the extent to which 'natural' structures emerge in totalitarian States within and beyond the deliberately imposed structures. Admittedly, the secrecy which surrounds 'real' political life in totalitarian systems makes the discovery of these natural structures sometimes difficult: little is known about the way in which demands are formulated by informal groupings, either outside the recognised groups or within recognised bodies such as trade unions or the officially permitted party. But the absence of readily available data is not the only reason for the model's limitation.

As the model stands at present, too much emphasis is given to the formal structures which totalitarian systems create and not enough place is left to the informal structures which may come to life beyond the formal arrangements. In effect, Almond treats the 'structural-functional' model which he developed in a much less flexible fashion than he might have done. If, as is postulated by the general framework, any function can be fulfilled by any type of structure, it could easily be assumed that there might be systems in which a function is fulfilled by totally different structures from those which fulfil that function in another system. Demands may be articulated in the Soviet Union in a fashion which bears no relationship to the way in which these demands are articulated in Britain or the United States. It may be that in this respect the characteristics of the Soviet Union resemble more closely those of a developing country — the Soviet Union *was* a developing country for a large part of this century. It may also be that the major distinction between the Soviet Union and a developing country lies in the modes of regulation of outputs, and not in the input processes.

Totalitarian systems could be reintroduced fully into the model without a profound reconstruction, let alone an abandonment, of the general framework. What seems to be needed is a much closer look at the way in which structures are used in the model: the concept of structure is used in a more so-phisticated fashion in the context of both Western and de-veloping societies than in the context of totalitarian societies. A detailed consideration of the structures of totalitarian coun-tries would probably reveal a much greater richness in pat-terns of group development than is suggested even in the characterisation given by Almond and Powell.[11] Moreover, patterns of relationships between structures and functions could also be described for the whole of the political system. Even if only rough indications could be given in a first ac-count, some of the present difficulties might be more easily overcome. Thus an abandonment of the framework is not suggested and would indeed constitute a setback: as we shall see from the next section and from the substantive accounts reproduced in this book, Almond's model constitutes a con-siderable advance over the current achievements of the partial theories which have been adequately tested and to which we now turn. But a refinement of the concept of structure and a close examination of the extent to which structures do leave certain functions only partially fulfilled might help to promote the more rapid development of a general theory.

III

The development of theory in comparative government ex-tends now over the whole range of structures, even if it does not often come to relate the characteristics of structures to specific functions. But the development has been somewhat uneven. There are definite growth points, while in other fields findings remained less significant. Perhaps the area in which the least advance has recently been made is that which at-tracted most interest traditionally, namely the field of constitu-tional government and of the behavioural patterns character-istic of States operating under constitutional rule. Meanwhile, the examination of the bases of political systems led to a de-tailed consideration of the relationship between patterns of government and socio-economic variables; political parties have been closely analysed and their anatomy is understood in some detail; totalitarian systems and forms of bureaucratic and military rule have come to be closely scrutinised and the

[11] Almond and Powell, op. cit., pp. 74–79. See extract 8 below, pp. 60–65.

latter type of regime has been the subject of comprehensive enquiries.

BASES OF POLITICAL SYSTEMS

We noted in the first section that the variables with which students of comparative government were to be concerned were both numerous and varied. We also noted that some variables of a socio-economic character lent themselves naturally to quantitative analysis. Attempts have indeed been made to measure the precise degree of association between political systems and socio-economic development. The Western type of liberal democracy appears generally associated with a high standard of living, while developing countries seem characterised both by greater instability and by a high propensity towards authoritarianism; but there are exceptions. Moreover, the analysis is complicated, as we noted, by the number of the variables which have to be taken into account and the relative imprecision or ambiguity of some of the concepts. Political stability, for instance, is an ambiguous concept which may refer to the stability of regimes or to the stability of governments: the distinction between the two components is not always as simple to draw as might be imagined. Liberal democracy is equally difficult to define, as the major components of a combined index (free elections, existence of an opposition, etc.) seem to defy rigorous operationalisation.

The measurement of the degree of association between liberal democracy and socio-economic development was attempted with some success, however. First, S. M. Lipset undertook to consider the relationship in the context of European, Anglo-Saxon and Latin-American countries: the classification was somewhat crude, as it was based on pairs of dichotomies.[12] In 1962, a more refined index was constructed by P. Cutright.[13] It included the whole world, except for African countries which had only recently acquired their independence; it also gave 'points' to each country meeting a number of objective conditions characteristic of democracy and these points were attributed on a yearly basis for the twenty-two years of the 1940–1961 period. The liberal character of countries came thus to be assessed on a flexible basis,

[12] *Political Man*, chap. 2, pp. 46–76.
[13] See below, extract 5, pp. 29–41.

and the overall performance was judged through a sequence of events extending almost over a generation.

Cutright was thus able to measure the precise degree of relationship between political development and a number of selected socio-economic indicators and to discover that a 'communications' index, not the standard of living index, accounted for most of the variations. This analysis also led to the measurement of degrees of *relative* political over- and underdevelopment for a given level of social or economic development. Relative over- or underdevelopment can be revealing for countries or groups of countries: Latin American States are usually thought to be politically underdeveloped because of their general instability: in fact, most of them are politically *over*developed in relation to their level of socio-economic attainment. What is surprising about Latin America, therefore, is not that the countries of the subcontinent should be periodically subjected to bouts of authoritarian rule, but that these periods should not be more frequent or prolonged.

The analysis of the relationship between general socio-economic indicators and patterns of government has thus come to be precise. By contrast, the analysis of the relationship between cultural factors and political life is much less advanced. Almond and Verba's work on the *Civic Culture* showed, as was noted in the first section, that the precise measurement of culture was possible. But the study covered five countries only and a general coverage must take place before a Cutright-type analysis of cultural variables can be undertaken. But Cutright's work at least showed that a substantial part of the variations (about one-third) remained unaccounted for by socio-economic indicators: specific cultural patterns and 'historical accidents' have thus a large part to play. The way in which these patterns could be found and these 'accidents' ordered was shown by S. M. Lipset, whose examination of the differences in historical development of a number of Western European countries constitutes one of the first attempts at incorporating 'culture' in the comparative study of types of governments.[14]

Indicators of socio-economic development and of the political culture of countries can thus be found to 'explain' the

---

[14] See extract 7, below, pp. 52–59.

general framework within which governments operate. But the concrete means by which society activates political action is constituted by groups: these have different characteristics in different types of polities. Developed political systems are subjected to the pressure of large numbers of associations while, in other societies, the same demands may originate from kinship groups, even tribes, or 'institutions' such as the army or the church. Almond was the first to attempt to relate an overall classification of groups to various types of political systems.[15] As we noted, his classification could be more refined and a precise measurement of the impact of each type of group could directly help to characterise a type of polity. But, by undertaking the first classification of groups in relation to political systems, Almond prepared the ground for an analysis of the concrete linkages between political development and social development.

POLITICAL PARTIES

Political parties are the modern type of political structure *par excellence*. Although they had numerous forerunners in pre-modern societies, their growth was one of the major characteristics of the nineteenth century. Parties have acquired legitimacy in all political systems and even appear to be synonymous with 'modernity'. Developing countries are as anxious to have parties (or at least one party) as to have a modern bureaucracy and a modern communications system. As we noted in the previous section, totalitarian States used parties rather than abolished them: the one-party system seems to be as important to modern dictatorships as the parliamentary or presidential system of government was to the development of liberal democracies. In so doing, totalitarian States do not only pay tribute to the role of parties in democracies: they show that parties have truly become one of the universal political structures of modern societies.

Having become universal, parties are naturally diverse in character. A special effort had therefore to be made in order to find regularities behind the large number of concrete differences. Interest in parties had started early in the twentieth century and the work of Ostrogorski and Michels had directed

---

[15] See extract 8, below, pp. 60–65.

the study of parties towards the discovery of general trends.[16] But the first truly cross-national study of parties (at least in the West and East) was that of M. Duverger, *Political Parties*.[17] An attempt was made to classify parties in terms of two poles, the party of 'cadres' (or committees) and the mass party, the former being defined by a traditional and elitist origin and base, a small or non-existent membership, a relatively low level of ideology and a tendency towards sectional appeal, while the mass party had all the converse characteristics.[18] This theory led to considerable controversy: it became increasingly clear that Duverger had given too much emphasis to individual membership as the determining factor; the real stress needed to be placed, not on the presence or absence of followers willing to pay dues, but on the national character of the party's appeal and on the extent to which broad 'images' were evoked in the minds of the electors. Moreover, the distinction had to be conceived more definitely in polar terms: existing political parties needed to be measured on the basis of the *extent* to which they were mass parties or parties of committees. This would facilitate the integration of parties of developing countries into a theory which had originally been conceived in order to account for the rise of Western and Eastern parties only.

The broad contention of Duverger's thesis does remain valid, however, despite the fact that new parties have been created in many new countries. Most detailed parts of the analysis also remain valid, in so far as they describe the role of followers, 'inner circles', and leaders in various types of organisations.[19] In particular, the theory of the oligarchical nature of the leadership in democratic and socialist parties, first discussed by Ostrogorski in terms of an 'iron law of oligarchy', was shown by Duverger to have a wide extension. Moreover, Duverger also accounted for the tendency displayed both by Western and non-Western parties to move towards 'monarchical' leadership (of a charismatic character in many cases).[20] The formal structure of the political parties

---

[16] Ostrogorski, *Democracy and the Organisation of Political Parties*, 2 vols., 1902; Michels, *Political Parties*, 1914.

[17] Methuen, 2nd ed., 1959.

[18] See below, extract 10, pp. 77–85.

[19] See below, extracts 12 and 13, pp. 96–111.

[20] See below, extract 14, pp. 112–16.

is less important than the extent to which the party needs to create and maintain a 'positive' image if it is to mobilise the mass of its supporters at the polls or in other forms of political and social action.

The study of the *anatomy* of political parties thus made substantial advances, though the use of truly rigorous indicators would be of great value, as both Western and non-Western parties could be ranked and compared with greater accuracy. The study of *party systems* is much more embryonic, however. Duverger did not attempt to define the elements which enter into the composition of a party system. Even the one basic component of a party system, the number of parties, is not carefully operationalised. As a result, Duverger's celebrated 'law' of the relationship between electoral systems and party systems (according to which a single ballot majority system leads to the development of a two-party system with the converse effect in the case of other electoral systems) does not receive any real empirical testing.[21] Moreover, while the number of parties is clearly an important factor, other variables, such as the relative strength of the parties, their place on the ideological spectrum, their type and structure (mass or non-mass) have not been taken into account. Overall, Duverger was so anxious to relate electoral systems to the number of parties that he made little attempt to develop for party systems a general theory which could be compared with his general theory of party structures.

Some advance has been made since Duverger wrote *Political Parties*, however, particularly in the field of one-party systems. These have been shown to be numerous and complex and the degree of association between one-party systems and totalitarian government is markedly lower than is generally assumed. Most totalitarian systems do use the one-party system, but some rely on other forms of control, and others function on the basis of permanent coalitions in which one of the parties plays a predominant or hegemonic part.[22] Conversely, a degree of pluralism and liberalisation has taken place in some cases within the framework of a one-party system. Thus, as we noted in the previous section, parties do fulfil very different functions and embody very different norms, even in the context of one-party systems. What is

[21] See below, extract 17, pp. 138–41.
[22] See below, extract 16, pp. 127–37.

therefore required is a consideration of the broad patterns of relationships between types of party systems (defined by using a number of indicators) and types of political systems. This will, in a second stage, facilitate the examination of the relationship between types of party systems and types of socio-economic structures. Though the theory of party systems is thus not as advanced as the theory of the structure of political parties and the theory of the relationship between political development and social development, the direction in which further studies should take place has become clear.

CONSTITUTIONAL GOVERNMENT

Constitutional government deserves to be analysed separately, not only because it has occupied a special place in the history of Western countries since the end of the eighteenth century, but because it is placed, as we noted, at a particularly critical point between outright 'imposed' government and 'natural' political systems. Indeed constitutional structures have given rise to a special kind of theory which might be defined as 'institutional theory'. This was one of the oldest aspects of the study of comparative government; for a long time, it constituted the only 'positive' aspect of the study of politics, even though the logical analysis which characterised much of the work of constitutional lawyers of the nineteenth and twentieth centuries was often concerned merely with the purely structural aspects of constitutions: as long as constitutions were assumed to be implemented, such an institutional theory was both practically very important and theoretically very revealing about the nature of political systems.

As D. Verney shows in the *Analysis of Political System*, institutional theorists developed three models of constitutional systems of government.[23] These three models can be deduced from one general definition, a postulate and a corollary. First, the definition states simply that a governmental system can be deemed to be constitutional only if the electoral body takes part in the selection of the rulers. Second, the postulate stems directly from the writings of the constitutional theorists of the seventeenth and eighteenth centuries, Locke and Montesquieu. It states that a constitutional government implies the distinction between a legislature and an executive (a distinc-

---

[23] Free Press, 1959. See below, extract 19, pp. 160–69.

tion which does not mean that there is technically to be a 'separation of powers', as we shall see), because there are general policies which can be dealt with at some leisure and should be examined by a large body, and more detailed matters which are best left to a smaller and permanent body, also empowered to act in cases of emergency. The distinction between general policies and detailed implementation has come under severe criticisms, but it does constitute even now the basis for the allocation of powers between legislatures and executives in constitutional government. Finally, the corollary states that the system cannot be deemed to be constitutional if the legislature is inferior to the executive: as the legislature deals with general matters and the executive deals with detailed questions and emergency situations, it would be inconsistent to allow the executive to be superior to the legislature.

On the basis of the postulate and the corollary it follows that there can be three, and only three 'constitutional' systems of government. These can be deduced in the following way. First, the legislature can be either equal or superior to the executive. If the latter obtains, the executive proceeds from the legislature. If the former obtains, there are two further possibilities: either the legislature and the executive are in a reciprocal power relationship or they are completely separated; in the latter case, the executive has to proceed directly from the electoral body. The three systems have been given characteristic names, which have therefore a technical meaning in institutional theory. When the executive is inferior to the legislature, the system is known as *convention* government; when the executive is in an equal, but reciprocal relationship, the system is known as *parliamentary;* when, finally, the executive is separated from the legislature and they both proceed directly from the electoral body, the system is known as *presidential* or as a *separation of powers* form of government.

Institutional theorists considered a number of further consequences from the postulate. For instance, the right of dissolution 'should not' exist in convention type systems or in a presidential form of government, but 'should' exist in parliamentary regimes: if convention type systems included dissolution, the legislature would not be superior to the executive; if dissolution did exist in presidential forms of government, the legislature and executive would not be truly separated; but if dissolution did not exist in parliamentary systems, the

arrangements for reciprocal influence could not be established. This is because, in a similarly logical fashion, parliamentary systems and convention systems must give the
legislature the right to dismiss the executive (motion of censure), while presidential regimes should not give this right.
These rules, and many others which can be similarly deduced
constitute 'instructions' to constitution-makers. They were indeed generally obeyed by the framers of most nineteenth-
century constitutions and of the constitutions of the early
part of the twentieth century. They were more commonly
disobeyed in the middle part of the twentieth century, but
the constitutions which have seriously contravened the principles have also had either a limited life or a limited 'real' implementation.

Institutional theory was thus given considerable attention
by political scientists and constitutional lawyers. But much less
attention was given to the relationship between structure and
behaviour within the framework of a constitutional system.
Only recently have political scientists begun to recognise that
patterns of behaviour in constitutional systems could vary
markedly. Studies of legislative and executive behaviour have
remained rare, except in the United States: even commonly
accepted theories, for instance about the role of dissolution
on the behaviour of legislatures, have not been tested on a
cross-national basis. More general propositions about the decline of legislatures or the increased role of executives have
been normally accepted without empirical testing over a fairly
long time period or on the basis of a broad cross-national
analysis. Studies of executive structure, of the role of coalitions, or of the relative importance of governmental stability
on executive efficiency have not been given either the comparative basis or the systematic character which they require, if hypotheses are to be tested and general conclusions
drawn.[24]

Of the various branches of the study of comparative government, that of constitutional government thus remains the
only one in which institutional-cum-normative theory is sin-
gularly more advanced than positive theory. This is in part
due to the fact that, for a fairly long period, institutional
theory appeared to obviate for the need of a positive theory;
the study of constitutional government was also in part ham-

[24] See below, extracts 20 and 21, pp. 170–75 and 176–83.

pered by the very development of other branches of comparative government, in which patterns had remained hitherto undiscovered and immediate advances appeared more imperative. Studies of patterns of behaviour in constitutional government have started to take place, however, following behavioural analyses of constitutional structures in the United States. Indeed, the analysis of party systems will probably lead to the behavioural study of constitutional government as parties constitute the major structural variable accounting for differences in performance between governmental systems.

POLITICAL RULE OUTSIDE CONSTITUTIONAL SYSTEMS

The study of non-constitutional forms of rule, either 'imposed' and totalitarian or 'natural' and wholly behavioural constitutes on the contrary an area to which contemporary students of comparative government devoted considerable attention. Efforts have taken place in three major directions, those of totalitarian government in general, of military rule and of bureaucratic influence. For the last two of these fields at least, studies were prompted by the interest shown in and the importance attributed to developing societies, though the extension of totalitarianism from Communist to Third World countries also led to an enlargement of the base of the theory as more data could be obtained and a wider range of experiments could be analysed.

Yet, as we noted, totalitarian government is both difficult to interpret in terms of a general theory of government and difficult to assess in view of the secrecy which surrounds its operation. Detailed analyses of behavioural patterns on a cross-national basis have therefore not always sufficiently backed general theories; reliable indicators have often been difficult to construct.[25] Gradually, however, it has become possible to integrate totalitarian government within a general model of the polity. Empirical evidence drawn from Communist and developing States has corroborated the hypothesis that totalitarianism was an intermediate stage in political development. The increased social and economic development of Eastern European States and of the Soviet Union in the 1950s and 1960s has been accompanied by increased pluralism and increased liberalisation. In the new States, totali-

---

[25] See below, extracts 22 and 23, pp. 187–99 and 200–7.

tarianism appeared as a means to break traditional social structures and the authority of traditional forms of government. There is no clear evidence that totalitarian government itself quickens the pace of development, though members of 'new elites' in developing countries often believe that this is the case; there is indeed evidence that totalitarianism can be accompanied by stagnation. But there is also evidence that the social tensions produced by economic development can be mastered by totalitarian government.

The study of totalitarian government requires a thorough analysis of the variables which account for the apparently accidental distribution of totalitarianism throughout the world both in developing and economically advanced countries: an analysis of the range of cultural patterns of societies might well increase the understanding of the conditions leading to these variations. At the other end of the spectrum, the movement towards pluralism and the break-up of totalitarian tendencies in Communist States needs to be studied with equal precision: contemporary developments in Eastern Europe show a variety of patterns and of rates of liberalisation, which need to be measured with more precise indicators than those which have hitherto been at the disposal of students of totalitarian government.

Progress has been faster in the field of military government. No systematic work on the military was undertaken before the 1950s: by the early 1960s, the conditions likely to maximise the probability of military rule were fairly well established and the relationship between types of military rule and levels of political culture had been clarified. Like totalitarian government (with which military rule has some, but only some connections), military rule tends to develop in intermediate stages of development, after 'take-off', but before the society becomes fully developed. Indeed, the type of ideology of the military can be shown to be closely related to the level of development: military governments which take over countries at a relatively early level of development are more likely to be ideologically 'progressive' than military governments which take over countries at a later stage of development.

However, military intervention in politics must be seen as a general phenomenon: it can be shown to extend to developed societies as well as to developing countries. While military *rule* and military take-over are extreme cases of intervention, other forms of action, such as ordinary pressure on the civilian government in order to increase expenditure or even to shift policy, are quite common in the most 'advanced' societies. Even less 'constitutional' modes of intimidation are used on occasion. But these forms of intervention are closely related to the degree of pluralism of the polity: the major variables at play are the degree of complexity of the society, the legitimacy of the regime and the social and economic tensions leading to clashes between traditional and new elites.[26] Thus Latin America or Africa are no more predestined to military intervention than any other area: the specific forms which this intervention takes can be analysed by reference to the characteristics of the social development and of the political culture of the countries concerned. What modern studies of the military have shown is that military intervention as such no longer requires explanation: future studies therefore need to concentrate on the means by which military intervention can be limited and ceases to become a danger for the stability of the polity.

Bureaucracies, as well as armies, exist under all types of government. But, unlike armies, bureaucracies had earlier been thought to be associated with highly advanced industrial societies only: the 'bureaucratic State' had therefore sometimes been considered to be the last stage of political development. This was seen as a threat, as various negative characteristics can be shown to develop if bureaucracies are uncontrolled and become the main source of policy decisions.[27] But contemporary analysis has also shown that bureaucracies play an early and large part in developing as well as developed nations, partly because, as well as armies, they constitute one of the 'modern structures' (or 'institutional groups', to use Almond's terminology) through which demands for a modern social and economic system are processed. Thus the 'bureaucratic State' could menace any society: the menace needs to be measured, not by the absolute number of public officials in a given country, nor even by the percentage of the population in public employment, but as a ratio of public servants to other managers and leaders of interest groups in the wide sense; (in a Communist country, this ratio would be that of public servants in the narrow sense to managers of commerce and industry and party offi-

---

[26] See below, extract 24, pp. 208–16.
[27] See below, extract 25, pp. 217–25.

cials, even though all these leaders are legally employed by the State). Moreover, and conversely, the danger represented by bureaucracies seems in fact to decrease, rather than increase, with the development of societies: bureaucracies, as well as armies, tend to expand their influence if and where the civic culture is low and if and where demands are numerous, strongly voiced and mutually exclusive. Moreover, as well as armies, bureaucracies lack a legitimate foundation to maintain themselves in power: they need to rely on the authority of political leaders; while military rulers need to 'civilianise' their regime in order to remain in office, bureaucratic leaders can really expand their influence only if they act in the shadow of a political group.

Comparative studies of government thus greatly expanded their scope in the course of the 1950s and 1960s. Admittedly, the political development of societies still remains in large part unexplained: it is therefore not possible to predict with certainty what political direction countries will take in the future. We do not know how widespread the move towards democracy will be, nor which States will go through a phase of totalitarian or authoritarian government if the aim is a rapid increase in levels of social or economic development. Indeed, it is futile to expect the answers to such questions to be given in a broad and uniform manner: answers have to be given in terms of alternative developments related to various sets of conditions. But the number of 'partial theories' has grown: a much clearer picture of the variables accounting for political development has been obtained. The 'structures' of political systems are being described in much greater detail; polities are no longer considered individually and compared haphazardly. Political systems are characterised by an increasingly large number of general variables which can be related to a general model of political life.

Unquestionably, the demand for 'political engineering' will increase as a result. It will become possible to 'manipulate' political systems more accurately than was possible in the past. This will lead to 'mistakes', similar to those for which economists were criticised when they started 'manipulating' national economies. This will also contribute arguments for the view that man has ceased to be 'free', if government can be predicted not only in its general framework, but in the concrete forms of political structures and types of political action. Yet the will to manipulate government is not new: supporters of constitutional rule, as well as dictators, often tried in the past to change the conditions under which politics was to take place. What was often lacking was not the desire, but the ability to intervene effectively in the field of government. As in other subjects, a better knowledge of the conditions of development is no substitute for a concern for values and moral goals. A better knowledge of government will not prevent man from discussing what forms of government are best suited for human society: it will increase man's power of control over society by making clearer to leaders what consequences are likely to be drawn from the actions which are taken. By increasing our knowledge, comparative government can thus give future societies real opportunities to enable man to implement more fully political ideals which too often remained in the past formal or ill applied.

PART ONE

METHOD AND PRESENT STATE
OF
COMPARATIVE GOVERNMENT

1. A SURVEY OF THE FIELD
OF COMPARATIVE GOVERNMENT

R. C. MACRIDIS

MAJOR CHARACTERISTICS OF THE TRADITIONAL APPROACH

A brief account of the characteristics of the traditional approach and emphasis in the comparative study of government will reveal the source of the current dissatisfaction and will point to the need for reorientation. Comparative study has thus far been comparative in name only. It has been part of what may loosely be called the study of foreign governments, in which the governmental structures and the formal organization of state institutions were treated in a descriptive, historical, or legalistic manner. Primary emphasis has been placed on written documents like constitutions and the legal prescriptions for the allocation of political power. Finally, studies of foreign governments were largely addressed to the Western European democracies or to the political systems of Western Europe, Great Britain, and the Dominions.

It may be worthwhile to discuss briefly each of these characteristics of the traditional approach.

Essentially Noncomparative

The vast majority of publications in the field of comparative government deal either with one country or with parallel descriptions of the institutions of a number of countries. The majority of texts illustrate this approach. The student is led through the constitutional foundations, the organization of political power, and a description of the ways in which such powers are exercised. In each case 'problem areas' are discussed with reference to the country's institutional structure. The right of dissolution is often cited to explain political in-

From *The Study of Comparative Government*, pp. 7–12, Random House, 1955. We are grateful to the publishers for permission to reproduce this extract.

stability in France, and, conversely, political stability in England is discussed with reference to the prerogatives of the Crown, with particular emphasis, of course, on the Prime Minister's power of dissolution. The interest of the student is concentrated primarily on an analysis of the structure of the state, the location of sovereignty, the electoral provisions, and the distribution of the electorate into political parties whose ideologies and programs are described. This approach will be found in any standard text and in a number of monographs which aspire to be more comparative in character.

Essentially Descriptive

It may well be argued that description of the formal political institutions is vital for the understanding of the political process and that as such it leads to comparative study. If so, we hardly ever have any comparison between the particular institutions described. A reading, for instance, of one of the best texts, *Governments of Continental Europe,* edited by James T. Shotwell, will reveal that as we pass from France to Italy, Switzerland, Germany, and U.S.S.R. there is no common thread, no criterion of why these particular countries were selected and no examination of the factors that account for similarities and differences. The same generally applies to Frederic Ogg's and Harold Zink's *Modern Foreign Governments,* and to Fritz M. Marx's *Foreign Governments.* In a somewhat different fashion John Ranney's and Gwendolen Carter's *Major Foreign Powers* has the virtue of addressing itself to only four political systems and of discussing them with reference to some basic problem areas, but again the connecting link and the criterion of selection are missing. Another pioneer book in the field, Daniel Witt's *Comparative Political Institutions,* abandons the country-by-country approach in favor of categories within which comparison is more feasible, but the author is satisfied to include under such categories as 'The Citizen and the Government' and 'The Electoral Process' separate descriptions of the institutions of individual countries, and fails to make explicit comparisons.

It should be clearly understood here that these remarks are not meant to reflect on the scholarly quality of the books cited, nor to disparage the descriptive approach. They are meant merely to point out that these books are limited primarily to political morphology or what might also be called political anatomy. They describe various political institutions generally without attempting to compare them; what comparison *is* made is limited exclusively to the identification of differences between types or systems, such as federal versus unitary system or parliamentary versus presidential system or the more elusive differences between democratic and totalitarian systems.

There are two typical approaches in the descriptive study of political institutions. The first is *historical* and the second is *legalistic*. The historical approach centers on the study of the origins and growth of certain institutions. We trace the origins of the British parliamentary system to Magna Carta and study its development through successive historical stages. It is assumed that parallel historical accounts of the evolution of the French parliament or the German representative assemblies will indicate similarities and differences. The approach followed is almost identical with that used by the historian. There is no effort to evolve an analytical scheme within which an antecedent factor is related in terms other than chronological to a particular event or development.

The second most prevalent approach is what we might call the legalistic approach. Here the student is exposed primarily to the study of the 'powers' of the various branches of government and their relationships with reference to the existing constitutional and legal prescriptions. This is almost exclusively the study of what can be done or what cannot be done by various governmental agencies with reference to legal and constitutional provisions. Again, this approach, like its historical counterpart with which it often goes hand in hand, describes the political system in a very narrow frame. It does not seek the forces that shape the legal forms, nor does it attempt to establish the causal relationships that account for the variety in constitutional prescriptions from one system to another or from one period to another. A typical illustration of this approach are two recent studies on post-World War II constitutional developments in Western Europe: Arnold Zurcher's *Constitutionalism and Constitutional Trends since World War II*, and Mirkine Guetzevitch's *Les Constitutions Européennes*. To a great extent Ivor Jenning's works on the *British Cabinet* and the *British Parliament* rely on the legalistic approach with particular emphasis on the search for precedents that 'explain' the powers of various governmental organs.

The combination of the historical and the legalistic approaches is found in the great majority of books published on foreign systems that purport to be comparable. Even though they give us a cameralike picture of the development and relationships of the various political organs in a system, and point to parallel historical development, they do not attempt to devise a general frame of reference in which we can get broad hypotheses about the development and operation of institutions.

Essentially Parochial

The great number of studies on foreign political systems has been addressed to the examination of Western European institutions. Accessibility of the countries studied, relative ease of overcoming language barriers, and the availability of official documents and other source materials, as well as cultural affinities, account for this fact. France, Great Britain, Germany, Switzerland, and to a lesser extent the Scandinavian countries and the British Dominions have been the countries to which writing and research has been directed and which are being included in the various comparative government courses in the greater number of American universities. Again, however, no systematic effort has been made to identify the similarities and the differences among these countries except in purely descriptive terms. No effort has been made to define in analytical terms the categories that constitute an 'area' of study. True, most authors seem to identify these countries in terms of a common historical and cultural background and they often pay lip service to some other common traits, such as their advanced economic systems, particularly institutions, and democracy. What is meant by 'advanced' economic systems, however, and, more specifically, what is the relationship between political institutions and the existing economic system? We often find the statement that Germany did not develop a democratic ideology and parliamentary institutions because capitalism developed 'late,' but no effort is being made to test the validity of such a generalization comparatively — for, after all, capitalism developed 'late' in the United States and in some of the British Dominions. Often statements about the existence of a common ideology are made without attempting to define what is 'common' and how ideology is related to political institutions.

There is no doubt that references to social and economic configurations, political ideologies, and institutions that can be found in texts should be interrelated into a system that would make comparative analyses of these Western European countries possible. No such effort, however, with the exception of Carl Friedrich's *Constitutional Government and Democracy*, has been made, and even Professor Friedrich is concerned only with the interplay between ideology and institutions. There is no systematic synthesis of the various 'characteristics' or 'traits' of different political systems. Yet without such a conceptualization no variables can be identified and compared, and as a result no truly comparative analyses of the Western governmental systems have been made by political scientists.

Some notable exceptions, in addition to Professor Friedrich's and Professor Herman Finer's books, are Michel's book on *Political Parties* and the recent comparative analysis of the structure and the organization of political parties and the relationship between structure and ideology by Professor Maurice Duverger. Another good illustration of a more sophisticated study is a current essay on the French political system by François Goguel in which he points out that political, economic, and social instability in France is due to the uneven development of various regions in the country, thus suggesting a relationship between political stability and uniformity of economic development within a country.

Concentration on Western systems cannot be exclusively attributed to some of the considerations suggested above. An even more important factor was the belief at one time shared by many political scientists that democracy was the 'normal' and durable form of government and that it was destined to spread throughout the world. In fact, 'comparative study' would embrace more political systems only as they developed democratic institutions. James Bryce put this in very succinct terms:

> The time seems to have arrived when the actualities of democratic government in its diverse forms, should be investigated, and when the conditions most favorable to its success should receive more attention than students, as distinguished from politicians, have been bestowing upon them.

It was natural that such a point of view should limit comparative study to the democratic systems and that it would call for the study of other systems only for the purpose of identifying democratic institutions and forms. As we shall see, such a preoccupation distorted the analysis and study of non-Western systems by centering upon patterns and institutions that were familiar to the Western observer, such as constitutions and legislatures, but whose relevance to the political process of non-Western countries was only incidental.

Essentially Static

In general the traditional approach has ignored the dynamic factors that account for growth and change. It has concentrated on what we have called political anatomy. After the evolutionary premises of some of the original works in the nineteenth century were abandoned, students of political institutions apparently lost all interest in the formulation of other theories in the light of which change could be comparatively studied.

The question of sovereignty and its location occupied students of politics for a long time; the study of constitutional structures became a favorite pastime, though no particular effort was made to evaluate the effectiveness of constitutional forms in achieving posited goals or to analyze the conditions underlying the success or failure of constitutionalism. The parallel development of administration was noted, but again its growth was studied with reference to a constitutional setting, as Dicey's work amply illustrates. The growth of political parties was studied, but aside from descriptions of their legal status little consideration was given by political scientists to the radical transformation parties were to bring about in the organization of political power. Henry Maine's and William Lecky's bold hypotheses about the impact on democracy of the development of party government and of the extension of the franchise were abandoned in the light of contrary evidence and were never replaced with new ones. Indeed, Walter Bagehot's analysis of the British Cabinet remained standard until the turn of the century, though the word 'party' rarely appears in it, and Dicey's formal statement of the limitations of parliamentary sovereignty were considered for a long time to the most definitive formulation of the problem. The British people, it was pointed out by Dicey, constituting the 'political sovereign' body limited the 'legal sovereignty' of the parliament and such limitation was institutionalized through the courts. Federalism and its development in the various dominions was also discussed with reference to the legal organization of power and to its relationship with the concept of sovereignty. In all cases the studies made were a dissection of the distribution of powers in terms of their legal setting and left out of the picture altogether the problem of change and the study of those factors—political or other—that account for change.

Essentially Monographic

The most important studies of foreign systems, aside from basic texts, have taken the form of monographs that have concentrated on the study of the political institutions of one system or on the discussion of a particular institution in one system. Works such as those by John Marriott, Arthur K. Keith, Joseph Barthelemy, James Bryce, Ivor Jennings, Harold Laski, A. V. Dicey, Frank Goodnow, W. A. Robson, Abbott L. Lowells, Woodrow Wilson, and many others were addressed generally to only one country or to a particular institutional development within one country. The American presidency, the British parliamentary system, the congressional form of government were presented in studies in which the particular institutional forms were placed in the context of the whole tradition and legal system of the country involved. Sometimes such monographs represented great advances over the legalistic approach because they brought into the open nonpolitical factors and institutions or attempted to deal analytically with some of the problems facing the democratic systems. They had a focal point and the description of the institutions was always related to a common theme or was undertaken in the light of a common political problem, such as the relationship between executive and legislature, the growth of administrative law and the institutions of administration, the relationship between national characteristics and political ideology, and the like. The relationships established between political and nonpolitical factors, however, hardly attain a systematic formulation that can be used for comparative study, i.e., for identifying variables and attempting to account for them. Nor is the suggestion ever explicitly made that the particular way in which a problem is studied or certain institutional developments discussed is applicable to parallel phenomena in other countries.

2. THE POLITICAL SYSTEM

G. A. ALMOND AND G. B. POWELL

The term 'political system' has become increasingly common
in the titles of texts and monographs in the field of comparative politics. The older texts used such terms as 'government', 'nation', or 'state' to describe what we call a political
system. Something more is involved here than mere style of
nomenclature. This new terminology reflects a new way of
looking at political phenomena. It includes some new names
for old things, and some new terms to refer to activities and
processes which were not formerly recognized as being parts
or aspects of politics.

The older terms — state, government, nation — are limited
by legal and institutional meanings. They direct attention to
a particular set of institutions usually found in modern Western societies. If one accepts the idea that the study of such
institutions is the proper and sole concern of political science,
many problems are thereby avoided, including the thorny
question of limiting the subject matter of the discipline. However, the costs of such a decision are very high. The role
played by formal governmental institutions such as legislatures and courts in different societies varies greatly; in many
societies, particularly in those outside the Western world,
their role may not be so important as that of other institutions
and processes. In all societies the role of formal governmental
institutions is shaped and limited by informal groups, political
attitudes, and a multitude of interpersonal relationships. If
political science is to be effective in dealing with political
phenomena in all kinds of societies, regardless of culture, degree of modernization, and size, we need a more comprehensive framework of analysis.

The concept of 'political system' has acquired wide cur-

From *Comparative Politics: A Developmental Approach,* by Gabriel A.
Almond and G. Bingham Powell, Jr., pp. 16–21. Copyright © 1966 by
Little, Brown & Co., Inc. and reprinted with their permission.

rency because it directs attention to the entire scope of political activities within a society, regardless of where in the society such activities may be located. What is the political system? How do we define its boundaries? What gives the political system its special identity? Many political scientists have dealt with these questions; while the precise language of their definitions varies considerably, there is some consensus. Common to most of these definitions is the association of the political system with the use of legitimate physical coercion in societies. Easton speaks of *authoritative allocation of values;* Lasswell and Kaplan, of *severe deprivations;* Dahl, of *power, rule, and authority.*[1] All these definitions imply legitimate, heavy sanctions; the rightful power to punish, to enforce, to compel. We agree with Max Weber[2] that legitimate force is the thread that runs through the action of the political system, giving it its special quality and importance, and its coherence as a system. The political authorities, and only they, have some generally accepted right to utilize coercion and command obedience based upon it. (Force is 'legitimate' where this belief in the justifiable nature of its use exists.) The inputs which enter the political system are all in some way related to legitimate physical compulsion, whether these are demands for war or for recreational facilities. The outputs of the political system are also all in some way related to legitimate physical compulsion, however remote the relationship may be. Thus, public recreation facilities are usually supported by taxation, and any violation of the regulations governing their use is a legal offense. When we speak of the political system, we include all the interactions which affect the use or threat of use of legitimate physical coercion. The political system includes not only governmental institutions such as legislatures, courts, and administrative agencies, but *all structures in their political aspects.* Among these are traditional structures such as kinship ties and caste groupings; and

[1] David Easton, *The Political System* (New York: Alfred A. Knopf Inc., 1953), pp. 130 ff., and his *A Framework for Political Analysis* (Englewood Cliffs: Prentice-Hall Inc., 1965), pp. 50 ff.; Harold D. Lasswell and Abraham Kaplan, *Power and Society* (New Haven: Yale U.P., 1950); Robert A. Dahl, *Modern Political Analysis* (Englewood Cliffs: Prentice-Hall Inc., 1963), pp. 5 ff.

[2] See Max Weber, 'Politics as a Vocation', in his *From Max Weber: Essays in Sociology,* ed. Hans H. Gerth and C. Wright Mills (New York: Oxford U.P., 1946), pp. 77-78.

anomic phenomena such as assassinations, riots, and demonstrations; as well as formal organizations like parties, interest groups, and media of communication.

We are not, then, saying that the political system is concerned solely with force, violence, or compulsion; rather, that its relation to coercion is its distinctive quality. Political elites are usually concerned with goals such as national expansion or security, social welfare, the aggrandizement of their power over other groups, increased popular participation in politics, and the like; but their concern with these values as politicians is related to compulsory actions such as law making and law enforcement, foreign and defense policy, and taxation. The political system is not the only system that makes rules and enforces them, but its rules and enforcements go all the way to compelling obedience or performance.

There are societies in which the accepted power to use physical compulsion is widely diffused, shared by family, by clan, by religious bodies, or other kinds of groups, or taken up privately, as in the feud or the duel. But we consider even these as political systems of a particular kind, and still comparable with those polities in which there is something approaching a monopoly of legitimate physical coercion.

If what we have said above defines the 'political' half of our concept, what do we mean by 'system'? A system implies the interdependence of parts, and a boundary of some kind between it and its environment. By 'interdependence' we mean that when the properties of one component in a system change, all the other components and the system as a whole are affected. Thus, if the rings of an automobile erode, the car 'burns oil'; the functioning of other aspects of the system deteriorates, and the power of the car declines. Or, as another example, there are points in the growth of organisms when some change in the endocrine system affects the over-all pattern of growth, the functioning of all the parts, and the general behavior of the organism. In political systems the emergence of mass parties, or of media of mass communication, changes the performance of all the other structures of the system and affects the general capabilities of the system in its domestic and foreign environments. In other words, when one variable in a system changes in magnitude or in quality, the others are subjected to strains and are transformed; the system changes its pattern of performance, or the unruly component is disciplined by regulatory mechanisms.

A second aspect of the concept of 'system' is the notion of boundary. A system starts somewhere and stops somewhere. In considering an organism or an automobile, it is relatively easy to locate its boundary and to specify the interactions between it and its environment. The gas goes into the tank, the motor converts it into revolutions of the crankshaft and the driving wheels, and the car moves on the highway. In dealing with social systems, of which political systems are a class, the problem of boundary is not that easy. Social systems are made up not of individuals, but of roles. A family, for example, consists of the roles of mother and father, husband and wife, sibling and sibling. The family is only one set of interacting roles for its members, who also may have roles outside the family in schools, business firms, and churches. In the same sense a political system is made up of the interacting roles of nationals, subjects, voters, as the case may be, with legislators, bureaucrats, and judges. The same individuals who perform roles in the political system perform roles in other social systems such as the economy, the religious community, the family, and voluntary associations. As individuals expose themselves to political communication, form interest groups, vote, or pay taxes, they shift from nonpolitical to political roles. One might say that on election day as citizens leave their farms, plants, and offices to go to the polling places, they are crossing the boundary from the economy to the polity.

Another example of a shift in the boundary of the political system might occur when inflation reduces the real income of certain groups in the population. When such a change in the economic situation of particular groups gets converted into demands for public policy or for changes in political personnel, there is an interaction between the economy and the polity. Certain psychic states resulting from changes in the economic situation are converted into demands on the political system. Demands are made on trade-union or other pressure-group leaders to lobby for particular actions by the legislature or by executive agencies. Somewhere in this process a boundary is crossed from one system to another — from the economic system to the political system.

The boundaries of political systems are subject to relatively large fluctuations. During wartime the boundaries become greatly extended as large numbers of men are recruited into military service, as business firms are subjected to regulations, and as internal security measures are taken. In an election the boundaries again are greatly extended as voters become politicians for a day. With the return to more normal conditions, the boundaries of the political system contract.

The problem of boundaries takes on special significance because systems theory usually divides interaction processes into three phases — input, conversion, output. Any set of interacting parts — any system — which is affected by factors in its environment may be viewed in this fashion. The inputs and outputs, which involve the political system with other social systems, are transactions between the system and its environment; the conversion processes are internal to the political system. When we talk about the sources of inputs, their number, content, and intensity, and how they enter the political system, and of the number and content of outputs and how they leave the political system and affect other social systems, we shall in effect be talking about the boundaries of the political system.

3. THE FUNCTIONAL ASPECTS OF
POLITICAL SYSTEMS

G. A. ALMOND AND G. B. POWELL

This discussion of flows of inputs and outputs leads logically
to a consideration of the *functions* of political systems. *Functionalism* is an old theme in political theory. In its modern
form, the stress on functionalism is derived from anthropological and sociological theory. The chief social theorists associated with functionalism are the anthropologists Malinowski
and Radcliffe-Brown and the sociologists Parsons, Merton,
and Marion Levy.[1] Although these men differ substantially
in their concepts of system and function, essentially they have
said that the ability to explain and predict in the social sciences is enhanced when we think of social structures and
institutions as performing functions in systems. By comparing
the performance of structures and the regulatory role of political culture as they fulfill common functions in all systems,
we may analyze systems which appear very different from
one another.

The functioning of any system may be viewed on different
levels. One level of functioning is the system's *capabilities*,
that is, the way it performs as a unit in its environment. Ani-

---

From *Comparative Politics: A Developmental Approach*, by Gabriel A.
Almond and G. Bingham Powell, Jr., pp. 27–33. Copyright © 1966, by
Little, Brown & Co., Inc., and reprinted with their permission.
[1] Bronislaw Malinowski, *Magic, Science and Religion and Other Es-
says* (Garden City: Doubleday & Company Inc., 1954); A. R. Radcliffe-
Brown, *Structure and Function in Primitive Society* (New York: The
Free Press of Glencoe, 1957); Talcott Parsons, *Essays in Sociological
Theory Pure and Applied* (New York: The Free Press of Glencoe,
1959) and *The Social System* (New York: The Free Press of Glencoe,
1951); Talcott Parsons and Edward Shils (eds.), *Toward a General
Theory of Action* (Cambridge: Harvard U.P., 1951); Robert K. Merton,
Social Theory and Social Structure (New York: The Free Press of
Glencoe, 1957); Marion Levy, *The Structure of Society* (Princeton U.P.,
1952).

mals move while plants do not. Some machines process data; others produce power. An economy produces and distributes physical goods and services. Families produce children and socialize them into adult roles and disciplines. At this level we are focusing on the behavior of the system as a unit in its relations to other social systems and to the environment.

When we speak of the capabilities of a political system, we are looking for an orderly way to describe its over-all performance in its environment. The categories of capability which we use grow directly out of our analysis of types of inputs and outputs. Some political systems are primarily *regulative* and *extractive* in character. Totalitarian systems suppress demands coming from their societies and are unresponsive to demands coming from the international environment. At the same time, they regulate and coerce behavior in their societies, and seek to draw maximum resources from their populations. Communist totalitarianism differs from fascist totalitarianism in having a strong *distributive* capability as well. This means that the political system itself actively shifts resources from some groups in the population to other groups. In democracies outputs of regulation, extraction, and distribution are more affected by inputs of demands from groups in the society. Thus we may speak of democracies as having a higher *responsive* capability. These concepts of *regulative, extractive, distributive,* and *responsive* capability are simply ways of talking about the flows of activity into and out of the political system. They tell us how a system is performing in its environment, how it is shaping this environment, and how it is being shaped by it.

The second level of functioning is internal to the system. Here we refer to *conversion processes.* Physiological examples would be the digestion of foods, the elimination of waste, the circulation of the blood, and the transmission of impulses through the nervous system. The conversion processes, or functions, are the ways systems transform inputs into outputs. In the political system this involves the ways in which demands and supports are transformed into authoritative decisions and are implemented. Obviously the capabilities and the conversion processes of a system are related. In order for an animal to be able to move, hunt, and dig, energy must be created in the organism, and the use of the energy must be controlled and directed.

The conversion processes of one political system may be

analyzed and compared with those of other systems according to a sixfold functional scheme. We need to look at the ways in which (1) demands are formulated (interest articulation); (2) demands are combined in the form of alternative courses of action (interest aggregation); (3) authoritative rules are formulated (rule making); (4) these rules are applied and enforced (rule application); (5) these applications of rules are adjudicated in individual cases (rule adjudication); and (6) these various activities are communicated both within the political system, and between the political system and its environment (communication).

Finally, we shall speak of *system maintenance and adaptation functions.* For an automobile to perform efficiently on the road, parts must be lubricated, repaired, and replaced. New parts may perform stiffly; they must be broken in. In a political system the incumbents of the various roles (diplomats, military officers, tax officials) must be recruited to these roles and learn how to perform in them. New roles are created and new personnel 'broken in'. These functions (in machines, maintenance and replacement of parts; in political systems, *socialization* and *recruitment* of people) were discussed earlier in this chapter. They do not directly enter into the conversion processes of the system, but they affect the internal efficiency and propensities of the system, and hence condition its performance.

THE COMPARISON OF POLITICAL SYSTEMS

When we compare classes of political systems with one another, or individual political systems with one another, we need to compare *capabilities, conversion functions,* and *system maintenance and adaptation functions,* and the interrelations among these three kinds, or levels, of functions. When we talk about political development, it will also be in these same terms. A change in capability will be associated with changes in the performance of the conversion functions, and these changes in turn will be related to changes in political socialization and recruitment.

While the individual categories of functions which we use may turn out to be inappropriate when fully tested in empirical cases, this threefold classification of functions is important for political analysis; we believe it will hold up under testing and examination. The theory of the political system will consist of the discovery of the relations between these different levels of functioning — capabilities, conversion functions, and system-maintenance and adaptation functions — and of the relation of the functions at each level.

In country studies we deal with a wide variety of political systems. If we extend our perspective to include the whole of man's experience with politics, we are overwhelmed by the variety of forms, the differences in size and structural pattern, and in kinds of public policy and performance. It may be useful to suggest several common dimensions and characteristics so that we can begin to think about how we can compare, classify, and characterize these systems.

The first common characteristic can be stated concisely: All political systems can be compared in terms of the relationship between functions and structures. That is, in a particular political system at a particular interval of time, there is a given probability that function A will be performed by structure X (*e.g.,* that political demands will be made by associational interest groups). This proposition assumes that all the political functions can, *in some sense,* be found in all political systems, and that all political systems, including the simplest ones, have political structure.

There is no such thing as a society which maintains internal and external order without a political structure of some kind. In very simple political systems the interactions, or the structures, may be occasional or intermittent. They may not be clearly visible, but to say there are no structures would be to argue that the performance of the political functions is random. We may find that in some systems one or a very few structures perform all political functions. The leader of a primitive band may occupy such a dominant position. At the other extreme, in a highly differentiated system, such as that of the United States, political functions may be performed by a very large number of highly specialized structures: communication is dominated by the mass media; political recruitment, by the electoral and party structures; interest articulation, by a large variety of interest groups. However, the great differences between the United States and the primitive band merely represent extreme cases of the range of differentiation of structures. Both systems possess political structures performing political functions, and may be compared in such terms.

Any particular structure may perform more than one function. Just as we must be aware of the presence of political structures in relatively undifferentiated societies, we must also be cautious about assuming that a structure will perform only those functions which the formal rules lead us to expect. Political structures, in short, tend to be *multifunctional,* although the degrees of multifunctionality depends on many factors.

A simple example of multifunctionality can help to illustrate the problem. Typically, public schools are viewed in relation to the political system in terms of their effect on the formation of attitudes and the development of skills among the young. This is, unquestionably, a major impact which the educational structures may have upon the political system. However, schools also affect the recruitment of political elites by expanding or limiting the society's reservoir of skilled manpower. Schools give rise to informal, inter-elite communication patterns through the formation of 'old school ties', and play a key role in communications processes in general, especially in nations with no powerful and independent mass media. Finally, they play important 'input' roles in the political system by giving rise to special communities of interest and laying the basis for interest-group organization. Teachers' unions are an example. Student riots, which have played such an important role in such countries as Turkey, Indonesia, and Korea, illustrate the impact of another school or university-based group.

One can infer from this example that in a nation with relatively few formal and differentiated structures, such organized structures as do appear are likely to be quite multifunctional. While multifunctionality is more obvious in simple, less differentiated societies, it is a universal phenomenon, and is a characteristic of modern bureaucracies and courts as well as of kingships and chieftainships in primitive and traditional societies.

In the discussion of cultural patterns, too sharp a line is often drawn between societies characterized by traditional cultures and those characterized by modern cultures. The modern societies have been presented as secular and rational. Their cultures have been represented as embodying attitude patterns which treat individuals in universalistic fashion, according to their formal and relevant roles rather than according to personal relationships and attributes. The bureaucrat looks with equal favor upon all applicants for services; he does not favor his brother or his cousin. Traditional societies, on the other hand, have been viewed in terms of ascription of particular statuses, and diffuse and particularistic relationships. That is, individuals attain position according to criteria other than their merit (such as status of parents), and personal relationships and informal communication patterns permeate the political process.

However, modern social science research has demonstrated the continuing significance of primary groups (*e.g.,* families, peer groups) and informal organizations in the social processes of Western societies. The first attitude-survey studies of voting provide a classic example.[2] The researchers expected to find that political voting attitudes in modern America were shaped by the modern media of mass communication and by the opinions of those with expertise in relevant areas. Such would be the expected rational pattern. But these studies showed how exaggerated and oversimplified our conception of modern political culture was. We now know that face-to-face communication channels have a continuing vital role in opinion formation, in spite of the presence of the mass media. The typical opinion leader, moreover, is not an expert in a relevant field, but a trusted individual whose political influence is often a diffuse consequence of other roles. (For example, the opinion of a wealthy member of the leading social circle is likely to have great weight with individuals in certain strata, quite apart from any qualifications of special knowledge or even proven judgment.)

Thus, while one cannot question the fact that important differences do exist in the cultural characteristics of traditional and modern systems, any analysis of modern political systems must take account of the continuing importance of the informal and traditional relationships which shape the attitudes and actions of individuals. Therefore, our second major characteristic is: All political systems have mixed political cultures. The most primitive societies have threads of instrumental rationality in their structure and culture. The most modern are permeated by ascriptive, particularistic, and informal relationships and attitudes. They differ in the relative dominance of one against the other and in the pattern of mixture of these components. Secularization is a matter of degree and of the distribution of these 'rational' aspects.

---

[2] See Paul F. Lazarsfeld, Bernard Berelson, and Hazel Gaudet, *The People's Choice* (New York: Duell, Sloan & Pearce Inc., 1944).

4. CHOICES BETWEEN POLITICAL SYSTEMS

D. E. APTER

The analysis that follows brings together the three approaches [normative, structural, behavioral] by centering on models of government, described in terms of two main criteria; degree of hierarchy and type of values. The first is the measure of stringency of control and is structurally visible in the degree of centralization of authority. The second criterion is the degree to which ultimate ends are employed in action, with ultimate ends understood as 'religion' and intermediate ends as 'secularity', following Durkheim's distinction between sacred and secular ends. The extremes of these factors combine to form four models, of which two, the secular-libertarian and the sacred-collectivity, are the most interesting. These two normative models are in perpetual conflict and are constantly in danger of being transformed into each other.

Although we insist on the normative characteristics of these models, with all that that implies in terms of types of authority, the distinctions we will use here accord with most of the comparative schemes that have gained currency today that are based on the degree of pluralism. What might be called the 'pluralism-monism' continuum has proved to be a better basis for determining types of polities than the 'democracy-totalitarianism' continuum because it is somewhat broader and is based on forms of differentiation rather than on the explicit method of government. Competition is another useful criterion. As James S. Coleman has suggested: 'Competitiveness is an essential aspect of political modernity, but not all competitive systems are "modern". . . .'[1] Edward A. Shils has developed a similar classification, in which the modernization

---

[1] See Gabriel Almond and James S. Coleman, *The Politics of the Developing Areas* (Princeton U.P., 1960), p. 533.

process is described as a progressive sharing by the public in an understanding of modern life in such a way that, no longer passive agents acted upon by outside forces, they can utilize their potentialities and their creativity.[2]

These two factors, pluralism and participation, form the basis of almost all the typologies of 'political systems' or 'polities', and each student adopts some variant of these to suit his particular purposes. Morris Janowitz, for example, in his recent study of the military in the developing countries, notes five types: (1) authoritarian-personal control; (2) authoritarian-mass party; (3) democratic competitive and semicompetitive systems; (4) civil-military coalition; and (5) military oligarchy.[3]

The typology I have used accepts the same principles and to that extent is not different from the others. By stressing values and hierarchy, however, I want to emphasize the way people organize society and feel its pull in terms of durable proprieties, rights and wrongs. This approach will reinforce the point that has recently been made by Gabriel Almond and Sidney Verba in their study of the civic culture. The importance of their book for me lies in its advance from typologies based purely on matters of structural differentiation to a typology based on the forms of cognition and meaning that exist in a particular culture. This leads them to the analysis of 'fit' or congruence between the ideals and values of the community and the forms by which it is organized.[4] The problem of congruence, which emerges most clearly in roles, has been the central point of my analysis. Since roles are institutionalized forms of behavior defined by function, both the structural and the behavioral approaches are employed in analysis. The structural deals with the organization of roles and their functional relationships. The behavioral deals with the ideas of right conduct embodied in the roles and the consequences

[2] See Shils, *Political Development in the New States* (The Hague: Mouton, 1962), *passim*. A useful variant of the pluralism-monism continuum is Chalmers Johnson's typology for situations of radical change; see his *Revolution and the Social System* (Stanford, Calif.: Hoover Institution on War, Revolution, and Peace, 1964), no. 3.

[3] See Morris Janowitz, *The Military in the Political Development of New Nations* (Chicago U.P., 1964), p. 5.

[4] See Almond and Verba, *The Civic Culture: Political Attitudes and Democracy in Five Nations* (Princeton U.P., 1963), chap. i.

of those ideas in the formation of personalities.[5] Any complete analysis necessarily includes both these aspects. As I use the terms, the behavioral approach deals with *which* choices are made by groups or individuals and *why;* the structural approach delineates *what* choices are possible.

To incorporate both structural differentiation and cognitive evaluation in a highly generalized manner is a difficult task. The following approach seems feasible. If we consider the two main variables discussed above, hierarchy and values, we obtain the typology of authority types given in Figure 1.

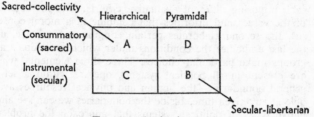

FIG. 1. — Authority types

Types *A* and *B* are derivative of the pure normative models, the sacred-collectivity and the secular-libertarian, and are the polar opposites in this general formulation. As I have already suggested, they are more often than not in conflict with one another. The other two, *C* and *D*, may be described as historically significant, and perhaps practical, alternatives to the two major conflicting forms. Type *A* may be called a mobilization system, and *B* a reconciliation system. Category *C* does not have a convenient name. Subtypes might be called modernizing autocracies or neomercantilist societies. Category *D* is equally difficult to label, but its subtypes may be called theocracies. The last model is most helpful in analyzing traditional societies and will be used explicitly in [this work],

---

[5] The best discussion of the explicitly structural aspect of roles is S. F. Nadel, *The Theory of Social Structure* (Glencoe: Free Press of Glencoe, Ill., 1957). Discussion of the behavioral aspect is to be found in T. M. Newcomb, *Social Psychology* (New York: Dryden Press, 1950), chap. ix. The most important effort to combine these two dimensions of analysis remains Talcott Parsons', *The Social System* (Glencoe: Free Press of Glencoe, Ill., 1951), *passim;* and T. Parsons, Robert F. Bales, and Edward A. Shils, *Working Papers in the Theory of Action* (Glencoe: Free Press of Glencoe, Ill., 1953).

whereas the other three can be used in the study of most modernizing cases. Type *C*, for example, would include 'Kemalism' and the 'Neo-Bismarckian' types now gaining considerable currency in the literature. Type *D* includes feudal systems.

Each of these types is first a normative system organized around certain structural features and incorporating particular styles of political life and civic action. Most important of all, each of these political systems defines the conditions of choice differently. Three approaches can be used to examine such conditions — normative, structural, and behavioral — each imposing different evaluative criteria. The first consists of the values and priorities that combine in a moral consensus, the second elaborates certain conditions of choice, and the last embodies the conditions under which individuals and groups make particular choices. These three elements, which are present in all political systems, operate within a set of general boundaries — the human and physical resources available at any given time. Inside the boundaries we can see alternative types of political systems that approach the problems of modernization somewhat differently. The extreme model, type *B*, may, as we have said, be called the secular-libertarian; *it is a perfect information model.* Its opposite, type *A*, is the sacred-collectivity, *a perfect coercion model.* Between these two extremes the other types have proved to be accommodated or mixed systems of choice.[6]

Let me consider type *B* as a normative system. It can be observed to be analogous to the marketplace. Individual minds within the system become independent units that act upon the external world in order to make it conform to their perception of meaning. Individual minds are, in summation, the means by which the external world is given subjective meaning; yet the objectification of these subjective meanings is the basis of scientific knowledge. Toleration, leading to debate

---

[6] The best short introduction to the immediate problems of analysis is contained in Karl W. Deutsch's *The Nerves of Government* (New York: Free Press of Glencoe, 1963). See also Wilbert E. Moore, *Social Change* (Englewood Cliffs, N.J.: Prentice-Hall Inc., 1963). The most important and explicit statement of structural-functional requisite analysis is in Marion J. Levy, Jr., *The Structure of Society* (Princeton U.P., 1952). See also Juan J. Linz, 'An Authoritarian Regime: Spain', in E. Allardt and Y. Littunen (eds.), *Cleavages, Ideologies and Party Systems* (Helsinki: Westermarck Society, 1964), pp. 291–301.

and competition in ideas, is the way to discover truths. Policy is a form of truth for the members of a community. Just as one's person is property and must be safeguarded, so one's mind is sacred and must be free. Ideas are derivations from empirical phenomena and must be tested competitively with other ideas in order to establish truth. And the establishment of truth is the aim of science. Hence, the libertarian model is essentially an extension of the rationalism of the market-place, with the atomistic, competitive, and free play of ideas controlled only by a legal constitutional mechanism that prevents any group from obtaining a monopoly of power.[7] Its principle of legitimacy is *equity,* and its main emphasis is on allocation.

The limits on this normative type are many. Just as the pure theory of competition in economics does not accurately describe the real world, neither does the secular-libertarian model correspond to an existing political system. Just as, in the first instance, there are monopolies and oligopolies through which a few firms control the market, so, in the case of politics, there are classes and interest groups that wield superior power and give exceptional opportunities to some at the expense of others.

The structural defect in this normative type in large-scale and complex societies is the ineffectiveness of individual representation. Indeed, the liberal critique of modern society is that modern industrial enterprise has created such conditions of political inequality that individual representation is rendered meaningless. Early Marxism, for example, is essentially an attack on inequalities; it ascribes the failure of the representational system to inequalities arising in the economic sphere. Workers have become subdued to the discipline of the machine, subordinated in political as well as in economic terms, brutalized, and alienated from society. Marx's fame was instantaneous because his critique of the prevailing system was not only drastic but intellectually very powerful. For him, the problem was not merely that the liberal market system did not work in practice; he came to feel it could not work, in

---

[7] The idea of power in this system is the zero-sum approach. There is a given amount of it in the system, and if one group gains more, that of others decreases correspondingly. See Talcott Parsons, 'On the Concept of Political Power', *Proceedings of the American Philosophical Society,* CVII (June 1963).

either economic or political life. Indeed, even the ethic appeared a vast deception — not scientific but antiscientific. Accordingly, the new science would begin by formulating certain principles of political and social conduct that would serve as universal rules for analyzing the evolutionary aspects of history. The morality of society was to be realized in an evolutionary way when economic groups were deprived of their special privileges, or more specifically, when economic classes disappeared. Indeed, liberal toleration of other systems than the libertarian begins with this critique. Today we can see that there are other problems than the ineffectiveness of the representation system.

In fact, the Marxist critique created a new moral ideology that concedes that some men, having gained a superior insight into themselves and their institutions, both as scientific and moral beings, must realize this superior knowledge in a system of authority. Men of superior intellect who emancipate themselves from the limitations of their own class outlook and the knowledge of their day — by having a scientific understanding of social life — are the ones who must establish the new collectivity. To be scientific is to know these principles and to work for their realization.

This is the basis of the modern collectivist community (the sacred-collectivity type): the generation of new power through unity, the unfolding of a moral and scientific personality through the mystique of developing toward a higher plane. Politically, one would not want to represent the people as they are, because 'as they are' is debased by the imperfections of the society. Here the principle of legitimacy is *potentiality*, and its main emphasis is on development. It is not surprising, therefore, that many political leaders of modernizing nations are attracted to the Marxian view.

PART TWO

BASES OF POLITICAL SYSTEMS

5. NATIONAL POLITICAL DEVELOPMENT: MEASUREMENT AND ANALYSIS*

P. CUTRIGHT

Large scale comparative studies of national political systems offer the social scientist a methodology of great analytic power if only proper use can be made of the material at hand. In this article we examine in some detail a single sociological effort to apply the comparative method to national political systems.

Perhaps the best known and most articulate effort by a sociologist to deal empirically with a large number of contemporary national political systems is that of Seymour M. Lipset.[1] Lipset establishes two groupings of national political

From *American Sociological Review,* April 1963. We are grateful to the author and to the American Sociological Association for permission to reproduce this extract.

* It is a pleasure to acknowledge the support of the Faculty Research Committee of Dartmouth College. A Ford Foundation Public Affairs grant to Dartmouth College also aided the execution of this research. I was greatly stimulated by and am indebted to Robert A. Dentler for his advice, encouragement and helpful criticism during the initial and final stages of the study. Robert Sokol gave the manuscript a careful reading. My thanks to Robert Van Dam, Lawrence Stifler, Kimberly Holtorff and the other students who helped in the collection of some of the materials. The views expressed here in no way reflect the opinion of the Social Security Administration.

[1] Seymour M. Lipset, 'Some Social Requisites of Democracy: Economic Development and Political Legitimacy', *American Political Science Review,* 53 (March 1959), pp. 69–105. See also Lyle W. Shannon, 'Is Level of Development Related to Capacity for Self-Government?' *American Journal of Economics and Sociology,* 17 (July 1958), pp. 367–82, and a follow-up study also by Shannon, 'Socio-economic Development and Demographic Variables as Predictors of Political Change', *Sociological Quarterly,* III (January 1962), pp. 27–43. Leo F. Schnore's 'The Statistical Measurement of Urbanization and Economic Development', *Land Economics,* XXXVII (August 1961), pp. 229–45, contains an

systems, stable and unstable democracies, and popular and elite based dictatorships. He then poses the question: What differences in national economic development might explain why a nation would be in one group and not in the other?[2] To answer this question he offers a number of indicators of wealth, industrialization, education, and urbanization. (He does not combine indicators to form a scale of wealth or industrialization, or economic development, although development forms one-half of the central theme of the paper. The other half, 'democracy', is not scaled either.)

Lipset presents the statistical means for the nations in each of the two political groups (stable democratic as opposed to all other forms of government) in two areas of the world, the English-speaking and European areas and the Latin American area. A sample of his analysis of these means is instructive: Among the English-speaking and European stable democracies the average number of telephones per 1,000 persons (a 'wealth' indicator) is 205 compared to only 58 per 1,000 in 'European and English-speaking unstable democra-

---

assessment of the relationship among a number of different non-political indicators of national development we will use in this paper.

[2] Ratings by a single expert or by panels of experts, averaging the opinions of judges concerning their opinions on the condition of the press, political freedoms, etc., are of less value than a more objective indicator of political development. Careful examination of Russell H. Fitzgibbons, 'A Statistical Evaluation of Latin American Democracy', *Western Political Quarterly*, 9 (1956), pp. 607–19, as well as Lipset's attempt to place nations in 'democratic' or what amounts to 'undemocratic' clusters, reveal the problems of this method of subjective evaluation. The shift in the rank order (by experts) of the Latin American nations across time periods allows the person using the index to take his pick of the democratic and undemocratic nations. A more crucial point is the lack of agreement among raters concerning the rank order and, with larger numbers of nations, the necessity to abandon subjective evaluations and turn to objective indicators — what expert can be in intimate contact with the political histories of all the nations of the world and also be willing or able to order them on simple scales, let alone multiple dimensions? We can devise statistical and objective methods of measuring political development, just as the economist does when he asks about energy consumption per capita and not what an expert believes the whole economy of a nation has been doing over the past year. This implies that we can also remove ourselves from the world of ethnocentric judgments about the goodness or evil of political systems and turn to other aspects of political systems in order to understand them.

cies and dictatorships'. Similar differences favoring democratic nations is revealed for all of the indicators of wealth, industrialization, urbanization and education among the English-speaking and European groups and, also, among Latin American democracies and non-democracies.

Lipset seeks to show the effect of economic development on national political systems. This statistical effect is given as proof that a strong relationship exists. However, comparison of means between two groups may show a difference without telling us the strength of the association between the independent variables that are presumably responsible for the observed difference between the two groups. Thus Lipset notes that stable democracies have 205 telephones per 1,000 persons compared to only 58 per 1,000 in non-democratic nations and infers that there is a 'strong' relationship or association between this indicator of national wealth and the type of political system observed.

To give a little more depth to his claims, Lipset presents the ranges for each indicator. Here some curious findings appear. The first and most obvious is that the means between the two types of national governments differ, yet the spread in the values on almost every indicator is so extreme that it appears that it would be very difficult to place a single nation in either the democratic or non-democratic category knowing, for example, only its score on the number of telephones. In the European and English-speaking stable democracies a nation may have from 43 to 400 telephones per 1,000 population while a European dictatorship may have as few as 7 or as many as 196 per 1,000. One wonders about the stable European democracies that have only 43, 60, 90, 130, 150 or even 195 telephones. How do they manage while dictatorial European nations can at the same time have as many as 196 per 1,000? More striking is the case of Latin American *democracies* in which the average number of telephones is 25 and the range is from 12 to 58. The number of telephones in Latin American democracies seems paltry when compared to the number of telephones in European dictatorships. European dictatorships have, on the average, double the number of telephones (and 'wealth' and 'economic development') of Latin American democracies.

Such a peculiarity can exist for a number of reasons. The first may be a failure to develop a scale of 'democracy' that could approximate the scale on which all the independent variables are defined. A nation is either democratic or it is not, according to the Lipset scoring system. It makes little difference that in the verbal discussion of national political systems one talks about shades of democracy if, in the statistical assessment, one cannot distinguish among nations. However, one cannot distinguish among national political systems without a scoring system that assigns values to different nations according to some stated criteria. Although Lipset states his criteria he does not differentiate between France and Albania, Brazil or Chile. We would be better able to assess his descriptive statistics if the dependent variables — the national political system — had been indexed or scaled.

A second reason is a lack of adequate conceptualization of national political systems. A value laden curiosity about democracies and dictatorships is no substitute for theoretical focus. A theoretical focus means one has a hypothesis to test using a set of predicting variables that are 'given' by the theoretical scheme. Lipset seeks to test the hypothesis that democracy will flourish in nations where wealth is distributed rather equally and in which large masses of starving or near starving farmers and workers are not dominated by an elite of wealth and aristocracy. Do populations with a relatively high standard of living possess the 'self restraint' necessary to sustain 'democratic institutions'? Do impoverished masses languish under an elite dictatorship which further represses them or do they support tyrants (in which they give popular support to a dictatorship) who repress them? Lipset makes no distinction between the varieties of 'democratic' or non-democratic political systems. His working hypothesis asks only whether or not a significant difference on each economic indicator exists between nations with two types of political characteristics. When the hypothesis is confirmed he explains the finding through discussion of what people want or what the effects of education might be on self-restraint.

The concept of social change does not appear in Lipset's analysis of his data but he refers to studies by Schnore and Lerner in which statistical assessment of the interdependence of many of the same indicators used by Lipset is demonstrated and, in the case of Lerner, some links between education, communication, urbanization, economic development and individual political participation are tentatively established.[3] Lerner's analysis is, however, restricted to the Middle East.

RESEARCH OBJECTIVES AND HYPOTHESIS

In the first part of this paper we develop an index of political development. The index of political development is operationally defined. The concept that guided construction of the index can be stated simply — a politically developed nation has more complex and specialized national political institutions than a less politically developed nation. Degree of political development can be measured and each nation can be placed on a continuum of development, which will allow it to be compared with any other nation in the world. Operationally we bank heavily on the role played by political parties in national political life in measuring political development.[4]

The principal hypothesis tested is that political institutions are interdependent with educational systems, economic de-

---

[3] See Daniel Lerner, *The Passing of Traditional Society*, Glencoe: The Free Press, 1958.

[4] The index is, of course, heavily dependent upon available data. The selection among alternative items for the index was guided by the coherent interpretation of Max Weber's political sociology as given by Reinhard Bendix, *Max Weber: An Intellectual Portrait*, Garden City: Doubleday, 1960.

The primary source for the materials used in this study was the *Political Handbook of the World: Parliaments, Parties and Press,* published annually for the Council on Foreign Relations, New York: Harper and Brothers, from 1940 through 1961. Needed supplementary checks were secured by reference to the *Encyclopedia Britannica* and other reference works. Nations included for study are listed in Table 2. With the exception of nations located in Africa, nations recognized by the United Nations as being 'independent' nations in the 1960 *Statistical Yearbook* were included in this study. A few very small nations (Monaco, Liechtenstein, Andorra) were omitted. Nearly 100 per cent of the populations of all continents except Africa are thus included. The decision to omit Africa was based on the well known statistical effect of artificially inflated relationships when a large number of the cases cluster at one or both ends of the regression line. Including African nations would have inflated our correlations because they would have clustered in one corner of the scattergram. Until we develop a more sensitive measure of political development and also accumulate accurate information on the social and economic conditions in most African nations it seemed reasonable to exclude them from this initial study. A total of 77 independent nations are included.

velopment, communications systems, urbanization, and labor force distribution. A nation's economic system can develop only if its educational system keeps pace, if people concentrate in urban areas, if communication and transportation systems emerge and if changes occur in family and social life that induce people to fit into the demands of the unfolding system. Schnore has measured the interdependence among certain of these factors.[5] But to test the hypothesis that political institutions are not set apart from the rest of a society's social institutions we must construct an index of political development and then test the hypothesis by assessing the association between political development and other measures of national systems.

CONSTRUCTING AN INDEX OF POLITICAL DEVELOPMENT

The following items were selected and given the weights indicated. The time period covered by the data is 1940 through 1960. The score each nation received for the first year was added to the score it received the following year to get a cumulative total score.

A scheme for scoring the nations (in which high scores mean high development) should penalize each nation for po-

---

[5] For a matrix of rank order correlations of a number of indicators of these variables see Schnore, op. cit., p. 236. Schnore's correlations tend to be slightly higher than product moment correlations using the T scoring method, but slight differences in the case base included may account for such differences.

See also Alex Inkeles, 'National Character and Modern Political Systems', Francis L. K. Hsu (ed.), in *Psychological Anthropology*, Homewood, Illinois: The Dorsey Press, 1961, pp. 172–208. He reviews various approaches to this topic and cites studies which suggest connections between national character and modern political systems. However, no conclusions can be drawn from this body of work in part because it lacks a standard measure of political systems against which different national characters might be associated. For a definite point of view on the subject of the importance of personality to social change generally and economic and political change in particular, see Everett E. Hagen, *On the Theory of Social Change*, Homewood, Illinois: The Dorsey Press, 1962. Hagen's theory has the virtue of being testable but he presents little supporting evidence himself—again, in part, because the evidence simply does not exist. In rejecting economic theories of social change Hagen swings to psychological explanations, but does not completely bypass sociological perspectives.

litical instability which represents 'backsliding' and reward it for achieving or retaining more complex political forms of organization. Points for any one year were awarded in the following manner.

1. Legislative Branch of Government.

> Two points for each year in which a parliament existed in which the lower or the only chamber contained representatives of two or more political parties and the minority party or parties had at least 30 per cent of all seats. One point for each year in which a parliament existed whose members were the representatives of one or more political parties, but where the '30 per cent rule' was violated. No points for each year no parliament existed or for years when either of the above types of parliaments was abolished or discarded by executive power. Parliaments whose members are not members of political parties are given a zero. Parliaments that are not self-governing bodies (e.g., the mock parliaments of colonial governments) are given a zero.

2. Executive Branch of Government.

> One point for each year the nation was ruled by a chief executive who was in office by virtue of direct vote in an open election where he faced competition or was selected by a political party in a multi-party system, as defined by the conditions necessary to get 2 points on the legislative branch indicator above. If the parliament ceased being a multi-party parliament because of executive action, the chief executive stopped getting points. One half point each year the chief executive was not selected by virtue of his hereditary status but was selected by criteria other than those necessary to attain one point as given above. Colonial governments receive one half point per year. No points if the nation was governed by a hereditary ruler.

It is possible for a nation to acquire no points, one half or 1 point depending on the selection of the chief executive. The combined index has a range of zero to 3 points per year. Over the 21 year period of our study it would be possible for a nation to have a total raw score between zero and 63 points.

RELATIONSHIP OF POLITICAL TO OTHER MEASURES OF NATIONAL DEVELOPMENT

This study began with the aim of measuring the degree of association between political development and other types of socio-economic development. The objective was a statistical assessment of the degree of association between educational development, urbanization, communication development, economic growth and labor force characteristics and the measure of political development.[6] A statistical statement of the proportion of the variation around the mean of the political development index that could be accounted for by covariation with selected independent variables was also sought. Finally, if the association was reasonably close one might build a prediction equation which would describe for each nation whether its level of political development was commensurate with the values it had on the independent variables in a prediction equation.

Of the several independent variables considered, the communications development index[7] had a Pearson zero order association with political development of .81.[8] The communica-

---

[6] Social-economic statistics used in this report were drawn from the last reporting year from the following United Nations sourcebooks: *Demographic Yearbook, 1960, Statistical Yearbook, 1960,* and *Report on the World Social Situation, 1957. The Yearbook of Labor Statistics, 1960,* was the source for labor force statistics.

Statistical assessment followed T scoring of all data. A simple technique for computing the T score is given in Allen E. Edwards, *Statistical Methods for the Behavioral Sciences,* New York: Holt, Rinehart & Winston, 1954. For a single item, T scoring of the raw data will yield a mean of 50 and a standard deviation of 10. If we add items together to form an index, four items with a sum of 200 represents a subject (or nation) with an average index score. All single item indicators and combined indices in this paper have been T scored. The original T scoring was done for all independent and territorial political divisions in the world (excluding most Pacific Island dependent territories) for which data was available. Thus the T score for newsprint consumption is based on a case base of 93 and not the 77 nations reported here. This fact accounts for the small departures in Table 1 of means and standard deviations one would expect from T scoring.

[7] The communications development index is formed by summing the T scores a given nation received on newspaper consumption, newsprint consumption, telephones and the number of pieces of domestic mail per capita. If one or two indicators of the four were missing we took the average of the two or three available indicators and added their scores to estimate the total index score. Five of the 77 nations had less than two communications indicators and their scores were estimated and used in the prediction equation developed later in the paper.

[8] Variables considered but not included in the matrix because of high intercorrelations with variables in the matrix were an economic develop-

tions development index is tightly related to an index of economic development (.95) but is a better predictor of political development than is economic development.[9] The communications index reflects the ability and the need of national systems to maintain differing types of communication systems depending on the varying degrees of literacy of their population and varying levels of integration of the economic and social order.

The relationship between national communications development and political development may be seen in graphic form in Figure 1.

This scattergram makes the correlation coefficient more meaningful. The communication development scores on the horizontal axis increase from left to right. The political development scores are on the vertical axis and increase vertically.

The most striking thing about the Figure 1 is the steady increase in the level of political development as the level of communication development increases. The main diagonal is the *regression line*. If every nation's scores were such as to put it exactly on that line, the correlation coefficient would be 1.00. We see, however, that some nations are above the line and some are below. What is the difference? A nation below the line is politically underdeveloped relative to its given level of communication development.[10] The difference

---

ment index and the industrial labor force index. Economic development was measured by combining the T scores for a given nation of per capita measures of: energy consumption, steel consumption, income in U.S. dollars and the number of motor vehicles. These items are all highly intercorrelated: See Schnore, op. cit. p. 236.

[9] Product moment correlation of communication development against political development was .81 compared to .68 for economic development against political development.

[10] Our use of the terms politically over- or underdeveloped should not be understood as a judgment of what the nation should have from a moral or ethical point of view. A politically underdeveloped nation lacks sufficient points which it could obtain only if it met the criteria set by our political development index. In severe cases it may lack any political party or even a parliament. Our statements of whether or not a nation is underdeveloped or overdeveloped are not made with sole reference to its score of the political development index — a nation is either high, low or in between on the index. This judgment is made with reference to the political development score the nation should have *relative* to its level of communications development. Thus a nation with a one party

between the communication index scores that the politically overdeveloped nations (above the line) really have and what they would have if they were on the regression line may represent the extent of possible imbalance in the social system of the nation.

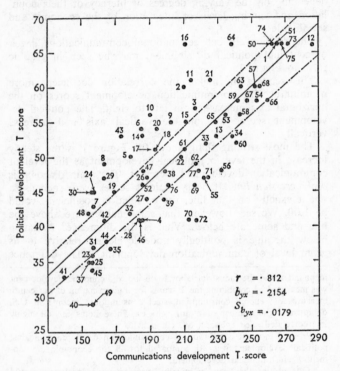

FIG. 2. — *Relationship of Communications Development to Political Development*

Nations below the line face alternative routes to the line. They can increase their level of political development and rise vertically to the line or they can decrease their communi-

system may actually be overdeveloped politically relative to its communications system or its level of urbanization and other measures of national growth.

cations and move to the left until they meet the line — maintaining or perhaps decreasing their level of political development. Such movements as this may seem unlikely to people living in a society in which communication systems are believed to increase steadily, but alternative (even 'impossible') movements can occur during revolutions, civil wars and territorial occupation by a foreign power, or through economic disasters. Internal social change may be violent or not, but in any case should result in movement of predictable direction.

Mathematical models have been considered[11] which might be applied to data like these to test the notion that there will be movement toward the line. Empirical testing would be the only way to state whether nations do in fact increase or decrease either variable in order to come into equilibrium. However, if measurements are made each year for a period of

TABLE 1. Matrix of Correlations of National Measures of Political Development, and Levels of Communication, Urbanization, Education and Employment in Agriculture: N = 77

	2	3	4	5	Means	S.D.
1. Communication	74	88	−86	81	204.5	36.4
2. Urbanization	—	77	−75	69	49.9	8.2
3. Education		—	−78	74	105.8	16.7
4. Agriculture			—	72	53.1	10.5
5. Political Development				—	49.9	9.7

$$\hat{Y} = 3.7 + 0.172X_1 + 0.232X_2 + 0.003X_3 + -0.014X_4$$
$$R_y 0.1234 = 0.82$$

Modified prediction equation used:

$$\hat{Y} = 1.97 + 0.1789X_1 + 0.2274X_2$$
$$R_y 0.12 = 0.82$$

The communications index summed the T scores of newspaper readers *per capita,* newsprint consumption *per capita,* the volume of domestic mail *per capita* and the number of telephones *per capita.*

The urbanization index is the T score of the proportion of the population of the nation living in cities over 100,000. The education index was formed by combining T scores of literacy with T scores of the number of students per 100,000 enrolled in institutions of

[11] See James S. Coleman, 'The Mathematical Study of Small Groups', in Herbert Soloman (ed.), *Mathematical Thinking in the Measurement of Behavior,* Glencoe: The Free Press, 1960, pp. 26–30.

higher education, and the proportion of the economically active labor force employed in agriculture was also T scored.

Political development scores were T scored.

Correlations in this matrix use estimated values when no data was available. Although political development values were available for each nation, urban data was missing in 2 of the 77 cases, communication scores in 5, education lacked 4 national scores and agriculture was missing in 18 cases. Estimates were based on the regression of a known value for a nation on the unknown, using regression weights for all of the nations on which data was available. These estimates were then used in the prediction equation.

years, the movement of nations can be precisely plotted. If empirical tests do not show nations moving toward their equilibrium point, then it is also possible that the same test will reveal different equilibrium points for nations in different socio-economic conditions. We have conveniently assumed a common set of equilibrium points rather than several (one could have had several equilibrium points simply if different clusters of nations had different regression lines, a possibility to be explored in later research).

The inability of our index to actually distinguish for every nation the refinements of political development, the missing data and substitution of estimates for five communication scores, the mis-reporting of political information — all of these types of error exist and should be considered before refined explanations of minor deviations from the line are attempted.[12] For the benefit of students who may wish to consider these possibilities, the nations that lie between the two broken lines

---

[12] In Figure 1 we have drawn broken lines on either side of the regression line we actually observed for the 77 nations. For these data the sample estimate of the standard error of the regression coefficient can be applied to describe what is a 'small' and what is a 'large' departure from the regression line. The broken lines on each side of the regression line represent the range of alternative regression lines that would be likely to occur if we were drawing a sample of 77 from a larger population. Although these statistical conditions are not met in this case, the use of a high and a low estimate of alternative regression coefficients establishes a hypothetical band which may help us sort out errors of measurement and other types of error that may result in moving a nation several points away from the line when actually it should be closer to it. Measurement errors may also place a nation on the line when it ought not to be there, but this is less likely than the former movement which decreases   correlations.

in Figure 1 may be considered as being off the regression line because of measurement and other errors; hence attention may be devoted to nations that are outside the bands for deviant case analysis or comparison of extreme cases on either side of the line.

6. IMPLICATIONS OF SOCIAL MOBILIZATION FOR THE POLITICS OF DEVELOPMENT

K. W. DEUTSCH

In whatever country it occurs, social mobilization brings with it an expansion of the politically relevant strata of the population. These politically relevant strata are a broader group than the elite: they include all those persons who must be taken into account in politics. Dock workers and trade union members in Ghana, Nigeria, or the United States, for instance, are not necessarily members of the elites of these countries, but they are quite likely to count for something in their political life. In the developing countries of Asia, Africa and parts of Latin America, the political process usually does not include the mass of isolated, subsistence-farming, tradition-bound and politically apathetic villagers, but it does include increasingly the growing numbers of city dwellers, market farmers, users of money, wage earners, radio listeners and literates in town and country. The growth in the numbers of these people produces mounting pressures for the transformation of political practices and institutions; and since this future growth can be estimated at least to some extent on the basis of trends and data from the recent past, some of the expectable growth in political pressures — we may call it the potential level of political tensions — can likewise be estimated.

Social mobilization also brings about a change in the quality of politics, by changing the range of human needs that impinge upon the political process. As people are uprooted from their physical and intellectual isolation in their immediate localities, from their old habits and traditions, and often from their old patterns of occupation and places of residence, they experience drastic changes in their needs. They may now

From the *American Political Science Review*, September 1961, pp. 497–502. We are grateful to the author and editors of the *Review* for permission to reproduce this extract.

come to need provisions for housing and employment, for social security against illness and old age, for medical care against the health hazards of their crowded new dwellings and places of work and the risk of accidents with unfamiliar machinery. They may need succor against the risks of cyclical or seasonal unemployment, against oppressive charges of rent or interest, and against sharp fluctuations in the prices of the main commodities which they must sell or buy. They need instruction for themselves and education for their children. They need, in short, a wide range and large amounts of new government services.

These needs ordinarily cannot be met by traditional types of government, inherited from a precommercial and preindustrial age. Maharajahs, sultans, sheikhs and chieftains all are quite unlikely to cope with these new problems, and traditional rule by land-owning oligarchies or long established religious bodies most often is apt to prove equally disappointing in the face of the new needs. Most of the attempts to change the characteristics of the traditional ruling families — perhaps by supplying them with foreign advisers or by having their children study in some foreign country — are likely to remain superficial in their effects, overshadowed by mounting pressures for more thoroughgoing changes.

In developing countries of today, however, the increasingly ineffective and unpopular traditional authorities cannot be replaced successfully by their historic successors in the Western world, the classic institutions of 18th and 19th century liberalism and laissez-faire. For the uprooted, impoverished and disoriented masses produced by social mobilization, it is surely untrue that that government is best that governs least. They are far more likely to need a direct transition from traditional government to the essentials of a modern welfare state. The developing countries of Asia, Africa and parts of Latin America may have to accomplish, therefore, within a few decades a process of political change which in the history of Western Europe and North America took at least as many generations; and they may have to accomplish this accelerated change almost in the manner of a jump, omitting as impractical some of the historic stages of transition through a period of near laissez-faire that occurred in the West.

The growing need for new and old government services usually implies persistent political pressures for an increased scope of government and a greater relative size of the government sector in the national economy. In the mid-1950s, the total government budget — national, regional and local — tended to amount to roughly 10 per cent of the gross national product in the very poor and poorly mobilized countries with annual per capita gross national products at or below $100. For highly developed and highly mobilized countries, such as those with per capita gross national products at or above $900, the corresponding proportion of the total government sector was about 30 per cent. If one drew only the crudest and most provisional inference from these figures, one might expect something like a 2.5 per cent shift of national income into the government sector for every $100 gain in per capita gross national product in the course of economic development. It might be more plausible, however, to expect a somewhat more rapid expansion of the government sector during the earlier stages of economic development, but the elucidation of this entire problem — with all its obvious political implications — would require and reward a great deal more research.

The relationship between the total process of social mobilization and the growth of the national income, it should be recalled here, is by no means symmetrical. Sustained income growth is very unlikely without social mobilization, but a good deal of social mobilization may be going on even in the absence of per capita income growth, such as occurs in countries with poor resources or investment policies, and with rapid population growth. In such cases, social mobilization still would generate pressures for an expansion of government services and hence of the government sector, even in a relatively stagnant or conceivably retrograde economy. Stopping or reversing in such cases the expansion of government or the process of social mobilization behind it — even if this could be done — hardly would make matters much better. The more attractive course for such countries might rather be to use the capabilities of their expanding governments so as to bring about improvements in their resources and investment policies, and an eventual resumption of economic growth. To what extent this has been, or could be, brought about in cases of this kind, would make another fascinating topic for study.

The figures just given apply, of course, only to non-Communist countries; the inclusion of Communist states would make the average in each class of government sectors higher. It would be interesting to investigate, however, whether and to what extent the tendency toward the relative expansion of the government sector in the course of social mobilization applies also, *mutatis mutandis,* to the Communist countries.

A greater scope of governmental services and functions requires ordinarily an increase in the capabilities of government. Usually it requires an increase in the numbers and training of governmental personnel, an increase in governmental offices and institutions, and a significant improvement in administrative organization and efficiency. A rapid process of social mobilization thus tends to generate major pressures for political and administrative reform. Such reforms may include notably both a quantitative expansion of the bureaucracy and its qualitative improvement in the direction of a competent civil service — even though these two objectives at times may clash.

Similar to its impact on this specific area of government, social mobilization tends to generate also pressures for a more general transformation of the political elite. It tends to generate pressures for a broadening and partial transformation of elite functions, of elite recruitment, and of elite communications. On all these counts, the old elites of traditional chiefs, village headmen, and local notables are likely to prove ever more inadequate; and political leadership may tend to shift to the new political elite of party or quasi-party organizations, formal or informal, legal or illegal, but always led by the new 'marginal men' who have been exposed more or less thoroughly to the impact of modern education and urban life.

Something similar applies to elite communications. The more broadly recruited elites must communicate among themselves, and they must do so more often impersonally and over greater distances. They must resort more often to writing and to paper work. At the same time they must direct a greater part of their communications output at the new political strata; this puts a premium on oratory and journalism, and on skill in the use of all mass media of communication. At the same time rapid social mobilization causes a critical problem in the communications intake of elites. It confronts them with the ever present risk of losing touch with the newly mobilized social strata which until recently still did not count in politics. Prime Minister Nehru's reluctance to take into account the strength and intensity of Mahratti sentiment in the language conflict of Bombay in the 1950s and his general tendency since the mid-1930s to underestimate the strength of communal and linguistic sentiment in India suggest the seriousness of this problem even for major democratic leaders.

The increasing numbers of the mobilized population, and the greater scope and urgency of their needs for political decisions and governmental services, tend to translate themselves, albeit with a time lag, into increased political participation. This may express itself informally through greater numbers of people taking part in crowds and riots, in meetings and demonstrations, in strikes and uprisings, or, less dramatically, as members of a growing audience for political communications, written or by radio, or finally as members of a growing host of organizations. While many of these organizations are ostensibly non-political, such as improvement societies, study circles, singing clubs, gymnastic societies, agricultural and commercial associations, fraternal orders, workmen's benefit societies, and the like, they nevertheless tend to acquire a political tinge, particularly in countries where more open outlets for political activities are not available. But even where there are established political parties and elections, a network of seemingly nonpolitical or marginally political organizations serves an important political function by providing a dependable social setting for the individuals who have been partly or wholly uprooted or alienated from their traditional communities. Such organizations may serve at the same time as marshalling grounds for the entry of these persons into political life.

Where people have the right to vote, the effects of social mobilization are likely to be reflected in the electoral statistics. This process finds its expression both through a tendency towards a higher voting participation of those already enfranchised and through an extension of the franchise itself to additional groups of the population. Often the increase in participation amongst those who already have the right to vote precedes the enfranchisement of new classes of voters, particularly in countries where the broadening of the franchise is occurring gradually. Thus in Norway between 1830 and 1860, voting participation remained near the level of about 10 per cent of the adult male population; in the 1870s and 1880s this participation rose rapidly among the enfranchised voters, followed by extensions of the franchise, until by the year 1900, 40 per cent of the Norwegian men were actually voting. This process was accompanied by a transformation of Norwegian politics, the rise to power of the radical peasant party *Venstre,* and a shift from the earlier acceptance of the existing Swedish-Norwegian Union to rising demands for full Norwegian independence.[1] These political changes had been preceded or accompanied by a rise in several of the usual indicators of social mobilization among the Norwegian people.

Another aspect of the process of social mobilization is the shift of emphasis away from the parochialism and internationalism of many traditional cultures to a preoccupation with the supralocal but far less than worldwide unit of the territorial, and eventually national, state.

An as yet unpublished study of American communications before the American Revolution, which has been carried on by Richard Merritt, shows how during the years 1735–1775 in the colonial newspapers the percentage of American or all-colonial symbols rose from about 10 to about 40 per cent, at the cost, in the main, of a decline in the share of symbols referring to places or events in the world outside the colonies and Britain, while Britain's share in American news attention remained relatively unchanged. Within the group of American symbols, the main increase occurred among those which referred to America or to the colonies as a whole, rather than among those referring to particular colonies or sections.[2]

More recent experiences in some of the 'development countries' also suggest a more rapid rise of attention devoted to national topics than of that given to world affairs, on the one hand, and to purely local matters, on the other. This, however, is at present largely an impression. The nature and extent of attention shifts in mass media, as well as in popular attitudes, in the course of social mobilization is a matter for research that should be as promising as it is needed.[3]

Some data on the flow of domestic and foreign mails point

---

[1] See Raymond Lindgren, *Norway-Sweden: Union, Disunion, Reunion* (Princeton U.P., 1959); and K. W. Deutsch *et al., Political Community and the North Atlantic Area* (Princeton U.P., 1957).

[2] Richard Merritt's monograph, 'Symbols of American Nationalism, 1735–1775', which is to cover eventually one or more newspapers from Massachusetts, New York, Pennsylvania and Virginia, respectively, will be published in due course. [*Symbols of American Community, 1735–1775* (Yale U.P., 1966)—ed. note.]

[3] For examples of pioneering contributions of this kind, see the series of Hoover Institute Studies by Harold Lasswell, Ithiel Pool, Daniel Lerner, and others, and particularly Pool, *The Prestige Papers* (Stanford U.P., 1951).

in a similar direction. Of five development countries for which data are readily available the ratio of domestic to foreign mail rose substantially in four — Egypt, Iran, Nigeria, and Turkey — from 1913 to 1946–51; the fifth, Indonesia, was an exception but was the scene of internal unrest and protracted warfare against the Dutch during much of the latter period. The trend for Egypt, Iran, Nigeria, and Turkey is confirmed in each case by data for the intermediate period 1928–34, which are also intermediate, in each case, between the low domestic-foreign mail ratio for 1913 and the high ratios for 1946–51. Many additional development countries — including the Gold Coast (now Ghana), the Belgian Congo, Malaya, French Morocco, Kenya-Uganda, Tanganyika, Mozambique, and Malaya — for which data were found only for the 1928–34 to 1946–51 comparison, show upward trends in their ratios of domestic to foreign mail.[4] Here again, a relatively moderate investment in the further collection and study of data might lead to interesting results.

According to some data from another recent study, a further side effect of social mobilization and economic development might possibly be first a substantial expansion, and then a lesser but significant reduction, of the share of the international trade sector in the national economy. Thus, in the course of British development, the proportion of total foreign trade (including trade to British overseas possessions) rose from an average of 20 per cent in 1830–40 to a peak of 60 per cent in 1870–79, remained close to that level until 1913, but declined subsequently and stood at less than 40 per cent in 1959. Similarly, the proportion of foreign trade to national income rose in Germany from about 28 per cent in 1802–1830 to a peak of 45 per cent in 1870–79, declined to 35 per cent in 1900–1909, and by 1957 had recovered, for the much smaller German Federal Republic, to only 42 per cent. In Japan, the early proportion of foreign trade to national income was 15 per cent in 1885–89, rising to peaks of 41 per cent in 1915–19 and 40 per cent in 1925–29; but by 1957 it stood at only 31 per cent. Data for Denmark, Norway, France and Argentina give a similar picture, while the same foreign-trade-to-

---

[4] See charts 1, 3, and 4 in Karl W. Deutsch, 'Shifts in the Balance of Communication Flows: A Problem of Measurement in International Relations', *Public Opinion Quarterly*, 20 (Spring 1956), pp. 152–55, based on data of the Universal Postal Union.

national-income ratio in the United States fell, with minor fluctuations, from 23 per cent in 1799 to less than 9 per cent in 1958.[5] Here again the evidence is incomplete and partly contradictory, and the tentative interpretation, indicated at the beginning of this paragraph, still stands in need of confirmation and perhaps modification through additional research.

The problem of the ratio of the sector of internationally oriented economic activities relative to total national income — and thus indirectly the problem of the political power potential of internationally exposed or involved interest groups *vis-a-vis* the rest of the community — leads us to the problem of the size of states and of the scale of effective political communities. As we have seen, the process of social mobilization generates strong pressures towards increasing the capabilities of government, by increasing the volume and range of demands made upon the government and administration, and by widening the scope of politics and the membership of the politically relevant strata. The same process increases the frequency and the critical importance of direct communications between government and governed. It thus necessarily increases the importance of the language, the media, and the channels through which these communications are carried on.

Other things assumed equal, the stage of rapid social mobilization may be expected, therefore, to promote the consolidation of states whose peoples already share the same language, culture, and major social institutions; while the same process may tend to strain or destroy the unity of states whose population is already divided into several groups with different languages or cultures or basic ways of life. By the same token, social mobilization may tend to promote the merging of several smaller states, or political units such as cantons, principalities, sultanates or tribal areas, whose populations already share substantially the same language, culture and social system; and it may tend to inhibit, or at least to make more difficult, the merging of states or political units whose populations or ruling personnel differ substantially in regard to

[5] See Karl W. Deutsch and Alexander Eckstein, 'National Industrialization and the Declining Share of the International Economic Sector, 1890–1957', *World Politics*, 13 (January 1961) pp. 267–99. See also Simon Kuznets, *Six Lectures on Economic Growth* (Glencoe, 1959), esp. the section on 'The Problem of Size' and 'Trends in Foreign Trade Ratios', pp. 89–107.

any of these matters. Social mobilization may thus assist to
some extent in the consolidation of the United Arab Republic,
but raise increasing problems for the politics and administration of multilingual India — problems which the federal government of India may have to meet or overcome by a series
of creative adjustments.[6]

In the last analysis, however, the problem of the scale of
states goes beyond the effects of language, culture, or institutions, important as all these are. In the period of rapid social
mobilization, the acceptable scale of a political unit will tend
to depend eventually upon its performance. If a government
fails to meet the increasing burdens put upon it by the process of social mobilization, a growing proportion of the population is likely to become alienated and disaffected from the
state, even if the same language, culture and basic social institutions were shared originally throughout the entire state
territory by rulers and ruled alike. The secession of the United
States and of Ireland from the British Empire, and of the
Netherlands and of Switzerland from the German Empire
may serve in part as examples. At bottom, the popular acceptance of a government in a period of social mobilization
is most of all a matter of its capabilities and the manner in
which they are used — that is, essentially a matter of its responsiveness to the felt needs of its population. If it proves
persistently incapable or unresponsive, some or many of its
subjects will cease to identify themselves with it psychologically; it will be reduced to ruling by force where it can no
longer rule by display, example and persuasion; and if political alternatives to it appear, it will be replaced eventually
by other political units, larger or smaller in extent, which
at least promise to respond more effectively to the needs and
expectations of their peoples.

In practice the results of social mobilization often have
tended to increase the size of the state, well beyond the old
tribal areas, petty principalities, or similar districts of the

---

[6] For more detailed arguments, see Deutsch, *Nationalism and Social
Communication,* and Deutsch *et al., Political Community and the North
Atlantic Area;* see also the discussions in Ernst B. Haas, 'Regionalism,
Functionalism and Universal Organization', *World Politics,* 8, (January
1956), and 'The Challenge of Regionalism', *International Organization,*
12 (1958), pp. 440–58; and in Stanley Hoffmann, *Contemporary Theory
in International Relations* (Englewood Cliffs, N.J., Prentice-Hall Inc.,
1960), pp. 223–40.

traditional era, while increasing the direct contact between government and governed far beyond the levels of the sociologically superficial and often half-shadowy empire of the past.

This growth in the size of modern states, capable of coping with the results of social mobilization, is counteracted and eventually inhibited, however, as their size increases, by their tendency to increasing preoccupation with their own internal affairs. There is considerable evidence for this trend toward a self-limitation in the growth of states through a decline in the attention, resources and responsiveness available for coping with the implicit needs and explicit messages of the next marginal unit of population and territory on the verge of being included in the expanding state.[7]

The remarks in this section may have sufficed to illustrate, though by no means to exhaust, the significance of the process of social mobilization in the economic and political development of countries. The main usefulness of the concept, however, should lie in the possibility of quantitative study which it offers. How much social mobilization has been occurring in some country per year or per decade during some period of its history, or during recent times? And what is the meaning of the differences between the rates at which some of the constituent subprocesses of social mobilization may have been going on? Although specific data will have to be found separately for each country, it should be possible to sketch a general quantitative model to show some of the interrelations and their possible significance.

---

[7] *Cf.* Karl W. Deutsch, 'The Propensity to International Transactions', *Political Studies*, 8 (June 1960), pp. 147–55.

7. SOCIAL CONFLICT, LEGITIMACY, AND DEMOCRACY

S. M. LIPSET

LEGITIMACY AND EFFECTIVENESS

The stability of any given democracy depends not only on economic development but also upon the effectiveness and the legitimacy of its political system. Effectiveness means actual performance, the extent to which the system satisfies the basic functions of government as most of the population and such powerful groups within it as big business or the armed forces see them. Legitimacy involves the capacity of the system to engender and maintain the belief that the existing political institutions are the most appropriate ones for the society. The extent to which contemporary democratic political systems are legitimate depends in large measure upon the ways in which the key issues which have historically divided the society have been resolved.

While effectiveness is primarily instrumental, legitimacy is evaluative. Groups regard a political system as legitimate or illegitimate according to the way in which its values fit with theirs. Important segments of the German Army, civil service, and aristocratic classes rejected the Weimar Republic, not because it was ineffective, but because its symbolism and basic values negated their own. Legitimacy, in and of itself, may be associated with many forms of political organization, including oppressive ones. Feudal societies, before the advent of industrialism, undoubtedly enjoyed the basic loyalty of most of their members. Crises of legitimacy are primarily a recent historical phenomenon, following the rise of sharp cleavages among groups which are able, because of mass communication, to organize around different values than

From *Political Man*, pp. 77–83. Copyright © 1960 by Seymour Martin Lipset. Reprinted by permission of Doubleday & Co. Inc. and Heinemann, Ltd.

those previously considered to be the only acceptable ones.

A crisis of legitimacy is a crisis of change. Therefore, its roots must be sought in the character of change in modern society. Crises of legitimacy occur during a transition to a new social structure, if (1) the *status* of major conservative institutions is threatened during the period of structural change; (2) all the major groups in the society do not have access to the political system in the transitional period, or at least as soon as they develop political demands. After a new social structure is established, if the new system is unable to sustain the expectations of major groups (on the grounds of 'effectiveness') for a long enough period to develop legitimacy upon the new basis, a new crisis may develop.

Tocqueville gives a graphic description of the first general type of loss of legitimacy, referring mainly to countries which moved from aristocratic monarchies to democratic republics: '. . . epochs sometimes occur in the life of a nation when the old customs of a people are changed, public morality is destroyed, religious belief shaken, and the spell of tradition broken . . .' The citizens then have 'neither the instinctive patriotism of a monarchy nor the reflecting patriotism of a republic; . . . they have stopped between the two in the midst of confusion and distress'.[1]

If, however, the status of major conservative groups and symbols is not threatened during this transitional period, even though they lose most of their power, democracy seems to be much more secure. And thus we have the absurd fact that ten out of the twelve stable European and English-speaking democracies are monarchies.[2] Great Britain, Sweden, Norway, Denmark, the Netherlands, Belgium, Luxembourg, Australia, Canada, and New Zealand are kingdoms, or dominions of a monarch, while the only republics which meet the conditions of stable democratic procedures are the United States and Switzerland, plus Uruguay in Latin America.

---

[1] Alexis de Tocqueville, *Democracy in America,* I (New York: Alfred A. Knopf, Vintage ed., 1945), pp. 251–52.

[2] Walter Lippman in referring to the seemingly greater capacity of the constitutional monarchies than the republics of Europe to 'preserve order with freedom' suggests that this may be because 'in a republic the governing power, being wholly secularized, loses much of its prestige; it is stripped, if one prefers, of all the illusions of intrinsic majesty'. See his *The Public Philosophy* (New York: Mentor Books, 1956), p. 50.

The preservation of the monarchy has apparently retained for these nations the loyalty of the aristocratic, traditionalist, and clerical sectors of the population which resented increased democratization and equalitarianism. And by accepting the lower strata and not resisting to the point where revolution might be necessary, the conservative orders won or retained the loyalty of the new 'citizens'. In countries where monarchy was overthrown by revolution, and orderly succession was broken, forces aligned with the throne have sometimes continued to refuse legitimacy to republican successors down to the fifth generation or more.

The one constitutional monarchy which became a fascist dictatorship, Italy, was, like the French Republic, considered illegitimate by major groups in the society. The House of Savoy alienated the Catholics by destroying the temporal power of the Popes, and was also not a legitimate successor in the old Kingdom of the Two Sicilies. Catholics were, in fact, forbidden by the church to participate in Italian politics until almost World War I, and the church finally rescinded its position only because of its fear of the Socialists. French Catholics took a similar attitude to the Third Republic during the same period. Both the Italian and French democracies have had to operate for much of their histories without loyal support from important groups in their societies, on both the left and the right. Thus one main source of legitimacy lies in the continuity of important traditional integrative institutions during a transitional period in which new institutions are emerging.

The second general type of loss of legitimacy is related to the ways in which different societies handle the 'entry into politics' crisis – the decision as to when new social groups shall obtain access to the political process. In the nineteenth century these new groups were primarily industrial workers; in the twentieth, colonial elites and peasant peoples. Whenever new groups become politically active (e.g., when the workers first seek access to economic and political power through economic organization and the suffrage, when the *bourgeoisie* demand access to and participation in government, when colonial elites insist on control over their own system), easy access to the *legitimate* political institutions tends to win the loyalty of the new groups to the system, and they in turn can permit the old dominating strata to maintain their own status. In nations like Germany where access was denied for prolonged periods, first to the *bourgeoisie* and later to the workers, and where force was used to restrict access, the lower strata were alienated from the system and adopted extremist ideologies which, in turn, kept the more established groups from accepting the workers' political movement as a legitimate alternative.

Political systems which deny new strata access to power except by revolution also inhibit the growth of legitimacy by introducing millennial hopes into the political arena. Groups which have to push their way into the body politic by force are apt to overexaggerate the possibilities which political participation affords. Consequently, democratic regimes born under such stress not only face the difficulty of being regarded as illegitimate by groups loyal to the *ancien régime* but may also be rejected by those whose millennial hopes are not fulfilled by the change. France, where right-wing clericalists have viewed the Republic as illegitimate and sections of the lower strata have found their expectations far from satisfied, is an example. And today many of the newly independent nations of Asia and Africa face the thorny problem of winning the loyalties of the masses to democratic states which can do little to meet the utopian objectives set by nationalist movements during the period of colonialism and the transitional struggle to independence.

In general, even when the political system is reasonably effective, if at any time the status of major conservative groups is threatened, or if access to politics is denied to emerging groups at crucial periods, the system's legitimacy will remain in question. On the other hand, a breakdown of effectiveness, repeatedly or for a long period, will endanger even a legitimate system's stability.

A major test of legitimacy is the extent to which given nations have developed a common 'secular political culture', mainly national rituals and holidays.[3] The United States has developed a common homogeneous culture in the veneration accorded the Founding Fathers, Abraham Lincoln, Theodore Roosevelt, and their principles. These common elements, to which all American politicians appeal, are not present in all democratic societies. In some European countries, the left and the right have a different set of symbols and different

---

[3] See Gabriel Almond, 'Comparative Political Systems', *Journal of Politics*, 18 (1956), pp. 391–409.

historical heroes. France offers the clearest example of such a nation. Here battles involving the use of different symbols which started in 1789 are, as Herbert Luethy points out, 'still in progress, and the issue is still open; every one of these dates [of major political controversy] still divides left and right, clerical and anti-clerical, progressive and reactionary, in all their historically determined constellations'.[4]

Knowledge concerning the relative degree of legitimacy of a nation's political institutions is of key importance in any attempt to analyze the stability of these institutions when faced with a crisis of effectiveness. The relationship between different degrees of legitimacy and effectiveness in specific political systems may be presented in the form of a fourfold table, with examples of countries characterized by the various possible combinations:

EFFECTIVENESS

LEGITIMACY

	+	-
+	A	B
-	C	D

Societies which fall in box A, which are, that is, high on the scales of both legitimacy and effectiveness, have stable political systems, like the United States, Sweden, and Britain.[5] Ineffective and illegitimate regimes, which fall in box D, are by definition unstable and break down, unless they are dictatorships maintaining themselves by force, like the governments of Hungary and eastern Germany today.

The political experiences of different countries in the early

---

[4] Herbert Luethy, *The State of France* (London: Secker & Warburg, 1955), p. 29.

[5] The race problem in the American South does constitute one basic challenge to the legitimacy of the system, and at one time did cause a breakdown of the national order. This conflict has reduced the commitment of many white southerners to the democratic game down to the present. Great Britain had a comparable problem as long as Catholic Ireland remained part of the United Kingdom. Effective government could not satisfy Ireland. Political practices by both sides in Northern Ireland, Ulster, also illustrate the problem of a regime which is not legitimate to a major segment of its population.

1930s illustrate the effect of other combinations. In the late 1920s, neither the German nor the Austrian republic was held legitimate by large and powerful segments of its population. Nevertheless, both remained reasonably effective.[6] In terms of the table, they fell in box C. When the effectiveness of various governments broke down in the 1930s, those societies which were high on the scale of legitimacy remained democratic, while such countries as Germany, Austria, and Spain lost their freedom, and France narrowly escaped a similar fate. Or to put the changes in terms of the table, countries which shifted from A to B remained democratic, while those which shifted from C to D broke down. The military defeat of 1940 underlined French democracy's low position on the scale of legitimacy. It was the sole defeated democracy which furnished large-scale support for a Quisling regime.[7]

Situations like these demonstrate the usefulness of this type of analysis. From a short-range point of view, a highly effective but illegitimate system, such as a well-governed colony, is more unstable than regimes which are relatively low in effectiveness and high in legitimacy. The social stability of a nation like Thailand, despite its periodic *coups d'état*, stands out in sharp contrast to the situation in neighboring former colonial nations. On the other hand, prolonged effectiveness over a number of generations may give legitimacy to a political system. In the modern world, such effectiveness means primarily constant economic development. Those nations which

---

[6] For an excellent analysis of the permanent crisis of the Austrian republic which flowed from the fact that it was viewed as an illegitimate regime by the Catholics and conservatives, see Charles Gulick, *Austria from Hapsburg to Hitler* (Berkeley: University of California Press, 1948).

[7] The French legitimacy problem is well described by Katherine Munro. 'The Right wing parties never quite forgot the possibility of a counter revolution while the Left wing parties revived the Revolution militant in their Marxism or Communism; each side suspected the other of using the Republic to achieve its own ends and of being legal only so far as it suited it. This suspicion threatened time and time again to make the Republic unworkable, since it led to obstruction in both the political and the economic sphere, and difficulties of government in turn undermined confidence in the regime and its rulers'. Quoted in Charles Micaud, 'French Political Parties: Ideological Myths and Social Realities', in Sigmund Neumann (ed.), *Modern Political Parties* (University of Chicago Press, 1956), p. 108.

have adapted most successfully to the requirements of an industrial system have the fewest internal political strains, and have either preserved their traditional legitimacy or developed strong new symbols.

The social and economic structure which Latin America inherited from the Iberian peninsula prevented it from following the lead of the former English colonies, and its republics never developed the symbols and aura of legitimacy. In large measure, the survival of the new political democracies of Asia and Africa will depend on their ability to meet the needs of their populations over a prolonged period, which will probably mean their ability to cope with industrialization.

LEGITIMACY AND CONFLICT

Inherent in all democratic systems is the constant threat that the group conflicts which are democracy's lifeblood may solidify to the point where they threaten to disintegrate the society. Hence conditions which serve to moderate the intensity of partisan battle are among the key requisites of democratic government.

Since the existence of a moderate state of conflict is in fact another way of defining a legitimate democracy, it is not surprising that the principal factors determining such an optimum state are closely related to those which produce legitimacy viewed in terms of continuities of symbols and statuses. The character and content of the major cleavages affecting the political stability of a society are largely determined by historical factors which have affected the way in which major issues dividing society have been solved or left unresolved over time.

In modern times, three major issues have emerged in Western nations: first, the place of the church and/or various religions within the nation; second, the admission of the lower strata, particularly the workers, to full political and economic 'citizenship' through universal suffrage and the right to bargain collectively; and third, the continuing struggle over the distribution of the national income.

The significant question here is: Were these issues dealt with one by one, with each more or less solved before the next arose; or did the problems accumulate, so that traditional sources of cleavage mixed with newer ones? Resolving tensions one at a time contributes to a stable political system; carrying over issues from one historical period to another makes for a political atmosphere characterized by bitterness and frustration rather than tolerance and compromise. Men and parties come to differ with each other, not simply on ways of settling current problems, but on fundamental and opposed outlooks. This means that they see the political victory of their opponents as a major moral threat, and the whole system, as a result, lacks effective value-integration.

8. INTEREST ARTICULATION STRUCTURES: INTEREST 'GROUPS'

G. A. ALMOND AND G. B. POWELL

A variety of structures, from an undisciplined mob to a businessmen's conference, may be involved in interest articulation. Such structures may be classified according to two major components: the type of *group* initiating the articulation, and the type of *access channel* through which it passes the message. It would be convenient, of course, if we could construct a typology which includes both of these features. We could speak of the associational groups as always articulating interests through regular and legal channels, and of the regional and kinship groups as always working through informal and intermittent channels. But in fact, associational groups, such as trade unions, may organize riots and strikes. All groups may and do utilize the channels of intermittent and informal personal contact. By the same token, speakers for unorganized, but important, language and ethnic groups may address party conventions.

Thus, although particular types of groups may be drawn by their organizational and representational nature to certain kinds of access channels, the general rule is that the interests will be articulated through those channels which are most available and which seem most likely to bring the demands to the attention of the relevant decision makers.

The term 'interest group' has become the object of considerable dispute among political scientists. We do not wish to engage in the polemic or to insist upon our own definition as of particular merit. By 'interest group' we mean a group of individuals who are linked by particular bonds of concern or advantage, and who have some awareness of these bonds. The structure of the interest group may be organized to include

From *Comparative Politics: A Developmental Approach*, by Gabriel A. Almond and G. Bingham Powell, Jr., pp. 74–79. Copyright © 1966, by Little, Brown & Co. Inc., and reprinted with their permission.

continuing role performance by all members of the group, or it may reflect only occasional and intermittent awareness of the group interest on the part of individuals. In subsequent discussion we shall attempt to identify some of the most important groups which may initiate interest articulation.

Perhaps we should begin by drawing attention to the importance of individuals as articulators of their own interests. Such individual self-representation, commonly cast in the guise of the articulation of more general societal or group interests, is a common feature of political systems. It may take the form of seeking to influence political decisions for financial or professional gain, or it may involve the articulation of interests perceived as more noble in scope.

In a society with group controls over individual elite behavior, such individual interest articulation is checked and ordered. But in societies where a small elite makes all the political decisions, where the articulation takes place from person to person or within a small group, it is a powerful factor in explaining the course of political decisions. Such interest articulation has been a common feature, for example, in the history of strongman dictatorships.

Somewhat akin to individual self-representation are the structures called *anomic interest groups*, the more or less spontaneous penetrations into the political system from the society, such as riots, demonstrations, assassinations, and the like. Of course, much of what passes for anomic behavior is really the use of unconventional or violent means by organized groups. But, particularly in cases where explicitly organized groups are not present, or where they have failed to obtain adequate representation of their interests in the political system, latent discontent may be sparked by an incident, or by the emergence of a leader, and may suddenly impinge upon the political system in unpredictable and uncontrollable ways.[1] Political systems may be marked by a high frequency of such violent and spontaneous group formation (as in France of the

---

[1] An analysis of the necessary prerequisites to anomic violence (and other types of mass action), and of the sequence of steps which lead to it, may be found in Neil J. Smelzer, *Theory of Collective Behavior* (London: Routledge & Kegan Paul, 1962). See also E. J. Hobsbawm, *Primitive Rebels: Studies in Archaic Forms of Social Movements in the Nineteenth and Twentieth Centuries* (New York: W. W. Norton & Co. Inc., 1959).

Fourth Republic, Italy, and the Arab nations), or notable for its absence. The peasant roadblocks in the French Fourth Republic, the Italian protests over the disposal of Trieste, and the British rural unrest and 'rick burning' in the period before the Reform Act of 1832 provide us with a few examples of anomic behavior.

Self-representation and anomic groups are marked by limited organization and a lack of constant activity on behalf of the group. To them we must add what we call *nonassociational interest groups*. By nonassociational interest groups we refer to kinship and lineage groups, and ethnic, regional, status, and class groups which articulate their interests intermittently through individuals, cliques, family and religious heads, and the like. Examples might include the complaint of an informal delegation from a linguistic group regarding language instruction in the schools, a request made by several landowners to a bureaucrat in a social club regarding the tariff on grains, or the appeals by kinsmen to a government tax collector for preferred treatment for the family business.

The distinguishing characteristics of such interest groups are the intermittent pattern of articulation, the absence of an organized procedure for establishing the nature and means of articulation, and the lack of continuity in internal structure. In highly differentiated modern societies, the influence of such groups is limited for two reasons. First, interest-groups studies have shown that organization is highly advantageous for successful interest articulation. In modern societies competition from numerous organized groups is too great to permit a high degree of successful articulation by nonassociational groups. Second, important nonassociational groups with continuing interests soon develop organized structures, and hence fall into one of the two following classes of interest groups.[2]

Institutional interest groups are found within such organizations as political parties, legislatures, armies, bureaucracies, and churches. These are formal organizations, composed of professionally employed personnel, with designated political or social functions other than interest articulation. But, either as corporate bodies or as smaller groups within these bodies

---

[2] LaPalombara finds this to be the case in Italy. Joseph LaPalombara, *Interest Groups in Italian Politics* (Princeton U.P., 1964), pp. 81–82. It also seems to be happening in the case of caste and language groups in India.

(such as legislative blocs, officer cliques, higher or lower clergy or religious orders, departments, skill groups, and ideological cliques in bureaucracies), these groups may articulate their own interests or represent the interests of other groups in the society.

We should note here that political parties may constitute the bases for institutional interest groups. In making such a statement we distinguish between the function of the party in representing and aggregating interests of its members, and the behavior of cliques within the party utilizing their institutional position to articulate particular interests. Conservative business interests have operated effectively within conservative parties, as have trade unions in Social Democratic parties.

Institutional interest groups may occupy particularly powerful positions in the society because of the strength provided by their organizational base. The prominent part played by military cliques, bureaucratic groups, and party leaders in articulating interests in underdeveloped areas, where associational interest groups are limited in number or ineffective in action, is obvious. Even in a society such as the United States, with its thousands of associational interest groups, one cannot ignore the role of the institutional military-industrial complex in articulating the numerous interests connected with defense industry.

The *associational interest groups* are the specialized structures for interest articulation — trade unions, organizations of businessmen or industrialists, ethnic associations, associations organized by religious denominations, and civic groups. Their particular characteristics are explicit representation of the interests of a particular group, a full-time professional staff, and orderly procedures for the formulation of interests and demands. As the importance of associational interest groups in interest articulation has been recognized, they have been the object of many studies in the more developed societies. Where these groups are present and are allowed to flourish, they tend to regulate the development of the other types of interest groups. Their organizational base gives them an advantage over nonassociational groups; their tactics and goals are often recognized as legitimate in the society; and by representing a broad range of groups and interests they may limit the influence of real or potential institutional interest groups and of self-representation.

Some knowledge of the internal dynamics of interest-group

behavior is useful in understanding the way certain groups perform their interest articulation functions. A group's ability to mobilize the support, energy, and resources of its members will surely influence its effectiveness. A loose, voluntary group may find it hard to mobilize support and resources. A tightly organized interest group may be very effective, but may represent its leaders' interests and not the interests of the group membership.[3]

One other characteristic of the interest-articulating groups should be stressed: the degree of differentiation and of autonomy among the groups. Of particular importance is the extent to which associational interest groups articulate autonomous goals of their leaders or members, or are subordinate to other groups and institutions. In France and Italy, for example, many associational interest groups, such as trade unions and peasant organizations, are controlled by the Communist Party or the Catholic Church. These associational groups may not articulate the needs felt and perceived by their members, but may serve only as instruments to mobilize support for the political parties or social institutions which dominate them. This lack of autonomy can have serious consequences for the political process. The denial of independent articulation to interests may lead to anomic outbreaks. Furthermore, the subordination of interest groups by political parties may limit the mobility of the political process, create monopolies in the 'political market', and even stalemate the political system.

Of course, the extreme case of lack of autonomy and differentiation in interest groups is to be found in totalitarian societies, where the dominating elite organizations penetrate all levels of the society and exercise close control over such interest groups as are permitted to exist. In systems such as those of Soviet Russia and Communist China, there is an effort to penetrate the entire society by the central party elite. Interest articulation takes the form of very low-level suggestions

---

[3] A much more inclusive analysis of these dynamics, an analysis beyond the scope of this discussion, may be found in Peter M. Blau, *Exchange and Power in Social Life* (New York: John Wiley & Sons Inc., 1964), especially in pp. 238–46 and in chap. 10. Among other significant analyses is the 'rational self-interest' problem raised by Mancur Olson, *The Logic of Collective Action* (Cambridge: Harvard U.P., 1965), chap. 1.

within specific bounds, or receives only latent expression. Important, overt interest articulation is limited to members of the elite, who can utilize their position in the various political institutions as a base from which to express their demands. The degree to which control is exercised over general interest articulation and over the processes of communication in a society provides an interesting way of classifying political systems.

PART THREE

POLITICAL PARTIES

9. TOWARD A COMPARATIVE STUDY OF POLITICAL PARTIES

S. NEUMANN

I. A PRELIMINARY DEFINITION

A definition of 'party' might as well begin with its simple word derivation. To become a 'party' to something always means identification with one group and differentiation from another. Every party in its very essence signifies *partnership* in a particular organization and *separation* from others by a specific program.

Such an initial description, to be sure, indicates that the very definition of party presupposes a democratic climate and hence makes it a misnomer in every dictatorship. A one-party system (*le parti unique*) is a contradiction in itself. Only the coexistence of at least one other competitive group makes a political party real. Still the fact remains that the term has been widely used by modern autocrats, and for a very obvious reason: to keep the semblance of a 'peoples' rule' in their postdemocratic dictatorships. But it is also true that even the totalitarian party depends upon a functioning opposition. If one does not exist, it must still be assumed by the dictators, since under monolithic rule the dictatorial parties must constantly justify their existence in view of the ever present threat of a counterrevolution, hidden or imaginary though its organization may be. The opposition party is the *raison d'être* of the dictatorial movement and its all-pervasive controls through institutions, propaganda, and terror.

Thus parties must prevail under the total structure, too. Yet here again, as in all other strata of the political pyramid, divergent political systems are hidden behind the same nomenclature. Just as 'leaders' and 'lieutenants' carry different meanings in democracies and dictatorships, so do 'parties' also.

Between the two extremes of 'democracy' and 'dictatorship' there are wide variations. The British, American, French, Indian, and Scandinavian democratic structures differ as greatly among themselves as do the totalitarian regimes of the Soviet Union, Fascist Italy, Nazi Germany, and Peronist Argentina. In short, the peculiar character of each party system must be defined in terms of the political order of which it is an integral part, if not its kingpin.

What is common to all parties, beyond partnership in a particular organization and separation from others, is their *participation* in the decision-making process, or at least the attempt at and a chance for such a mobilization for action. This ever present readiness alone makes them political in a genuine sense, for only in their fight for control and in their conscious influence on political forces, do parties gain meaning and importance. It is therefore not accidental that the beginning of modern political parties is closely tied up with the rise of a parliament. When political representation broadens and a national forum of discussion develops, providing a constant opportunity for political participation — wherever those conditions are fulfilled, political parties arise. This happened in England in the revolutionary seventeenth century; in France on the eve of the great Revolution of 1789; in Germany around 1848. Even where contingent influences may create political groups of an awakened intelligentsia, as in nineteenth-century tsarist Russia, they assume political dimensions only where some degree of participation is made possible.

While the hour of birth for the political party in every nation can well be defined by such a simple derivation from its original meaning, the same is true of the critical period of a party system. By its very definition, 'party' connotes not only the coexistence of different competing entities, with their characteristic partnership, separation, and participation, but also a fourth feature, most significant and yet often forgotten — the essential inclusion of every separate group as *a part in a whole*. Only where the specific interests of parties are imbedded in a common whole does the political struggle not lead to disintegration of the entire group. Only when essentials uniting the political adversaries are constantly reaffirmed can differences be balanced. Just as children are ready to accept the rules of the gang only as long as they are willing to continue their group life, so can sacrifices be asked from each political opponent as long as the preservation of the community seems worth while. A common field of activity, a basic homogeneity, a common language, are presuppositions for a functioning party system. Such a common basis alone makes compromise, sacrifice, and even defeat bearable. Wherever this body politic becomes questionable, the crisis of parties seems the necessary result. The viability of a party system becomes a test for the stability of a social and political order. The strength of the Anglo-American party system is founded largely upon a basic national unity which makes the differentiations of political groups 'differences in degree but not in kind'.

This interdependence of the fate of political parties with the fate of the national whole is the very result of their 'political' character; for political they are not only because of their claim to political power but even more so on account of their fulfilment of their political function of integration.

To summarize: we may define 'political party' generally as *the articulate organization of society's active political agents, those who are concerned with the control of governmental power and who compete for popular support with another group or groups holding divergent views.* As such, it is *the great intermediary which links social forces and ideologies to official governmental institutions and relates them to political action within the larger political community.*

A party's concrete character can be spelled out only in time and space. What 'this buckle' (to paraphrase Bagehot's description of the British cabinet) actually links up depends on a nation's specific constitution (i.e., the system of its correlated institutions) and its peculiar parallelogram of social forces. It is only in such a substantial situation that the functions, structure, and strategy of parties can be fully revealed.

II. FUNCTIONS OF POLITICAL PARTIES: DEMOCRATIC AND DICTATORIAL

It has often been stated that the primary task of political parties is to organize the chaotic public will. 'They bring order out of the chaos of a multitude of voters' (Lord Bryce). They are brokers of ideas, constantly clarifying, systematizing, and expounding the party's doctrine. They are representatives of social interest groups, bridging the distance between the individual and the great community. They maximize the voter's education in the competitive scheme of at least a two-party system and sharpen his free choice. The coexistence of a competitor, therefore, is paramount to an effective democratic party system which presupposes that the final compromise will reflect the reasonable decision of a free electorate.

In fact, the basic assumption of democracy is the inevitability of differing views and the free operation of conflicting opinions. 'The true democrat has a suspicion that he may not always be right', as W. Ivor Jennings remarked. Thus the opposition becomes the most important part of the parliament; its members are 'critics by profession'. It is not enough that Her Majesty's Opposition be highly respected by the ruling majority, but often its fruitful ideas are accepted — and, indeed, this is a wise course for the party in power to follow if it wants to remain there. Its political alternative represents not only the looming 'Shadow Cabinet' but also an active participant in actual control.

The open forum of parliament becomes the clearinghouse for the policies that a state should follow. The political parties are the proper engine of such continuous plebiscite. They make the voters choose at least the lesser of two evils, thus forcing political differentiations into a few major channels. Yet important as such machinery of political concentration may be, the political services of the parties do not stop at that. What is even more essential, parties transform the private citizen himself. They make him a *zoon politikon;* they integrate him into the group. Every party has to present to the individual voter and to his powerful special-interest groups a picture of the community as an entity. It must constantly remind the citizen of this collective whole, adjust his wants to the needs of the community, and, if necessary, even ask sacrifices from him in the name of the community. Nor can even the so-called 'class parties', which call upon only a specific part of the population, renounce this essential function. The outstanding example of such a class program, the *Communist Manifesto,* justifies its position with the claim that the united proletariat will represent the overwhelming majority and that its dictatorship will lead to a dissolution of all classes and therewith to the liberation of society as a whole. This second function differentiates the political party from a pressure group. Its specific interests must be fitted into the framework of the national collective. Wherever the policy-making parties do not succeed in this primary task, the modern state is in danger of deteriorating into a neofeudalism of powerful interest groups.

If the party in a democracy fulfils these two first functions of organizing the chaotic public will and educating the private citizen to political responsibility, then it can also lay claim to a third duty: *to represent the connecting link between government and public opinion.* Since democracies are pyramids built from below, the connection between leaders and followers becomes a necessity in the two-way traffic of democracy. It is the major function of the party to keep these lines of communication open and clear. Such a task makes the parties, if not the rulers, at least the controlling agencies of government in a representative democracy.

This crucial position is even more emphasized by the fourth function of a democratic party: *the selection of leaders.* Here as everywhere in a democracy, it is the competitive scheme, the choice between at least two oligarchies, which guarantees the quality of its leadership. Of course, such a selection presupposes an enlightened public, one qualified to make the right choice, and an intellectual climate appropriate to the functioning of democratic parties. Wherever these preconditions no longer prevail, the crisis of democracy is in the offing.

The crisis elements of democratic parties can be well perceived in the rise of dictatorial movements. In fact, dictatorial organizations often grow up within the democratic party system itself. They constitute a state within the state, alienated from its basic principles. And yet their rise is the expression of a basic lack within the society. They can recruit followers because there are those who no longer regard themselves as a part of the predominant society that does not seem to answer their essential desires and needs. No doubt every functioning group has and can bear some 'outsiders' in its midst. So long as they do not represent a considerable number, they do not constitute a serious threat to the existing order. If, however, they succeed in recruiting an appreciable following, then the democratic process enters a critical stage. The rise of dictatorial parties within modern states is a storm signal for the democratic party system. From now on, the argument between parties concerns fundamentals and a fight over ultimate issues. For these integrated political groups compromise becomes increasingly difficult, and so does any coalition with another party.

The main purpose of the fully developed totalitarian parties becomes the fight for a new political order, for a new society. Speaking a different language and living according to a different set of values, the partisans have to be segregated from the political and social body of the ruling class and society, so the party leaders decree. Otherwise the partisans may be enchanted and taken in by the old order, the destruction of which is the essential purpose of the 'guarantors' of the new morrow.

With the rise of the dictatorial party, its competitors in politics necessarily become more inflexible too. Struggle assumes the quality of a religious war; the only possible outcome for any contestant seems to be overwhelming victory or ultimate annihilation. Such a situation explains the revolutionary functions of a dictatorial party before its seizure of power: it is, above all, the *revolutionary vanguard* of the future state.

The functions of the dictatorial parties in power, outwardly at least, do not appear to be different from the four features of their democratic counterparts. They, too, have to organize the chaotic public will and integrate the individual into the group; they equally have to represent the connecting link between government and public opinion and, above all, guarantee the selection of leaders. Yet as their concepts of leaders and followers differ diametrically from democratic ideas, the meaning of these functions changes fundamentally. Organization of the chaotic will is fulfilled by a 'monolithic control'; integration of the individual means 'enforcement of conformity'; and, though these tasks are often directed by a 'Ministry of Education and Enlightenment', the maintenance of communication between state and society is assured by a mere one-way propaganda stream from above. True, dictatorships also have to concern themselves with 'public opinion'. They must listen to the 'voice of the people', especially since this is muted under the tyrant's rule. Thus the party serves through its secret agencies as a necessary listening post. Through such diverse services this leviathan apparatus, which claims at the outset to be the party to end all parties, becomes in fact the key instrument of modern totalitarianism.

All three functions, if successfully administered, secure the fourth and crucial purpose: the selection of leaders. Yet it is especially on this level of the creation, preservation, and extension of the ruling elite that the basic differences between the party systems become obvious.

Lenin's fight at the turn of the century for a small centralized revolutionary elite, as opposed to the Mensheviks' idea of a loose democratic mass organization, laid the foundation for a disciplined castelike order. He thus anticipated what revolutionary parties experienced a generation later when they had to choose between thoroughly revolutionist cadres and a mass following.

Only in a 'revolutionary situation' — i.e., when complete victory or the prospect of impending success brings a rush of adherents to the revolutionary cause — is it possible for such a radical party to win and to hold the masses. Revolutionary parties reckoning with a long struggle can count on only a small elite of unrelenting fighters who do not care for rewards today and who are ready to make the revolution their life's calling. Masses are in need of visible rewards. If they cannot reap the fruits now — or at least have reasonable expectation of doing so in the near future — they will leave the ranks. This fact explains the extraordinary fluctuation in membership to be observed in radical parties everywhere. The Fascist followers of yesterday are turning up today as communism's most reliable fighters; and the reverse may be true tomorrow. Whoever delivers the spoils has the confidence of the fluctuating masses; but if he cannot do so by tomorrow, another liberator will be sought out.

How different from the rank-and-file reaction are the attitudes of the vanguard and the core members of the established movement, taking their orders from the central party organization, whether it means robbing a bank, organizing a party cell, or conceiving a new program. The revolutionary intellectual in his great flight into a future morrow and the revolutionary 'wire-puller' in his minute work, far apart though they be, have one thing in common: they do not expect rewards in this world. They have given their lives to the party, which in return becomes their own life. Discipline is the password of the movement. Said Lenin in 1900: 'We must train men and women who will devote to the revolution not merely their spare evenings but the whole of their lives'. This is the clarion call to the totalitarian party. It can appeal to the professional revolutionary at all times; yet to the masses it may be meaningful only during a revolutionary situation.

The Continental Communist parties in the interwar period opened their ranks to the masses partly because of their mistaken misapprehension of what they deemed a revolutionary situation (which had passed by 1920). They did not fare too well. In Soviet Russia, of course, they could offer their followers the spoils of the victor. In fact, many people joined the Bolshevik party for such reasons alone, and the early purges of the Soviet regime were partly to free the party from those 'opportunists' (and more often from those whose services were originally useful but which now could be performed by newly recruited 'reliable' followers).

The radical parties in the non-Communist countries did not have to eliminate 'job-hunters' because there were no jobs to be distributed. As quickly as the prospects of revolutionary changes attracted the driftwood of a political reserve army, so did this army move quickly on to new shores which seemed more promising. The fate of the Communist parties outside Russia in the interwar period hinged on the dilemma between their revolutionary character and their aspirations for mass following, between their uncompromising attitude as a party which did not want to sell the revolution for a 'mess of pottage' and the necessity of offering substantial results at once because the masses would not be satisfied with a promised millennium. They wanted higher wages, social security, political recognition — visible signs of success today. Thus they left the party that was preparing for a revolution not yet in sight.

A mass party cannot survive without foreseeable success. Its final fate becomes a race against time. The surprising staying power of the Communist parties in western Europe since 1945 seems to contradict such a statement; yet, as Charles Micaud's analysis convincingly shows, the left-wing radicals have learned some lessons from their earlier failures and have defined more realistically the function and place of the totalitarian party in what they regard as the preparatory stage of an oncoming revolution. In fact, the continued appeal of communism in France and Italy, despite the Marshall Plan and NATO, serves as a warning to the democratic powers in areas where they have not yet succeeded in reintegrating large segments of their national community. It is the claim of the Communist movements that they can give their followers a feeling of belonging, an active faith, and a promising direction for the future when the party will possess the whole community and seize the power of the state.

10. THE CONCEPT OF MEMBERSHIP

M. DUVERGER

CADRE PARTIES AND MASS PARTIES

The distinction between cadre and mass parties is not based upon their dimensions, upon the number of their members: the difference involved is not one of size but of structure. Consider, for example, the French Socialist party: in its eyes the recruiting of members is a fundamental activity, both from the political and the financial standpoints. In the first place, the party aims at the political education of the working class, at picking out from it an elite capable of taking over the government and the administration of the country: the members are therefore the very substance of the party, the stuff of its activity. Without members, the party would be like a teacher without pupils. Secondly, from the financial point of view, the party is essentially based upon the subscriptions paid by its members: the first duty of the branch is to ensure that they are regularly collected. In this way, the party gathers the funds required for its work of political education and for its day-to-day activity; in the same way it is enabled to finance electioneering: the financial and the political are here at one. This last point is fundamental: every electoral campaign represents considerable expense. The mass-party technique in effect replaces the capitalist financing of electioneering by democratic financing. Instead of appealing to a few big private donors, industrialists, bankers, or important merchants, for funds to meet campaign expenses — which makes the candidate (and the person elected) dependent on them — the mass party spreads the burden over the largest possible number of members, each of whom contributes a modest sum. This invention of the mass party is comparable with that of National Defence Bonds in 1914: before then Treasury Bonds were

From *Political Parties*, by M. Duverger, Methuen, 1955, pp. 63–71. We are grateful to the publisher for permission to reproduce this extract.

issued in large denominations and taken up by a few great banks which loaned to the state: in 1914 came the brilliant idea of issuing many more small bonds to be taken up by as many members of the public as possible. In the same way, it is characteristic of the mass party that it appeals to the public: to the paying public who make it possible for the electoral campaign to be free from capitalist pressures; to the listening, active public which receives a political education and learns how to intervene in the life of the State.

The cadre party corresponds to a different conception: the grouping of notabilities for the preparation of elections, conducting campaigns and maintaining contact with the candidates. Influential persons, in the first place, whose name, prestige, or connections can provide a backing for the candidate and secure him votes; experts, in the second place, who know how to handle the electors and how to organize a campaign; last of all financiers, who can bring the sinews of war. Quality is the most important factor: extent of prestige, skill in technique, size of fortune. What the mass party secures by numbers, the cadre party achieves by selection. Adherence to it has therefore quite a different meaning: it is a completely personal act, based upon the aptitudes or the peculiar circumstances of a man; it is determined strictly by individual qualities. It is an act that is restricted to a few; it is dependent upon rigid and exclusive selection. If we define a member as one who signs an undertaking to the party and thereafter regularly pays his subscription, then cadre parties have no members. Some do make a show of recruiting after the contagious pattern of mass parties, but this is not to be taken seriously. The problem of the number of members belonging to the French Radical Socialist party is susceptible of no precise answer, simply because the problem itself is meaningless. The members of the Radical party cannot be counted, because the Radical party recruits no members, strictly speaking: it is a cadre party. American parties and the majority of European moderate and Conservative parties belong to the same category.

This distinction, though clear in theory, is not always easy to make in practice. As we have just noted, cadre parties sometimes admit ordinary members in imitation of mass parties. In fact, the practice is fairly widespread: there are few purely cadre parties. The others are not in practice far removed from them, but their outward form is likely to mislead the observer who must look beyond the official clauses laid down in the constitution or the declarations of the leaders. The absence of any system of registration of members or of any regular collection of subscriptions is a fairly reliable criterion; no true membership is conceivable in their absence, as we shall see. The vagueness of the figures put out can also be considered presumptive evidence: in 1950, the Turkish Democratic party claimed before the elections that it had 'three or four million members'. Obviously, it was referring to supporters, in actual fact, it was essentially a cadre party. In the same way, the distinction seems contradicted by the existence of indirect parties: mass parties which have no personal members. Consider the example of the Labour party: it was founded in 1900 to make it financially possible for working-class candidates to contest elections; from the financial point of view, the system is a mass-party system, election costs being met by Trade Unions, collectively. But this collective membership remains quite different from individual membership: it involves no true political enrolment and no personal pledge to the party. This profoundly alters the nature of the party and of membership, as we shall attempt to show in detail later. On the other hand, let us take the example of American parties in States which operate the system of 'closed primaries' with registration of electors; they resemble mass parties from the political point of view. Participation in the primary, with the registration and pledges it involves, may be considered as an act of membership. Moreover, activity connected with the nomination of candidates presented at elections by a party constitutes one of the activities typical of party membership. But, in this particular instance, this is the sole activity: there is no activity which at all resembles the branch meetings of the mass parties. More particularly there is no regular system of subscription to provide for the financing of the party and of election campaigns: from the financial point of view these are clearly examples of the cadre party. All things considered, the indirect party and the American party with closed primaries should be classified as semi-mass parties, though these examples must not be held to constitute a third category distinct from the two others because of their heterogeneous nature.

The distinction between cadre and mass parties corresponds to a difference in social and political substructure. In the beginning, it coincided on the whole with the replacement of a

limited franchise by universal suffrage. In electoral systems
based on a property qualification, which were the rule in the
nineteenth century, parties obviously took on the form of
cadre parties: there could be no question of enrolling the
masses at a time when they had no political influence. Moreover, capitalist financing of elections appeared natural. Indeed, it has survived the property franchise. In point of fact,
the coming of universal suffrage did not immediately lead to
the arrival of true mass parties. The cadre parties simply attempted to make their organization more flexible by pretend-
ing to open their ranks to the masses. The Birmingham caucus
system in the British Liberal party, the Primrose League in
the Conservative party, the institution of primaries in America, correspond to this first stage. The problem was how to
give the masses some scope for political activity and how to
confer on the notabilities composing the caucus the air of
having been popularly invested. In the first two cases some
approach was made towards the mass party: there existed a
system of formal membership as well as a periodic subscription. But the real life of the party was lived independently
of the members: the Primrose League, an organization distinct from the party proper, aimed at social mixing; the primaries are limited to the nomination of candidates; the Birmingham caucus alone with its local branch foreshadowed
a true mass party, but it proved to be no more than a passing
experiment. The political and financial bases of the mass
party were lacking. There was no question of rescuing candidates and elections from the clutches of capitalist finance, nor
of educating the masses and making direct use in political
life of their activity. The question was rather how to use the
political and financial strength of the masses as an ancillary
force. The first step had been taken, but only the first step.

The introduction of universal suffrage led almost everywhere (the United States excepted) to the development of
Socialist parties which made the decisive transition, not always, however, at once (cp. Table 1). In France, for example,
the first Socialist groups were not very different from the
middle-class parties; registration of members, collection of
subscriptions, autonomous financing of elections, developed
only slowly. Development was even slower in Italy and in
politically less-developed countries. Yet, at the outbreak of
the 1914–18 War, the European Socialist parties constituted
great human communities profoundly different from the

earlier cadre parties. A notable example is the German Social Democratic party which, with more than a million members and an annual budget of nearly two million marks, constituted a veritable state more powerful than some national states. It was the Marxist conception of the class party that led to such massive structures: if the party is the political expression of a class it must naturally seek to rally the whole of the class, to form it politically, to pick out the élites capable of leadership and administration. This effort of organization also made it possible to free the working class from the tutelage of middle-class parties: in order to put up independent working-class candidates at elections it was necessary to become independent of capitalist financing (except perhaps as a makeweight, the roles being reversed) and this was possible only with collective finances. To establish, in opposition to the middle-class political press, a working-class political press, it was necessary to collect funds and organize the distribution of the newspaper. Only a mass party could make these things possible.

This explains why the distinction between cadre and mass parties also corresponds approximately with the distinction between Right and Left, Middle-class and Workers' parties. The middle-class Right had no need, financial or political, to seek the organized support of the masses: it already had its élites, its personages, and its financial backers. It considered its own political education to be adequate. For these reasons, until the coming of Fascism, attempts to create mass Conservative parties have generally failed. The instinctive repugnance felt by the middle class for regimentation and collective action also played some part in the failures, just as the opposite tendency amongst the working class favoured mass organization in Socialist parties. It would not be out of place to reiterate at this point some earlier observations. Nothing less than the development of Communism or of revolutionary tactics was required before the middle classes, realizing that cadre parties were inadequate, were to make serious attempts to create mass parties: in 1932, the National Socialist party had reached a membership of 800,000. This however really signified its breach with democracy. Under the electoral and parliamentary system cadre parties have generally been found sufficient by the Right; in the struggle against the electoral and parliamentary system mass parties of the Fascist type have rarely shown the balance and stability of proletarian

Table 1: Membership of European Socialist Parties, 1900-55.

	Germany	Austria	Denmark	France	Great Britain Trade Union Members	Great Britain Individual Members	Total	Norway	Holland	Sweden	Switzerland
1900									3,200	44,100	
1901					353,070		375,931		4,000	48,241	
1902			22,061		455,450		469,311		6,500	49,190	
1903					847,315		861,150	17,000	5,600	54,552	
1904					956,025		969,800		6,000	64,835	9,155
1905	400,000		29,651	34,688	885,270		900,000		6,816	67,325	8,912
1906	384,327			40,000	904,496		921,280	19,100	7,471	101,929	19,840
1907	530,466			52,913	975,182		998,338		8,423	133,388	20,337
1908	587,338		34,078	56,963	1,049,673		1,072,418	27,838	8,748	112,693	20,000
1909	633,309			57,977	1,127,035		1,158,565	27,789	9,504	60,813	20,439
1910	720,038			69,085	1,450,648		1,486,308		9,980	55,248	21,132
1911	836,562			69,578	1,394,402		1,430,539		12,582	57,721	20,671
1912	970,112			72,692	1,501,783		1,539,092		15,667	61,000	21,508
1913	982,850	89,628	48,985	75,192	1,858,178		1,895,498	43,557	25,708	75,444	27,500
1914	1,085,905		57,115	93,218	1,572,391		1,612,147	53,866	25,609	84,410	29,730
1915	585,898		60,072	25,393	2,053,735		2,093,365	62,952	25,642	85,937	29,585
1916	432,618		67,724	25,879	2,170,782		2,219,764		24,018	105,275	27,485
1917	243,061		78,320	28,224	2,415,383		2,465,131	94,165	24,893	114,450	31,307
1918	249,411		91,791	15,827	2,960,409		3,013,129		27,093	129,432	39,765
1919	1,012,299	332,391	115,900	133,277	3,464,020		3,511,290		37,628	151,364	52,163
1920	1,180,208	335,863	126,603	179,787	4,317,537		4,359,807		47,870	143,090	51,250
1921	1,028,574	491,160	129,756	50,449	3,973,558		4,010,361	45,946	37,412	134,753	40,483
1922	1,464,868	553,022	124,549	49,174	3,279,276		3,311,036		41,472	133,042	36,552
1923	1,261,072	514,273	130,371	50,496	3,120,149		3,155,911		42,047	138,510	34,000
1924	940,078	566,124	143,203	72,659	3,158,102		3,194,399	40,394	41,230	153,187	31,306
1925	844,495	576,107	146,496	111,276	3,337,635		3,373,870		37,894	167,843	31,788
1926	823,526	592,346	144,680	111,368	3,352,347		3,388,286		41,221	189,122	33,339
1927	867,671	649,586	148,472	98,034	3,238,939		3,293,615	68,016	43,196	203,338	36,727
1928	937,381	713,834	149,120	109,892	2,025,139	214,970	2,292,169		46,169	221,419	41,621
1929	1,021,777	718,056	163,193	119,519	2,044,279	227,897	2,330,845	76,579	53,395	234,962	43,867
1930	1,037,384	698,181	171,407	125,563	2,011,484	277,211	2,346,908	80,177	61,162	277,017	47,444

Year											
1931	1,008,953	653,605	173,890	130,864	2,024,216	297,003	2,358,066	83,071	69,263	296,507	50,722
1932		648,497	179,579	137,684	1,960,269	371,607	2,371,787	87,315	78,920	312,934	55,186
1933			190,070	131,044	1,899,007	366,013	2,305,030	95,327	81,914	326,734	57,227
1934			191,995	110,000	1,857,524	381,259	2,278,490	104,517	87,212	330,350	55,571
1935			195,142	120,083	1,912,924	419,311	2,377,515	122,007	84,269	346,786	52,881
1936			191,424	202,000	1,968,538	430,694	2,441,357	142,719	87,826	368,158	50,599
1937			199,283	286,604	2,037,071	447,150	2,527,672	160,245	87,312	398,625	45,039
1938			198,836	275,373	2,158,076	428,826	2,630,286	170,889	88,897	437,239	42,860
1939			206,995		2,214,070	408,844	2,663,067		82,145	458,831	37,129
1940			188,825		2,226,575	304,124	2,571,163			487,257	33,842
1941			193,599		2,230,728	226,622	2,485,458			498,209	31,742
1942			206,565		2,206,209	217,783	2,453,932			519,322	32,995
1943			216,816		2,237,307	235,501	2,503,240			538,747	34,606
1944			232,215		2,373,381	265,763	2,672,845			553,724	37,453
1945			243,532	335,705	2,510,369	487,047	3,038,697	191,045		563,981	40,956
1946	701,448	357,818	267,876	354,878	2,635,346	645,345	3,322,358	197,638	114,588	558,584	47,662
1947	875,479	500,181	287,736	296,314	4,386,014	608,487	5,040,299	202,043	108,813	588,004	51,342
1948	844,653	570,768	296,175	223,495	4,751,030	629,025	5,422,437	203,094	117,244	635,658	52,697
1949	736,218	616,232	294,969	157,897	4,946,207	729,624	5,716,947	204,055	109,608	668,817	52,983
1950	684,698	614,366	283,907	140,190	4,971,191	908,161	5,920,172	203,094	105,609	722,073	53,697
1951	649,529	607,283		126,858	4,937,427	876,275	5,849,002		112,000	739,474	53,852
1952	627,827	621,074		116,327	3,071,935	1,014,524	6,107,859		110,000	746,004	53,911
1953	607,456	657,042	283,221	113,455	5,056,912	1,004,685	6,096,022	178,004	111,000	753,785	54,346
1954	585,479	666,373		115,494			6,498,027		112,000	757,426	54,111
1955		689,040							125,000		

Germany: 1. Figures prior to 1919 from J. Longuet, 'Le mouvement socialiste international (Encyclopédie socialiste, syndicale et coopérative de l'Internationale ouvrière), Paris, 1913, pp. 231-32. Cf. also: Yearbook of the International Labour Movement, 1956-57, London, 1956.
2. 1946-50 figures relate to West Germany only (in the corresponding area, in 1931, the Socialist party numbered 610,212 members).

Belgium: The Belgian Socialist party claimed 150,000 members in 1951 (individual members) against 650,000 in 1931 (affiliated members: the two figures are not comparable because of dual or triple affiliations which magnify the real figures). In 1951 it claimed 222,669 (again individual members. Cf. J. Longuet, op. cit., pp. 115-16).

Great Britain: The total includes not only Trade Union and Individual members but also members affiliated through Co-operative, Friendly, and Socialist Societies.

Holland: Figures from 1946 onwards are for 31 December each year, except in 1950 when figures are for 30 September. The December figures are generally about 2,000 below those for September.

Except where otherwise indicated all statistics are taken from the official party handbooks.

parties. They tend, moreover, as we shall see, to lose their pure mass-party characteristics.

Finally this distinction between cadre parties and mass parties coincides with differences arising out of the various kinds of party organization. Cadre parties correspond to the caucus parties, decentralized and weakly knit; mass parties to parties based on branches, more centralized and more firmly knit. Differences in recruiting technique follow from the differences in the kind of community to be fashioned. As for parties based upon cells or upon militia, they too are mass parties, but less definitely so. It is true that Communist and Fascist parties enrol the masses in as great numbers as do Socialist parties, even before their seizure of power and their transformation into the sole party: the German National Socialist party numbered 800,000 members in 1932, the French Communist party one million members in 1945, the Italian Communist party two million members in 1950. A development can however be traced. Periodically, Communist parties indulge in internal 'purges', with the aim of banishing the lukewarm, the passive, the suspect; in this way quality again becomes more important than quantity. They tend moreover to exercise strict supervision of recruitment: some Socialist parties similarly provide for this kind of supervision, but the system is little applied by them whereas the Communists seem to be stricter. In Fascist parties the emphasis on quality is even more marked, more perhaps in their doctrine, which is clearly aristocratic, than in their practice: the enormous growth in numbers of the National Socialist party in the last years before the seizure of power can scarcely have permitted any serious 'screening' of members.

In any case the general tendency is undeniable. It raises the problem of whether we are still dealing with true mass parties or whether there is a gradual evolution towards a new conception, a third category: devotee parties, more open than cadre parties, but more closed than mass parties. In the Leninist conception the party should not include the whole of the working class: it is only the advance guard, the fighting wing, the 'most enlightened' section of the working class. This represents a change from the conception of the party as class; it is the party conceived as the élite. Fascist doctrines are even more definite on this point; anti-egalitarian and Nietzschean, fundamentally aristocratic, they view the party as an 'Order', made up of the best, the most faithful, the most brave, the most suitable. The age of the masses is gone: we are in the age of élites. In consequence the meaning given to the term 'member' tends to vary. Even within the party there are to be found concentric circles corresponding to different degrees of loyalty and activity. In the National Socialist party there was first of all the Party, then the S.A., then the S.S. In the Communist party the official doctrine is egalitarian and therefore opposed to such a hierarchy; however, it is possible to discern an 'inner circle' that is reliable and permanent and around which is grouped the mass of ordinary members, often quite unreliable (the difference was very marked in the pre-war French Communist party).

The extent of such phenomena must not be exaggerated; they are as yet restricted. We may still classify the Communist and Fascist parties as mass parties so long as we remember their rather particular character, especially in view of the fact that the Socialist parties, in their early days, presented some characteristics analogous with those under discussion: they were then very strict about the members they recruited; before old age made them less exacting, they sought to be devotee parties. This last concept is clearly too vague to constitute a separate category, but it corresponds to an undoubted fact. In analysing what is meant by 'participation' we shall be led to consider it from another aspect.

11. THE POLITICAL PARTY AS A MODERNIZING INSTRUMENT

D. E. APTER

Sigmund Neumann, in trying to segregate crucial elements of political parties, suggests the following:

> A definition of 'party' might as well begin with its simple word derivation. To become a 'party' to something always means identification with one group and differentiation from another. Every party in its very essence signifies *partnership* in a particular organization and *separation* from others by a specific program.
>
> Such an initial description, to be sure, indicates that the very definition of party presupposes a democratic climate and hence makes it a misnomer in every dictatorship. A one-party system (*le parti unique*) is a contradiction in itself.[1]

There are good reasons why political parties are so hard to define. Their genesis is difficult to disentangle from the evolution of the modern society and state; the role of a party often changes substantially as political conditions in a country change (particularly in modernizing societies, where various political developments may bring about an elaborate and complex polity from a rudimentary one); and in developing countries, a peculiar relationship exists between state and society — they are linked together by party solidarity. It is this last aspect more than any other that establishes the general basis of agreement on the rules of the polity.

In terms of one set of relationships, a primary function of parties is to organize public opinion and test attitudes and to transmit these to government officials and leaders so that

---

[1] Neumann, *Modern Political Parties* (University of Chicago Press, 1956), p. 395.

the ruled and rulers, public and government, are in reasonably close accord. The entire representative principle of government rests on this relationship. From this point of view, we may see parties, first, as intervening variables between the public and the government.

A second significant characteristic of political parties is that their form is determined by the entire sociopolitical framework of the society. They depend upon the degree of modernization in a society for their pluralism and diversity; they require a constitutional framework or political regime congenial to their functioning (no matter which type they are); and they depend upon the groupings in the society for their membership. In this sense, political parties are dependent variables, with society and governmental organization, election or co-optation procedures, and the like, the independent variables.

A third significant aspect of political parties is their obvious importance as subgroups in the system with their own means of generating power. In terms of this aspect, which is most critical in the new nations, where the party is often the microcosm of the future society, the party can be identified as an independent variable. Society and government become dependent on party organization, the decisions of party leaders, and the framework the party imposes on society.

If the observer does not sort out the three aspects of political parties — as intervening, dependent, or independent variable — the political situation in a country will seem confused and baffling.

THE MODERNIZING IMPACT

As political parties become organized in a modernizing society, they engage in a variety of activities, not all of which are familiar to Western observers. In order to arouse political interest (sometimes for the first time), they make use of technologically advanced artifacts. Political action means loudspeakers, mobile propaganda vans, and business suits. The briefcase becomes as much the mark of the politician as of the civil servant.[2]

---

[2] Speaking of Africa, Thomas Hodgkin emphasizes the special significance of improved transportation. 'A modern political party must be able to deploy, with reasonable ease and speed, its leaders and organis-

The relationship between party and modernization, whether modernization in technology or organization, appears clearly in the campaigns and manifestoes of the various political parties. As a goal, modernization is particularly effective since the desire for education is widespread throughout the developing areas.

The employment of all the mass media during political campaigns, the use of journalists, cartoonists, poster-makers, and pamphleteers, also helps to identify political action with modernity and to stress the instrumental role of party activity in change and innovation. Similarly, the registration of voters, compilation of lists, and appointment of polling officers, voting papers and ballot boxes, the use of school children as messengers and of schools as meeting halls, and even the organization of a country into voting constituencies, districts, and wards, all encourage the identification of the mechanics of politics with a modern culture.[3]

---

ers. It must ensure a reasonable degree of central or regional control over local branches and groups. It is highly desirable (and, in the political context of French Africa, essential) to enjoy means of rapid communication between the colonial territory and the metropolitan capital. These technical preconditions of effective party organisation, propaganda, and pressure, have been largely satisfied in post-war colonial Africa. It would be hard to exaggerate the revolutionary political consequences of the creation of an efficient internal and international air net work. In practice, this means that M. Mamadou Konaté [now deceased], deputy for the French Sudan [now independent Mali] can attend a meeting of his party executive in Bamako in the morning; take part in a session of the *Grand Conseil* at Dakar in the late afternoon; and speak in the National Assembly in Paris next day. Dr. Nkrumah, Mr. Awolowo and Isma'il al-Azhari can combine their party, parliamentary and ministerial duties in the same way. At a less exalted level, the improvement in road communications has made it possible for the middle-rank leadership of parties — national officials, regional and district secretaries and agents — to penetrate into obscure villages in lorries, private cars, party vans, or even on bicycles. Thus party propaganda and slogans can be widely diffused, local branches established, and local grievances ventilated. The gospel is preached; new converts are won; the faithful are confirmed — even in the remoter bush' (Hodgkin, *Nationalism in Colonial Africa* [London: Frederick Miller Ltd, 1956], p. 143).

3 See the fascinating account of the elections of May, 1956, and March, 1957, in Nigeria by Philip Whitaker (Western Region) and J. H. Price (Eastern Region), in W. J. M. Mackenzie and Kenneth E.

Because political activities bring the parties into direct contact with the population, they, more than the civil service, army, or even the government itself, have the most immediate impact in developing communities. The other primary carriers of modernization — schools, Christianity, Islam, business firms and commercial enterprises, the market, a cash economy, and so on — are all utilized (and in a widespread manner) by the contemporary nationalist political party. The party needs money and keeps books. It develops a press and printing establishments. The techniques of management are employed to hold followers and to regularize authority and leadership. The party penetrates churches and mosques. Intense movement, from country to city, and from rural hut to modern, air-conditioned offices, characterizes the activities of party leaders and, more important, their followers. Outside the party headquarters of virtually all nationalist parties congregations of people can be found who are hoping for a handout or benefit, buttonholing a politician in order to complain about something, or basking in the aura of modernity. Simply to be there, talking and chatting with others about politics and personalities, is exciting and cosmopolitan.

And what a strange combination of organizations fall under the general rubric 'political party'. Sometimes they are simply coalitions of different organizations, some directly political, others not. The Burmese (AFPFL) Anti-Fascist People's Freedom League, for example, was a coalition that included socialists and Marxists in the Socialist Party of Burma, the All-Burma Peasants Organizations, the Federation of Trade Organizations, the Trade Union Congress, the Women's Freedom League, Burma Muslim Congress, Kachin National Congress, the Union Karen League, Chin's Congress, the United Hill People's Congress, the All-Burma Fire Brigade, the All-Burma Teacher's Organization, and the St. John's Ambulance Brigade. In the national elections of 1956 it won 148 out of a total of 250 seats, after which it began to break apart because of internal corruption and conflicts in personalities and ideologies.[4]

Robinson (eds.), *Five Elections in Africa* (Oxford: Clarendon Press, 1960).

[4] See the description by Lucian Pye, in Robert E. Ward and Roy C. Macridis (eds.), *Modern Political Systems: Asia* (Englewood Cliffs, N.J.: Prentice-Hall Inc., 1963), p. 336.

In contrast to the loose structure of coalitions such as the Burma AFPFL are the strongly 'articulated', to use Maurice Duverger's phrase, or militant parties. An example is the Parti Démocratique of Guinea, a militant party dedicated to 'permanent revolution'. It is based on democratic centralism, with an elaborate local structure composed of 7,000 village and ward committees, 163 sections, assemblies, congresses, and auxiliaries under tight control of the party. It has a youthful membership (with a mean age of thirty-seven) and without doubt is the pre-eminent organization in that society. Government is its dependency and the public its raw material.[5]

In Guinea, as in some other African states like Mali and Ghana, the political party has become more than a substitute for the colonial power. It organizes power from 'below', where government might otherwise have no independent validity or vitality of its own. In a sense, we can say that the party actually generates power, shapes it, and applies it to government, which, one step removed, translates it into its various decisions and acts.

To a certain extent a party in a modernizing nation does not need to commit itself to a particular schedule of benefits on which it is periodically judged (as in the West). It has the advantage of being a window to a wider world for many in the villages, linking immediate effort with a wider purpose. The individual suddenly sees that he is more than a unit in a kinship structure. He may be elected as a representative of his fellows or be given a post. He may feel the flood of self-esteem that comes with authority. The diffusion of generalized power provides a *feeling* of participation, beyond that gained in regularly scheduled elections and periodic and rather formal referendums, that is immediate, local, and enjoyable.

Shared responsibility through the political party is most effective in single-party countries in which the major issues of state are excluded from public discussion. In such countries

---

[5] The best description of the PDG is Bernard Charles's 'Un Parti Politique Africain, Le Parti Démocratique de Guinee', *Revue Française de Science Politique*, XII (June 1962). See also L. Gray Cowan's useful discussion in Gwendolen M. Carter, *African One-Party States* (Ithaca, N.Y.: Cornell U.P., 1962). The best review of political parties in Africa is Thomas Hodgkin's *African Political Parties* (London: Penguin Books, 1961).

the local variations in policy bite most deeply into people's lives and become the focal points for experiment and heated debate. Quite often political trivia are the substance of developmental politics, with the wider issues of politics remaining remote from the individual and impossible for him to comprehend.

Under such conditions, the party attracts more of our attention than government. Leaders are almost always leaders of parties first and government officials second. There are powerful exceptions to this generalization. But the exceptions are made more interesting by the general rule. In Morocco, for example, it is surprising that El Mehdi ben Barka is in exile and Hassan is on the throne. In most such cases it would be the other way around. The kings and colonials depart, and the party leaders remain. Clearly then, modernizing political parties can go much further than their Western counterparts because they, in effect, serve as microcosms of the new societies. Even when the parties are monopolistic (that is, when the party's ideology is the foundation of legitimate authority in the state), their structures incorporate such diversity that the real instruments of bargaining and debate in the country — the 'legislatures' — are the party congresses, the presidium, or the national party executive rather than the formal governmental organization.

In modernizing systems, then, it is obvious that parties are rarely limited to the more or less passive role of transmitting private wants to the makers of public policies. Nor are they aggregative devices, collecting varying expressions of want, belief, and outlook in some faithful manner. Quite the contrary, the political parties of a modernizing society play an active entrepreneurial role in the formation of new ideas, in the establishment of a network of communication for those ideas, and in the linking of the public and the leadership in such a way that power is generated, mobilized, and directed.

Hodgkin has pointed out for Africa what is clearly also the case elsewhere. There 'mass parties' have developed a multiplicity of functions of a 'judicial, administrative, police, educational, and social welfare type' in addition to their 'conventional electoral and parliamentary functions. In the case of parties in opposition to a colonial regime, this is liable to mean that the party becomes, in effect, a parallel state. In the case of parties in power it may mean a blurring of the distinction between the functions and responsibilities of the party on the one hand and those of the government and administration on the other'.[6]

THE PARTY AND INTERMEDIATE POLITICAL ROLES

We have suggested that a distinct feature of modernization is the proliferation of roles in the areas between traditional and modern life. Political parties and their auxiliaries serve as the framework in which these intermediate or accommodationist groups are interrelated. This is an extremely important task if we consider how difficult it is, even in Western societies, for different functional groupings to have a common political language. If, as C. P. Snow has said, the technician and the intellectual are inarticulate in each other's presence, how much greater are the barriers to communication in a modernizing community between farmers and civil servants, laborers, lorry drivers, and intellectuals who have only some aspects of tradition in common.[7]

Modernization brings people together into different social clusters based on occupation and work, education, foreign travel, and religion. They may live together in residential areas or blocks of flats reserved for, say, civil servants or technicians. Primordial attachments to linguistic groups or particular ethnic associations give way in the more generalized modern complex of relationships. On the other hand, new tensions and conflicts leading to mutual antagonisms that are just as intense and divisive as any of those in the past may arise, as was suggested in the previous chapter, from the separation of the highly educated from the uneducated, the urban from the rural, and all those who come to represent the modern establishment from the general population. Moreover, these mod-

---

[6] Hodgkin, *African Political Parties*, p. 167.

[7] So different are the traditions in many cases, however, that a recounting of them may drive the community apart, particularly when the traditions are ethnically based. Thus, in Ghana, political conflict arose in the form of ethnic antagonisms between 1954 and 1957. The most extreme form of ethnic conflict occurred in the Congo and served to focus modern conflicts, for example, between rural and urban groups, ethnically advantaged and ethnically disadvantaged, socialist and Catholic. Older ethnic issues helped to concentrate newer forms of antagonism so that the lines of cleavage on all issues were similar. Modern political parties, particularly of the type that emphasizes solidarity by monopolizing loyalties, try to bridge these 'primordial' sentiments.

ern divisions may be linked with traditional ones, as, to some extent, occurred in the Congo, with disastrous results.

The differentiation brought about by modernity can thus drive wedges between peoples as well as link them. This is why the elite-mass relationship is so important. Men may join together to turn out a machine product or to build a road, but their mutual understanding may remain limited to matters connected with the machine or the road. Otherwise, their life styles, housing, kin relationships, and general intellectual orientation may diverge even more than before. In most traditional societies, after all, everyone understood what roles were available. The chief or king did not live so differently from the farmer, only a bit more elaborately. Not so today, when cultural differentiation follows economic differentiation and sets up barriers to an effective set of intermediate groupings.

It is the political party that links the various functional bodies together. Party groups may be organized in factories, schools, churches, clans, extended families, and co-operatives, which will then be linked together by their connection with the party. No matter how reluctant he may be, the civil servant with the overseas degree may be forced to communicate with a rural party official or with a taxi driver who may have an important position in the party. To this extent, channels of communication are opened up between otherwise hostile or non-communicating groups, bringing them into sets of relationships out of which the state is built. This, more than any other factor, is the basis of the success of the single-party state. Its monolithic structure helps create many intermediate groupings in the society and binds them together, even those parts that are likely to be hostile to each other. Hence the political party derives its significance in terms quite opposite to those of the elite.

Where such a function is not limited to political parties, as in the cases of the army in the Sudan and the civil service in Ethiopia, it may be possible to maintain the continuity of tradition into modernity or alter it to conform to a new perspective. Such political groups often become 'government'.[8]

---

[8] In Western societies, the situation is very different. The presence of several competing political parties distinguishes the democratic from the autocratic modes of government. Competition for votes is widely regarded as the best method of insuring accountability by the political leaders to those who elect them. Political virtue is maintained through

But their success is very rare in the absence of an effective mass party.

In the West, political parties are thought of primarily as representative instruments, a means of insuring peaceful and regular alternation of governments through the succession of leaders to public office. The democracy practised by a multiparty government is one of the few systems in which succession in public office is a regular and healthy feature of political life. Without bitter purges and internecine warfare between oligarchs (as occurred, for example, after the deaths of both Lenin and Stalin in the Soviet Union) or conflicts over leadership (as in countries as diverse as Turkey, Vietnam, South Korea, and the Dominican Republic), stable multiparty democracy has solved the problem of peaceful succession in public office.

Whatever the form parties are important not only in the 'circulation of elites', to employ Pareto's phrase, but also as an instrument of political education and socialization that shapes the habits and attitudes of a people toward government. Parties, for example, extract certain policy modalities, which can be understood by voters, from the discontinuous and chaotic practices of government. By distinguishing the important from that which is not and by identifying current and historical issues with popular figures, parties arouse interests and passions in the political process. Parties help people, from childhood on, assimilate values about government and the form of the political process.[9] This is particularly important in modernizing nations, where generational differences and political socialization often vary. By defining permissible forms of political behavior, the socialization function

_____

periodic elections at which the government and opposition parties present themselves to the electorate for popular approval.

[9] In many of the new states, the parties make particular efforts to attract youth and to influence their early training and education. Herbert Hyman has shown that in democratic societies even children adopt political prejudices and preferences very early in life, largely as a result of the influence of the family. In a sense, the political modernization process in which political parties engage in the developing areas begins with the transfer of political socialization from the family to youth auxiliaries or other bodies. During colonial periods, the same functions were performed by the Boy Scouts, as in our own society. See Hyman, *Political Socialization* (Glencoe: Free Press of Glencoe, Ill., 1959), chap. iii.

of political parties determines the nature of political tolerance in society and the orientation of leaders and followers.

Representation, peaceful succession in office, and the socialization of values intrinsic to democracy are the functions of parties in societies that are approaching the secular-libertarian model; but they are all means to an end. This end is the constant scrutiny and re-evaluation by citizens of the problems they face and the solutions they pose. As Karl Jaspers puts it, 'The democratic idea requires justice for human variety and for the scale of rank among men, which can never be objectively determined. In the democratic ethos of equality no one is either despised or idolized. The greater and more solid carry weight; self-restraint is practiced for the love of quality, yet no one demands recognition of his own superior quality'.[10] Multiparty democracy helps to institutionalize and continually reinforce the qualities stressed by Jaspers. It is fickle with heroes and hard on villains. In the restless search for issues and grievances, political parties do more than find a response that will propel them to public office; they also probe for weaknesses in persons in power and in policies and subject them to the spotlight of publicity. This itself is a humbling experience. It helps to maintain the attitudes of fraternalism and individualism that are fundamental to the democratic way of life.

In the sacred-collectivity model, on the other hand, those functions disappear and the parties become devices for mobilizing and disciplining the population. Public offices become sinecures and autocratic regimes alternate with purges, revolts, and other forms of instability. These qualities make orderly change difficult and may intensify contempt for law and constitutionality. Instead of socializing values of compromise and accommodation, the moral imperative of the state becomes all-important, to the point that it saps the individuality of the citizen by denying him his moral and political personality.

These, then, are some of the functions and influences of political parties and elections. More important than their class basis, or their ideological structures, or even the quality of the leadership they train, are their capacities to represent the people, effect peaceful transition, and make men into sober political beings capable of accepting responsibility.

---

[10] Jaspers, *The Future of Mankind* (University of Chicago Press, 1958), pp. 310–11.

12. BASES OF PARTIES

M. DUVERGER

THE BASIC ELEMENTS

A party is not a community but a collection of communities, a union of small groups dispersed throughout the country (branches, caucuses, local associations, etc.) and linked by co-ordinating institutions. The term 'basic elements' is used for these component units of the party organization. The contrasting of direct and indirect parties was in a 'horizontal' plane; the idea of basic elements refers to a 'vertical' plane. Each of the corporate or professional groups which compose an indirect party is itself a union of 'basic elements': Trade Unions, Co-operatives, Guilds of the Boerenbond, local middle-class Leagues, etc.; but these are not political by nature: the party only appears through their agglomeration, either at the summit alone, or at the different levels. Moreover there should be no confusion between the 'basic elements', the units from which the party springs, and the 'ancillary organizations', institutions which centre upon it, either to bring together supporters, or to strengthen the bonds of membership: youth movements, women's organizations, sports clubs, cultural organizations, etc. As a matter of fact it is not always easy to distinguish between them and the professional or corporate communities whose union forms the indirect parties: the Trade Unions, for example, are sometimes ancillary organizations of a direct party, sometimes a branch of an indirect party. Only a general analysis of the structure of a party makes it possible to distinguish between the two.

The basic elements of each party have their own particular form. The French Radical Socialist caucus, the branch of the

From *Political Parties*, by M. Duverger, Methuen, 1955, pp. 17–20, 23–24, 27–30. We are grateful to the publisher for permission to reproduce this extract.

French Socialist party, the caucuses and electoral agents of the American parties, the cells of the Communist parties, the 'fasces' of the Italian Fascist party: all these institutions are profoundly different one from the other. Each party has its own structure which bears little resemblance to that of other parties. In spite of everything four main types of basic element may be distinguished and most of the existing parties can be related to one of them. These elements are the caucus, the branch, the cell, and the militia.

The Caucus

Though this unit might equally well be called a committee, a clique, or a coterie, the English political term 'caucus' will be used here. The first characteristic of the caucus is its limited nature. It consists of a small number of members, and seeks no expansion. It does not indulge in any propaganda with a view to extending its recruitment. Moreover, it does not really admit members, for this limited group is also a closed group; you do not get into it simply because you desire to do so: membership is achieved only by a kind of tacit co-option or by formal nomination. In spite of this numerical weakness the caucus nevertheless wields great power. Its strength does not depend on the number of its members but on their quality. It is a group of notabilities, chosen because of their influence.

The caucus functions in a rather large geographical area, usually corresponding to the chief electoral division. In France the caucuses work really within the framework of the arrondissement, which was the basic political division under the Third Republic. In America they are especially important in the counties and municipalities within which take place the elections for the principal administrative posts available as 'spoils'. Moreover the activity of the caucus is seasonal: it reaches its peak at election times and is considerably reduced in the intervals between the ballots. In short the caucus is semi-permanent by nature: we no longer have an ephemeral institution, created for a single electoral campaign and destined to end with it: neither do we yet have a completely permanent institution, like the modern parties for whom agitation and propaganda never cease.

Underlying these general characteristics, several types of caucus can be distinguished. First, there is the distinction between the 'direct' caucus and the 'indirect' caucus. The French Radical Socialist caucuses are a good example of the first. They are composed of notabilities chosen for their individual qualities and their personal influence: influential tradesmen, small country landowners, notaries or doctors in the country or in small towns, civil servants, teachers, lawyers, etc. None of them formally represents a class or a group: they are not delegates but individuals. Moreover their selection does not depend on any precise rule: it is the result of a kind of tacit co-option. Let us consider on the other hand a Labour party caucus in an electoral constituency before there were individual members: it was composed of members elected respectively by the local branches of the Trade Unions, the Trades Councils, the Socialist societies, the Co-operative organizations, and so on. This basic element of the Labour party consisted in the meetings of the delegates of the local basic elements of each of the communities which collectively constituted the party: here was an 'indirect' caucus. However different it is from the French Radical caucus, a typical 'direct' caucus, it has in common with it the general elements just defined. Each of its members can be considered as a 'notability', no longer because of his own personal characteristics, but because of his special position as a delegate. This represents an abandonment of the idea of a traditional elite, outstanding through birth or natural selection, in favour of the idea of an 'institutional' elite, owing its position to the confidence of the organized masses.

With these caucuses of notabilities can be compared the caucuses of 'experts', composed of people chosen less for their personal influence than for their acquaintance with the methods of fighting an electoral campaign: American party caucuses for example. Nevertheless, the experts are met with less within the caucus itself than at the level of electoral agents, the representatives of the caucus in smaller local divisions, in which through them its influence permeates to the very foundations of the country. In France, the caucuses formed at the arrondissement level try to have an agent in each commune. In the United States the caucuses formed at the county or city level co-ordinate the action of the *precinct-captains* (there are about 3,000 counties and 140,000 precincts). These electoral agents must be distinguished from the voluntary propagandists who help the party caucuses during the electoral campaigns, for example the canvassers in England: the latter correspond to the idea of 'supporter' which will be defined later: the former constitute an element in the very framework of the party.

A detailed analysis of the position of electoral agents and the part they play would be very useful. They are rarely true employees of the caucus, paid by it and working full time for it. Neither are they purely voluntary assistants, like the supporters just mentioned. Generally they occupy an intermediate position, drawing certain material advantages from the party, but also having a private profession which gives them a certain independence. Nevertheless, in the United States the captains are sometimes supported entirely by the party, either directly or indirectly (the party giving them a more or less fictitious post which allows them to work for it). The important place held by liquor retailers in the cohort of electoral agents has often been remarked upon. What place could be more propitious for political propaganda than the bar, the tavern, or the pub, where people come to relax as well as to have a drink, and where people can meet in groups and have a free discussion? Who could be better placed than the manager to lead this discussion and to spread his ideas? With a little understanding of human nature he can exercise a great deal of influence: the parties know it and try to attract him. The bar tends to become the Agora of modern democracies. . . .

The Branch

In itself, the term 'branch' designates a basic element which is less decentralized than the caucus: a branch is only part of the whole, and its separate existence is inconceivable: on the other hand the word caucus evokes an autonomous reality, capable of living on its own. As a matter of fact, it will be seen that parties founded on branches are more centralized than those founded on caucuses. But the profound originality of the branch lies in its organization, and not in its connection with the other branches. In this respect, the branch can be described by contrasting each of its characteristics in turn with those of the caucus. The latter is restricted in nature, the branch is extensive and tries to enrol members, to multiply their number, and to increase its total strength. It does not despise quality, but quantity is the most important of considerations. The caucus formed a closed circle into which you could enter only by co-option or as a delegate; the branch is wide open. In practice you only need to wish to belong to be able to do so. Certainly most parties make rules of membership and define entrance requirements, as will be seen later; but these generally remain theoretical, at least in the branch system (this is less true for the cell system). The caucus is a union of notabilities chosen only because of their influence: the branch appeals to the masses.

Moreover it tries to keep in touch with them: which is the reason for its geographical basis being less extensive than that of the caucus. In France, for example, the caucuses function chiefly at arrondissement level: the branches are built up within the framework of the *commune*. In the large towns they even tend to multiply and to be based on the *quartier* or ward. Certain parties (but not all) also admit within the branch smaller subdivisions which make possible a closer-knit organization of members: German and Austrian 'block' and tenement units; French Socialist party 'groups'. Nevertheless, a certain mistrust of excessively small subdivisions, as leading to rivalry and disorder, can be seen: thus the constitution of the French Socialist party, when it was united in 1905, affirmed the precedence of the branch over the group by refusing the latter any kind of autonomy. This was a reaction provoked by the disputes between small groups which had weakened the earlier Socialist parties. Finally the permanence of the branch contrasts with the semi-permanent nature of the caucus. Outside the election period the latter lives through a period of hibernation in which its meetings are neither frequent nor regular. On the contrary the activity of the branches, obviously very great at election times, remains important, and above all regular, in the intervals between ballots. Socialist branches generally meet every month or every fortnight. Moreover the character of the meeting is not the same as that of the caucus: it deals not only with election tactics, but also with political education. Party speakers come to talk of problems to the branch members; their lecture is usually followed by a discussion. It is true that experience has shown that meetings have a strong tendency to wander on to petty local and electoral matters; but usually the parties make praiseworthy efforts to counter this tendency and to ensure an adequate place for discussions of doctrine and of general questions.

As the branch is a more numerous group than the caucus it possesses a more perfected internal organization. The caucus has a hierarchy of a very simple kind: usually the personal influence of a leader can be seen at work and that is all. It is sometimes predominant: in the United States the caucus often consists of none but the followers of the 'boss'. Sometimes there are offices and official titles: president, vice-president, treasurer, secretary, recorder. But they do not correspond to a very strict division of work; rather are they honorary distinctions (that of 'president' enjoys particular prestige). On the contrary the hierarchy of the branch is more definite and the division of duties more precise. An organized committee is necessary to direct the mass of members, and it must comprise at the very least a secretary to call meetings and draw up the agenda and a treasurer to collect individual subscriptions. Whence the setting up of a regular procedure for appointing the committee, generally by election. . . .

The Cell

Two fundamental features distinguish the cell from the branch: the basis of the group and the number of members. The branch, like the caucus, has a local basis, narrower than that of the caucus, but still geographical. On the contrary, the cell has an occupational basis; it unites all party members who work at the same place. There are factory, workshop, shop, office, and administration cells. The home of the members matters little: in the large towns, where many companies employ salaried workers who live in the suburbs, it is possible to find members of one cell who live quite a considerable way from one another. This dispersion is even greater in certain particular cases, notably that of 'shipboard cells', which unite the sailors of one ship. Nevertheless, area cells must of necessity exist side by side with workplace cells, either to unite isolated workers (in Communist parties you must have at least three members in a factory to form a cell) or to group the members of the party who do not work in a large undertaking: artisans, doctors, lawyers, tradespeople, industrialists, and landworkers. The area cell resembles the branch because of its geographical basis. It generally differs from it in the narrower character of the latter: instead of a branch for each *commune* we find district cells, a cell for each village and hamlet, street cells, and 'block' cells (in towns where there are large residential units). But area cells never have the same importance: the real cell is the workplace cell which unites party members working in the same place.

With regard to the number of its members, too, the cell is
a much smaller group than the branch. In an average district
a branch normally has more than a hundred members. Frequently there are branches with several hundred members,
and even with several thousand. Cell membership on the contrary must never reach a hundred. 'It was not without surprise
that we learnt that certain of our cells had more than a hundred members; there is no need to emphasize how impossible
it is for such cells to exert effective action', said M. Léon
Mauvais in his report on the problems of organization to the
French Communist party Congress in 1945.[1] Later he made a
more precise statement: 'There are cells of between fifteen
and twenty members which achieve three times as much work
as cells with fifty or sixty members.' So the optimum number
of members is between fifteen and twenty. Nevertheless, the
constitution of the Communist party does not fix any definite
ceiling because the number of members is not the only thing
that matters. There is also the question of finding additional
leaders. Dividing up an excessively large cell necessitates finding a second secretary capable of carrying out the duties involved. M. Léon Mauvais explains this very well when he
declares in the same report: 'As soon as circumstances allow
us to appoint a second secretary we must decentralize [that is
divide] the cells with too large a membership.'

The nature and size of the cell give it a much greater hold
on its members than has the branch. In the first place, we are
dealing with a group that is absolutely permanent since it is
set up at the very place where the party members meet daily
in their work. Apart from meetings proper, there is constant
contact between members. At the beginning or end of the
working day the secretary can easily circulate orders, share
out the work, and control the activity of each member. Action
is all the more effective for the average number of members
being low: in a branch of several hundred members the leaders can neither know each one personally nor keep in continuous contact with them all. In a cell of between fifteen
and twenty members this presents no particular difficulties.
The result is too that the members of the cells know each
other well and that party solidarity is stronger.

---

[1] *Le Parti communiste français, puissant facteur de l'union et la renaissance de la France*, brochure, Éditions du Parti communiste, 1945,
p. 10.

It is increased by the occupational nature of the cell which gives it a concrete direct basis: factory problems, conditions of work and salaries are an excellent point of departure for a sound political education. Certainly there is a danger here that the cell might become entirely taken up with vocational claims, to the exclusion of purely political questions, that is to say that it should do the usual work of a Trade Union. This 'economic' deviation is the permanent temptation of cells; on reading the reports on organization to the Communist party Congresses it can be seen that much effort is necessary to avoid succumbing to it.[2] But provided this can be avoided, what an admirable basis for the political formation of the masses! The major difficulty here is the inevitable divergence between principles and their daily application. The mass of the people soon loses interest in general ideas, even very attractive ones, unless the direct consequences are pointed out. For the masses politics are not a luxury. It is different in a large middle-class party, especially in Latin countries where ideas are cherished in their own right. Now, when the local group consists of a branch, this connection between principles and the realities of daily life is not encouraged. General politics have little direct connection with sewerage, the upkeep of local roads, or personal quarrels. On the other hand they have a close connection with wage increases, security of employment, conditions of work and business organization. These links are even closer if the party professes the Marxist doctrine which considers politics as but a superstructure of economics. If the party makes a constant effort to relate each particular claim to a general principle, to link each special problem to its policy as a whole and to give each question of detail a place in the pattern of its doctrine it will give its members a formation that is sound and unequalled; it will have an incomparable hold over them.

Certainly the bearing of this analysis is limited. It is especially valid for working-class parties: in the case of the others the cell pattern would weaken the political education and loyalty to the party rather than strengthen it. Working-class mentality in Europe considers the conditions of work and professional life to be the result of collective action of a political nature because it is only by collective action, usually political

---

[2] Cf. the interesting statements of M. A. Lecœur, in his report to the Twelfth Congress (1950), pp. 13 and 14.

in nature, that it has ever effectively succeeded in bettering them. On the other hand the upper and lower middle classes and the peasants tend to consider work and professional life as private matters because their progress is essentially the result of an individual personal effort (the American working class shares the same point of view); economic evolution, which is clearly heading for a planned economy, has not yet brought about any profound change in this attitude, precisely because the middle classes and the peasants refuse to acknowledge it. For the working-class parties themselves labour problems are not the only basis of political life. Many other factors come into play, notably passion, mysticism, and faith. None the less, the cell system remains very strong, all the more so as it makes it possible to link with the work of the factory political problems apparently far removed from working life: for example it makes possible the political strike either directly or through control of the trade unions.

13. OLIGARCHY IN LEADERSHIP

M. DUVERGER

The leadership of parties tends naturally to assume oligarchic form. A veritable 'ruling class' comes into being that is more or less closed; it is an 'inner circle' into which it is difficult to penetrate. The phenomenon is just as true of titular leaders as of the real leaders, of autocratic as of democratic rulers. In theory, the principle of election should prevent the formation of an oligarchy; in fact, it seems rather to favour it. The masses are naturally conservative; they become attached to their old leaders, they are suspicious of new faces. Socialist parties, in which the recruitment of leaders is more democratic than in others, find correspondingly greater difficulty in finding new leaders.

THE FORMATION OF THE 'INNER CIRCLE'

The electoral system of the State seems to exercise a certain influence upon the oligarchic nature of party leadership and the formation of 'inner circles'. In so far as no candidate has a chance of being elected without the approbation of the committees of the party, its leaders play an essential part in the selection of future parliamentary representatives: they are nominated by the inner circle. On the other hand, if free candidature is possible, or if the personality of the candidate plays an important part in the election, with the result that the party committees depend more upon the candidate than he upon them, then the recruitment of parliamentary representatives occurs outside the inner circle, and outside the party oligarchy. Since, under such circumstances, the parliamentary representatives too play a very important part in the leadership of the party, the inner circle opens and the elites

From *Political Parties*, by M. Duverger, Methuen, 1955, pp. 151–57. We are grateful to the publisher for permission to reproduce this extract.

become more mobile. In consequence, voting by lists, which is by its nature collective and dependent on the party, strengthens oligarchy, whereas single-member voting weakens it. The internal oligarchy reigns supreme in the P.R. system with fixed lists and the ranking of candidates in a strict order which determines their election, for here the parliamentary representatives are chosen by the inner circle; the party in this case is a closed circuit. The same effects are also observable in the two-party system because the quasi-monopoly of the two parties gives them preponderant power in the selection of candidates in spite of the single-member voting system.

From the point of view of their formation the classes of leaders and inner circles can be divided into several kinds. No doubt the simplest is to be seen in the *camarilla,* a small group which makes use of close personal solidarity as a means of establishing and retaining its influence. Sometimes it takes the form of a clique grouped around an influential leader: this leader's retinue has a monopoly of the positions of leadership and takes on the characteristics of an oligarchy. Some examples of cliques in Socialist parties have already been cited. They flourish best in conservative and moderate parties in which the rivalry between cliques takes the place assumed elsewhere by the struggles between 'wings' or 'tendencies'; control of the party is almost always in the hands of the dominant cliques. The structure of the party favours the development of cliques; we need only recall the composition of the central bodies of the Radical party to see that everything is so arranged as to allow of the interplay between personalities with their retinues. In American parties the way the machines are organized around the bosses shows similar characteristics.

There is a distinction to be made between such clans and 'teams of leaders' which are not united by any personal attachment to a dominant chief: the distinctive feature of the team is the comparative equality that rules among its members, the fact that its bonds develop horizontally and not vertically. Such teams are formed in very different ways. Sometimes it happens that they are the result of a deliberate compact entered into by a few men, generally belonging to a new generation, who unite in order 'to shake the fruit tree', to win the positions of control from those in possession, and to monopolize them for their own advantage: this is the phenomenon that in literary and artistic matters produces schools

and coteries, but it is to be seen occurring quite frequently
in politics. Sometimes they are mythomaniacs pursuing their
dream of 'synarchy', that is the formation of a secret team
uniting influential leaders from several different parties, in
which case they are not to be taken seriously. There are however serious teams set up within individual parties: round
about 1933–4 a team of this kind could be seen forming
around the French Radical Socialist party (around Pierre Cot,
Jean Mistler, Pierre Mendès-France, etc.), but the events of
6 February 1934 broke it up: its members were not averse to
being called 'Young Turks', with the 1908 Revolution in
mind. More frequently such teams are the result of a spontaneous fellowship arising out of shared origins or training:
there is the local group (e.g. 1792 Girondins), the old boys'
group (e.g. the former students of the École Polytechnique
in Paris), the group that arises from collaboration in one organization (e.g. the Treasury), the group knit by war (e.g.
Old Soldier of the — Regiment).

The first of these is the most important: in districts in which
parties have long held sway there naturally grow up local
teams which often play an important part in the life of the
party. Albert Thibaudet was ironical at the expense of Old
Sarrien and the Radical teams in the Department of Saône-et-
Loire; Daniel Halévy observed that the evolution of the Radical party at the beginning of the century was synonymous
with the decline of the Parisian teams and the rise of those
from the Centre and the South. In the history of the French
Socialist party during the last half-century the passage of the
various teams, from the North, from Languedoc and Pro-
vence, from the Centre, and from Toulouse and so on, has left
fairly clear traces. Similar phenomena can be observed in all
parties. Some, the Communist parties in particular, attempt to
prevent them by such measures as 'rotation' and 'uprooting',
which we shall study later. The other types of team are much
less common within parties. It is comparatively rare to find
in them traces of influence similar to that exercised by Treasury officials or by Old Polytechnicians upon certain French
ministries: one example that might be quoted is the part
played within the M.R.P. by teams that arose out of the
Catholic Association of French Youth. In many present-day
European parties there are to be found teams of leaders that
grew out of common action in the Resistance Movement during the Occupation: on occasion there has moreover been

some rivalry between the London team and the team from the internal Resistance. A similar state of affairs was to be seen in the Russian Communist party after its seizure of power. The recent purges in Western European Communist parties generally aimed at eliminating the London teams to the advantage of the internal Resistance (or the Moscow) team; it is also worth noting that some purges were directed against the teams brought together in the struggle against Franco during the Spanish war.

Teams and cliques are personal oligarchies. On the other hand bureaucracy provides us with a type of institutionalized oligarchy. Unimaginable in the old parties based upon caucuses linked by a weak system of articulation, it came to birth with the branch system and complex structure and has developed more especially in the parties that are linked with Trade Unions, Co-operative and Friendly Societies. Thus, the German Social Democratic party had 3,000 permanent officials in 1910 (that is approximately one official per 250 members).[1] These permanent officials tended to play a dominant role: since their duties put them in daily contact with the base, they easily secured appointment as delegates to Congress and were thus able to exercise a decisive influence upon the composition of the governing bodies. Moreover their position within the party gave them immediate authority over the members: the permanent secretary of a Departmental federation obviously became the king-pin of the federal committee in which the other members, taken up with their private work, could not play so active a part. As a result of this twin mechanism the growth of a bureaucracy, in the proper sense of the term, could be observed. Some parties sought to react against the tendency by limiting the number of permanent officials who could be sent as delegates to Congress. Thus the constitution of the Belgian Socialist party laid it down (Article 23) that federal delegates to the National Congress must be drawn as to at least one-half from outside the ranks of the party's parliamentary representatives and permanent officials. But the rule was relaxed for the General Council, which is in fact the most important organ of control: federations which send more than three delegates to it need to choose only a minimum of one-quarter of the delegates from out-

---

[1] According to a report on the 1910 Congress, *Revue politique et parlementaire,* 1910, p. 509.

side the ranks of the parliamentary representatives and permanent officials (Article 31); other federations may make up the whole of their delegation with representatives and officials: the restriction is slight.

Other parties on the contrary seek to develop into a system the use of permanent officials. In their view, the party resembles a professional army, at least so far as its leading strata are concerned. On this question Lenin wrote a few pages that are crucial for this question, particularly in *What is to be done?* He was impressed by the terrible restrictions imposed on revolutionary action by daily work in the factory, the shop, and the workshop. He thought total and permanent devotion to the party, with no interruption or hindrance due to external cares, was essential for the formation of the real agitators in the new party. Hence the idea which he expounded on many occasions of the creation of a veritable class of professional revolutionaries who would act as the central nucleus of the party and would provide its basic militant members. 'No working-class agitator', he said, 'who has talent and shows promise should work eleven hours a day in a factory. We must arrange that he be maintained by the party'.[2] He makes it clear that the party should 'rely upon people who devote to the revolution not their free evenings but their whole life',[3] 'people whose profession is that of a revolutionary'.[4]

The ideas of Lenin seem to concern not only the leaders but also the militants. In practice, in so far as the latter are maintained by the party, they are naturally given positions of control because they alone dispose of sufficient leisure to fill these positions effectively. To create a 'class of professional revolutionaries' is equivalent to creating a class of 'professional leaders of revolutionary parties', an inner circle which stirs up the masses and which is founded upon the official duties performed within the party; it is equivalent to creating a bureaucracy, that is to say an oligarchy. If the posts for the party's permanent officials were strictly elective bureaucracy could coincide with democracy. But this is not so and cannot be so: the militants who are capable of filling a permanent position and willing to do so are not very numerous;

---

[2] Op. cit. Cf. *Selected works*, London, 1947, vol. I, p. 240.
[3] *Iskra*, no. 1.
[4] *What is to be done?* op. cit. p. 225.

the leaders of the party are anxious to keep close control of them so as to be certain of their technical ability and of their political trustworthiness; the leadership, as we have seen, is largely made up of permanent officials already in office. Thus there is born an authentic oligarchy which exercises power, retains it, and transmits it by means of co-option.

Sometimes the bureaucratic oligarchy assumes the form of a technocratic oligarchy. 'Courses for leaders' are set up inside the party which one must attend before being given a post of leadership. The system was first used by the Socialist parties in an attempt to form a political elite within the working class. In 1906 the German Social Democratic party founded in Berlin the *Parteischule* which aimed at completing the training of the permanent officials already in office in the party and at training candidates for employment in the party or in Trade Unions.[5] In 1910–11 141 students attended its courses: 52 party officials and 89 candidates, of whom 49 found positions on finishing the course. The Communist parties developed such training courses systematically. In the French Communist party at the present moment there are three kinds of course: the central, federal, and elementary. The first is further subdivided into 'four-month courses' intended for the higher leaders (parliamentary representatives, members of the Central Committee, federal delegates; 96 militants attended them in 1947–8) and into 'four-week courses', more particularly intended for leaders in agricultural areas and in ancillary organizations (in 1947–8 at least, when 292 militants attended them). The second category, federal courses, which last a fortnight, are provided for members of the federal and section committees (2,071 in 1947–8).[6] Furthermore there are courses in Moscow for the training of the highest and most trusted leading strata: those who have attended them form the supreme aristocracy of the party.

The Fascist parties and the National Socialist party in particular adopted similar methods. After seizing power the latter created veritable 'leadership schools' for its higher and middle-ranking leaders. The machinery for selecting and training future leaders was very highly organized. A thousand individ-

[5] Roberto Michels, *Political Parties,* p. 34.

[6] Information taken from report of M. Casanova to Central Committee on 28 February 1949 and from article by A. Parinaud, *Cahiers du Communisme,* October 1949, p. 1241.

uals a year were chosen from the total membership of the Hitler Youth Movement. After a period of initial training in the 'Adolf Hitler Schools' a further drastic selection took place. A small number of future leaders was then admitted to a special course of training for three years. After a period of foreign travel intended to broaden the mind the first year of study was designed to test their resistance and their character, the second to form them spiritually, the third to provide them with technical knowledge. There was provision for a period of practical work with a party leader. Obviously a system so highly organized is possible only under a single-party regime when the selection of leaders for the party is tantamount to choosing the leading political strata of the state.

The present-day Austrian Socialist party has organized a very interesting system for the privileged category of militants that are called in its constitution the 'party co-operators' (*Parteimitarbeiter*). They must attend the central training courses organized by the party (Article 1 of the constitution). If they wish to 'rise to the highest posts in the party' (ibid.), they must attend the more advanced training courses. The list of 'co-operators' is drawn up by the district committees, which are themselves elected by the delegates of the local branches. But the latter can elect as members of their committee only 'co-operators'. Since the leaders of the branch are generally chosen by it as its delegates to the district conferences at which the district committees are elected the result is that everything takes place in a closed circuit: the 'co-operators' play the fundamental part in the appointment of the district committee which itself nominates the 'co-operators'. This is an oligarchy into which entrance is gained by co-option combined with attendance at leaders' training courses. This system reproduces, officially and with refinements, practices that other parties follow without acknowledgement. It corresponds moreover to an attempt to make the party democratic. There is a list of co-operators from which branches may choose their responsible officers; each branch has the right of proposing to the district committee names for the list; the co-operators are numerous (50,000 out of 614,000 party members in 1950). A remarkable effort is made to give the base an opportunity of choosing the oligarchs.

14. PERSONALIZATION OF POWER

M. DUVERGER

The form of authority becomes modified within parties: a double evolution can be seen. The first phase is one of a slow change from personal government to institutional government. In the second phase a certain reversal of the process can be seen. Authority has taken on a personal character again, while retaining the framework of the institutions. This evolution is moreover not confined to political parties: it is met with in other communities and first of all in the State.

The development of Socialist parties at the end of the nineteenth century and later imitation of their methods by others, notably the Christian Democratic parties, had as a consequence the perfecting of the governing institutions. Formerly they were often very sketchy. Locally authority belonged to the party representative in parliament, to a boss or to some influential notability who either occupied the official function of a President or who remained in obscurity. Nationally there were indeed official committees and offices, but effective government was ensured by recognized leaders. It was men who were obeyed: Disraeli, Gladstone, Gambetta. Official institutions remained either factitious or supple; factitious when they remained ornamental in character, their members exercising no effective authority; supple when they allowed free play to personal influences. On the contrary Socialist parties made a great effort to establish an organized, institutionalized leadership in which the office was more important than the person who held it. Two principles seem to have guided them here. On the one hand they gave authority a pyramidal character, so as to avoid concentrating the power in a few hands. Hence the usual differentiation between three superimposed organizations (with various names according to the country): the Central Office, a permanent organization consisting of very

From *Political Parties*, by M. Duverger, Methuen, 1955, pp. 177–82. We are grateful to the publisher for permission to reproduce this extract.

few members; the Committee, larger and semi-permanent, in which a few representatives from the federations are added to the Central Office ('General Council', 'National Council', etc.); finally the annual Congress, formed by delegates from the whole party. In principle the Congress has the power of decision; the National Committee may act in the interval between Congresses, within the limits set by them; the Central Office is only an executive body. In practice the Central Office plays a fundamental role. On the other hand, Socialist parties have established a kind of horizontal separation of powers, placing beside the administrative Committee and the Central Office, which are entrusted with political management and administration, a 'Control Committee', invested with a power of financial supervision: the creation of this body is a sign both of the desire to remove all temptation from the leaders and of the distrust the militant party members have of them. The establishment of party tribunals, of discipline committees, and disputes committees completes this separation of powers at the jurisdictional level.

There seemed therefore to be a very high degree of institutionalization, but in reality it was otherwise. To begin with this perfected organization was not set up without some difficulty. Some of the creators of Socialism were very authoritarian, very imbued with their personal power, and not much inclined to dilute it in institutional forms. The influence of Karl Marx was in actual fact preponderant in the First International. The creator of the first German Socialist party, Lassalle, had given it a definitely dictatorial structure in which his authority was predominant. Once the institutional organizations were set up the personal influence of one leader or another was always great: Stauning, Branting, Jules Guesde, Jaurès, Vandervelde, Léon Blum — the roles that these men played in their respective Socialist parties clearly exceeded their official functions. In fact, behind the institutional façade power tended to become just as personal in character in Socialist parties as in the earlier middle-class parties. The explanation lies in the massive structure of these parties: it is true, as M. Maurice Thorez has said, that 'the working class is not prone to the affliction that is particularly rife among the lower middle class: lack of recognition of the role of individuals'.[1] Their natural realism perceives the man behind

---

[1] Quoted by *Le Monde,* 23 December 1949.

the function, obeys the individual and not his title, and trusts in personal qualities rather than in ranks and uniforms. Belief in institutions is dependent on a certain abstract juridical culture and a respect for form and titles which belong to the middle class.

But it was precisely against this tendency towards the personalization of power that Socialist parties tried to struggle. In their structure they sought to limit it as far as possible. Here the collective character of all the executive bodies reinforced the division of responsibilities already described: in principle there were no 'leaders' or 'presidents', but only committees, officers, and secretaries entrusted with the responsibility of putting their decisions into practice. The first Communist parties acted in the same way. At that time the cult of the leader did not exist in Russia. The prestige of Lenin was immense, but Lenin himself tried to hold it within bounds and avoid the development of personal power. Proceedings in the Russian Communist party did actually remain collective; discussion in committees was real, decisions were indeed taken in common. It must not be forgotten that the sense of equality was so profoundly developed in the early days of Bolshevism that in the first place it was decided that all officials should receive the same salary, the People's Commissars being on the same footing as the others. Foreign Communist parties showed the same characteristics; there, too, an attempt was made to check the inclination of the masses towards personal power. The desire of the Comintern to banish the great figures of Socialism and to place reliable men in the posts of command was very effective in this respect: the parties found no leaders of first rank, no brilliant personalities like those who had worked in the early Socialist parties.

The tendency was reversed by the Fascist parties: they were the first to develop the cult of the leader, considered as a person and not as the holder of an office. They were the first to utilize the natural aspiration of the masses towards personal power, instead of keeping it in check, in order to strengthen the cohesion of the party and establish its framework. For them all authority comes from the leader and not from election; and the authority of the leader comes from his person, from his individual qualities, from his own infallibility, from his being a man of destiny. 'Mussolini is always right', the Fascists used to say. The Germans went further and invented a completely new juridical theory, that of the *Führung*, to explain and justify the sovereignty of Adolf Hitler. In the end Communist parties followed this example, and, for various reasons, reversed their previous policy. The transformation of the Russian Communist party and the evolution of power in the U.S.S.R. no doubt played an important part here, as each national party modelled its organization quite closely on that of the big brother. The growth of the cult of Stalin in Russia is a partial explanation of the development of tendencies towards the personalization of power in France, in Germany, in Italy, and in all the Communist parties in the world: it was on the occasion of Marshal Stalin's seventy-first birthday that M. Maurice Thorez sketched the analysis of the role of leaders in Marxism and in working-class mentality which was alluded to above.

The influence of the Resistance and of party martyrs should also be pointed out. After the Liberation the party based its propaganda to a large degree on the memory of those who had been lost by developing a real hagiography around them. The cult of dead heroes leads quite naturally to the cult of living heroes. Finally reasons of efficiency no doubt played a great part in this evolution, the successes of Fascist propaganda having made the Communists realize what sympathetic vibrations are aroused in the masses by the leader mystique: with its habitual realism the party deduced the lesson from the facts. At all events, since the Liberation the Communists have been systematically developing the personal loyalty of members to leaders. This they do not do in the same way as Fascist parties, at least for national leaders (apart from Stalin). They do not consider them as supermen: on the contrary they try to relate them carefully to their background, to give them an important place in daily life, by presenting them as nothing but models of all the virtues (the general tone of the biographies of Communist leaders recalls that of the edifying stories of the 'good little boy' at whom Mark Twain poked fun). This personalization of power can go very far. On the occasion of the fiftieth birthday of M. Maurice Thorez the party circulated special membership forms drawn up in the form of a letter: 'Dear Maurice Thorez, I wish you long life and good health, and on the occasion of your fiftieth birthday I am joining the French Communist party, etc.' At the top the form bore the words: 'I hereby join the party of Maurice Thorez' — and not 'to the Communist party'. The personalization of power is sometimes accompanied by a real deification of power. This is a revival of a very ancient form of authority, that of the Divine King. This is the case in Fascist parties and in Communist parties as far as Stalin is concerned. The leader is omniscient, omnipotent, infallible, and infinitely good and wise: every word that falls from his mouth is true; every wish emanating from him is party law. Modern techniques of propaganda make it possible to invest him with extraordinary ubiquity: his voice penetrates everywhere, thanks to the radio; his picture is in every public building, on every wall, and in the house of every active member. Sometimes this real presence is accompanied by invisibility of the person: everywhere in Russia the effigy of Stalin was to be seen, but Stalin rarely appeared in public. The extreme case would be the dictator, child of a novelist's imagination, the 'Big Brother' of George Orwell, whose voice and haunting image accompany each man at each instant of his life: but Big Brother is nothing but an image and a voice; Big Brother does not exist. In the end deified personal power becomes depersonalized: the leader becomes no more than an effigy, a name, a myth, behind which others give the orders. In a way the leader becomes in his turn an institution.

15. MASS PARTIES AND INDUSTRIALISED SOCIETIES

J. BLONDEL

While one quickly had to recognise many shortcomings in the
Duverger theory of party, the distinction between mass parties and parties of 'cadres' or of 'committees' appeared to
correspond to modern realities.[1] On the one hand, some parties are merely organisations of professional politicians, held
together in order to fill elective posts: on the other, some
parties bring within their fold hundreds of thousands of ordinary people who have no personal political aspirations but
simply want to promote a cause and help others to gain political power. Moreover, the distinction did not only help to
classify parties; it made it possible to relate parties more
closely to the type of society in which they develop. It seemed
realistic to claim that mass parties were characteristic of modern industrialised countries while parties of committees appeared to coincide with less developed societies. For a period,
both types of political parties could co-exist in industrial
countries: the growing mass parties were the new parties of
the people, the Socialist parties; traditionalist parties remained
of the committee type. Gradually, however, even right-wing
parties had to become mass parties, partly because of the
changing way of life, partly because they had to fight Socialist parties with a more efficient organisation. Christian
parties, helped and backed by the Catholic Church, were
among the first right-wing organisations to become mass parties and they took over from Conservative parties in many
Western countries; elsewhere Conservative parties became
much more 'open'. It seemed therefore reasonable to claim
that mass parties were at least a very common feature of
modern industrialised societies and to predict that the politics

---

[1] M. Duverger, *Political Parties*, pp. 62 and 88.

of modern industrialised countries would increasingly become the politics of mass parties.

Developments of the 1950s and 1960s — and indeed a more careful analysis of the developments of the previous decades — seem to throw some doubt on this generalisation, however; the distinction between mass parties and parties of 'committees' did not appear as precise as was originally thought. The Duverger analysis of the mass party was based mainly on one criterion, that of open membership, because mass parties had been conceived as organisations to which large numbers of people belonged; the fact that large numbers of people seemed prepared to pay regular subscriptions was considered both as a necessary and a sufficient condition for an operational definition of the mass party. Instead of taking the fact of paying subscriptions as a *symptom*, but perhaps only one symptom, of a mass party organisation, one simply equated mass party with open membership; this was perhaps because it was assumed that mass participation had to take the form of regular subscriptions in view of some logically necessary connection which was not, however, carefully analysed; this was perhaps also because it was unconsciously assumed that there were no other practical means of measuring mass party participation. But this operational definition had at least two major drawbacks. American parties had to be excluded because they did not have members in the sense of the definition; considerable reliance had to be placed on published figures and problems were likely to arise each time parties refused to release totals of membership. The definition of the mass party was so geared to the notion of 'card-carrying member' that any difficulties in the measurement of even conceptualisation of the latter reverberated on the classification.

The mass party is normally operationally defined, as we saw, by the criterion of 'adhesion': 'The absence of any system of registration of members or of any regular collection of subscriptions is a fairly reliable (*sic*) criterion'.[2] Although Duverger is aware of certain difficulties, he bases his distinction between the two types of parties on the criterion of membership. For him, this criterion follows logically (although this is assumed and not demonstrated) from the fact that universal suffrage led to mass participation in politics. His syllogism would appear to be the following: universal

---

[2] Duverger, op. cit. p. 64.

suffrage means popular participation and popular influence; popular participation and popular influence can *only* take place through the organisation of parties of the 'card-carrying member' type; thus universal suffrage leads to parties of the card-carrying member type. The link between industrialisation and mass parties of this kind is provided for by another syllogism: universal suffrage is the consequence of industrialisation; indeed, *real* (as distinct from formal) universal suffrage is the consequence of mass education which is in turn the product of industrialisation; thus parties of the card-carrying type are correlated with industrialisation.

The syllogism appears to be simple and the criterion appears to be precise. Yet an ambiguity needs to be clarified, as at least two different interpretations could equally be adopted. One can divide parties on the basis of the numbers of card-carrying members, or, more specifically, on the basis of the ratio of card-carrying members to voters; this may seem to be the most rational type of distinction, but the dividing line is necessarily arbitrary: one has to decide, for instance, that a party which has more than five per cent of its electors among its members is a mass party, but that a party which has less than five per cent of its electors among its members is not a mass party. But one may also distinguish parties on the basis of the concept of membership: the fact that the party allows card-carrying members, that it is open potentially to all citizens, becomes the criterion: no arbitrary dividing line has then to be drawn, but one is liable to include among mass parties many organisations which are in fact very exclusive, although potentially widely open. Yet if membership is to be the criterion, the ambiguity cannot be avoided. These difficulties can be by-passed only if one returns to the original basis for the distinction and reconsiders the link between membership and popular participation which is deemed to be necessary in the Duverger analysis.

In order to find a more acceptable operational definition, it is best, perhaps, to reconsider the original distinction between the two forms of parties. What the classification aims at doing is surely at separating two broad types of political societies, those where the mass is excluded (*de jure* or *de facto*) from national decision-making and those where the whole people, in some general fashion, can and does participate in governmental activities. On the one hand, there are groupings where 'notables' from each area can, without risking their seat, take all the decisions and follow any policy; on the other, there are groupings where leaders have to pay attention to large numbers of people, indeed to the whole electorate, if their seats are to be secure and their party is to stay in power.

Although Duverger uses the expression to refer to another type of situation, it would seem that the best way of stressing the opposition between the two types of parties is to describe parties of committees as parties of 'indirect rule' and mass parties as parties of 'direct rule'. 'Indirect rule' is what the Founders of the American Constitution had in mind in constituting the presidential electoral college: they wanted the people to elect 'good' men who, independently from pressure, would choose a President; indirect rule is thus the rule of a 'representative' in the Burkian sense. The election is, in reality, if not always in theory, a two-stage one: the popular stage consists merely in choosing 'good' men, who, in turn, elaborate policies and choose leaders. The 'direct' formula, on the other hand, is very different: representatives and leaders are chosen, not because they are 'good' men, but because they agree to operate within the same political framework as that of the people who elect them: this framework, the political party, is meant to unite them all; it is in some ways superior to any individual and in any case lasts longer than any of the leaders.

Indirect rule is what Duverger and other political scientists have in mind when they analyse parties of committees; direct rule is what they have in mind when they speak of mass parties. In the case of the parties of committees, the personal allegiance of the people to each of the notables is what is required: the bond is one of vassality in each of the localities. In the case of mass parties, the stress is on the common allegiance of the people and leaders to the party and what it represents, however vaguely; potential leaders will succeed only if they appear to wear the mantle of party authority and the insignia of the party: once they are stripped of them, they lose this authority.

What is therefore meant by the advent of mass parties and the disappearance of parties of committees, is that, because of various developments, the people cease to be prepared to accept personal rule of an indirect kind and that they become directly, without intermediaries, involved in politics: they link themselves, they associate themselves, to a group known as the political party and owe allegiance to individual leaders because the leaders temporarily represent the political party.

It follows that the real distinguishing factor between mass party and party of committees is not directly related to questions of membership; the type of allegiance is the crucial problem. One is therefore able to by-pass the difficulties arising out of the concept of membership and to concentrate on a rather different type of characteristic. One should retain the expression of mass party, because it indicates that the mass is involved as a mass, and not as sub-sets of individuals owing allegiance to different personalities. But one should define the mass party as one in which one can find evidence of direct recognition of the abstract notion of party among the followers of the organisation. Thus the crucial criterion in an operational definition has to be found in the area of the perceived relationship between citizen and party. Broadly speaking, mass parties are those with which one finds segments of the population *consistently* identified, the word consistently being very important in that, as we shall see, time plays a considerable part in the gradual building up of the mass party. If one asks British electors what party they associate themselves with, the chances are that they will mention the Conservative or Labour parties, even if the survey addresses itself to local problems in a town where a 'Ratepayers' Association' is flourishing. In France, the chances of finding electors identifying themselves with the *Entente Républicaine*, the *Concentration Républicaine*, or even the *Union Démocratique et Socialiste de la Résistance* are pretty slim. In most parts of Germany identification with some of the small parties whose leaders were gradually lured into the *Christlich-Demokcratische Union* by Dr. Adenauer is very limited or non-existent. Perception of a party and perception of one's identification with it is indicative of the direct character of the link between elector and the political system.

Having thus defined the mass party in terms of a direct link and operationally defined it by means of an examination of the perception and identification of the citizens, we can then consider a number of characteristics which are likely to follow from this identification process, although these characteristics may be affected by the special circumstances of the political life of certain countries. These characteristics seem to be mainly of six types:

1. STABILITY OF ELECTORAL SUPPORT

A party is a mass party if electors identify themselves with it. But identification is a slow process which takes place through gradual political socialisation in the family, among friends, in the job. Thus it follows that party identifiers are unlikely to change their political allegiance often; they will change it only under the influence of very extreme circumstances, such as when the leader of another party appears able to deal with a highly disturbing economic, social or political problem, a war or a depression for instance. In the case of 'indirect' parties or parties of committees, on the contrary, the allegiance of the elector is to the local notables; the elector tends to follow the man if the man changes parties. Marked fluctuations in party support are likely to ensue if local leaders find it tactically useful to associate themselves with a different political party: the electors of the Centre and Right-Wing parties in France thus tend to follow their local leaders if these emigrate into another party; similar circumstances may account for the disappearance of the small German parties in the 1950s: electors followed their local leaders into the CDU. On the contrary, party identifiers such as most electors of the Left-wing parties in France and of both the major parties in Britain will continue to vote for their party, whether their current M.P. chooses to be loyal or disloyal.

2. VOLUNTARY HELP IN CASH OR KIND

Mass parties are characterised by a high reliance on voluntary help, both in kind and cash, while parties of committees are essentially organised on the basis of small nuclei of clients paid by or otherwise dependent on the local leader. Voluntary help in kind is made possible because of party identification, although it is obviously very important for the survival of the organisation. Help in cash is not really different in character; it is in fact often conceived (and this is impressed upon potential donors) as a substitute for the refusal or impossibility of help in kind. Card-carrying membership and the payment of subscriptions must be understood in this context. Whether it takes the form of regular dues as in European Socialist parties or of help at election times as in American parties, the help in cash fulfils the same functions. What is important is the possibility to obtain donations, while, in parties of committees, leaders have to make gifts to the electors and often to bribe them. American and European parties are thus essentially similar in that they are based on a high level of party identification which leads many of the followers to recognise that, if they are prodded, they have to help by giving their time, giving their money, lending their cars, or assisting in some other way. Active participants agree that the party has a right to ask them to do these things. Even other identifiers do not deny the party at least the right to ask for such help; they simply find various reasons, or excuses, for justifying their refusal. Card-carrying membership is thus not really different from the help given by American voters at election times. The difference between the two techniques is not greater than the difference between the European form of permanent electoral registration and the American method of periodic registration: one is simply more regular, perhaps even more efficient, than the other; but they both have the same aim.

3. PERMANENT ORGANISATIONS

Mass parties are also characterised by the existence of permanent organisations, both at national and at local level. The bureaucratisation of the party structure is a consequence of the stability of the institution which, in turn, is characteristic of mass parties. Party oligarchies may develop in this way and some of the 'democratic' features which appear to be associated with mass parties may diminish as a result. But the identification of the citizens with parties makes it necessary for the local and national machines to exist, particularly as these local and national machines have a very important part to play, namely that of investing individual leaders with the authority to act on behalf of the party. Only through this process and through these machines can leaders emerge who will be acceptable to the party identifiers. The manner in which these machines operate may vary considerably from country to country: indeed it is probably at this level that one finds the greatest differences between political systems where 'ascription' plays a considerable part — and where contests for positions are relatively closed and therefore fairly easy to solve, as in Britain and, to a lesser extent, in Continental countries — and political systems where 'achievement' is more important — and where the contest is therefore more open and more prolonged, as in the United States. But in all cases, the contest is to take over the machine, particularly at the local level or, to take a weaker expression, to be in a position to act on behalf of the local organisation and thus to be recognised by the electors and party identifiers as 'representatives' of the party. The procedure is very complex; the machinery can be very sensitive. But this should not be surprising: it is at this level that popular intervention ceases in a party of committees and that the independent action of the 'representative' begins. 'Feudal' tendencies are rampant in all parties, admittedly; party leaders who have achieved popularity within a mass party are often tempted to try their luck. But the pressure of the party structure is exercised and prevents them from seceding.

4. NATIONALLY RESPONSIBLE LEADERSHIP

A nationally responsible leadership is also characteristic of a mass party. Leaders of parties of committees may be responsible to M.P.s in Parliament or to small groups of chiefs outside it; leaders of mass parties are responsible to the mass of the electors who identify themselves with the party and indeed to the mass of the electors whom the leaders would like to attract into the party. National leaders emerging outside mass parties may not be 'responsible' in this sense: they may not feel that their power is dependent on the extent to which they try to appeal to both the actual and potential identifiers of the party; we shall see that this type of leadership may sometimes be, as in the French Fifth Republic, a substitute for mass parties. But leaders of mass parties cannot afford to be 'irresponsible' in this way; indeed, they are conditioned into being responsible by the years spent moving up the ladder in the permanent organisations of the party. Their appeal is not a strictly personal one; it takes place within the framework of the party and in relation to certain party characteristics. They may try to avoid being limited in their initiatives by the party framework; they may sometimes be successful, particularly if they have greatly expanded their party's electoral appeal, as Adenauer or Eisenhower, and if it seems therefore that the party is dependent on them for its success. Yet party identification remains critically important.

If it were to dwindle and be gradually replaced by the personal national appeal of the leader, the mass party would cease to exist. Developments such as these are likely to be rare, however, if party identification was fairly strong originally, if only because the tenure of office of the leader is rarely long enough to allow for a total transfer of allegiance from the party to the man. As long as party identification exists, the leader, however popular, has to remain 'responsible'.

5. ACCESS TO AND UTILISATION OF THE MASS MEDIA

Mass parties need the mass media because the mass media are the means through which the 'image' of the party is presented to the citizens. Although studies of the influence of the mass media are still inconclusive on many points, they have shown that television is an instrument of political knowledge and of reinforcement of national party identification. This is not to say that mass parties could not develop before the mass media existed, although there were very few such parties before the advent of the popular press, one notable exception being perhaps Jacksonian Democracy. What seems inconceivable is for a mass party to develop, now that the mass media exist, without having access to them. Parties of committees may come without the mass media; mass parties, based on popular identification, cannot, except in the very peculiar case of a narrowly circumscribed geographical minority, develop and be maintained without press, radio and television. Both the requirement of identification and that of responsible leadership are dependent on mass media utilisation.

6. WIDESPREAD PARTY IMAGES

Party identification does not take place in a total intellectual vacuum. Although we do not know the precise mechanisms of formation of party identification, surveys have shown that respondents associate political parties with certain types of images of a very general, and often non-policy, character. Moreover, the success of party leaders among the electors often depends on the capability of these leaders to fit with the images which followers have of the political party. Party identification is thus associated with certain images and the existence of these images tends to affect party identification in the long run. These images play the part of flags and of myths. They lead to certain reactions. They also reinforce party identification and party allegiance against outside attack: they help to diminish the influence which leaders of other parties could otherwise have on the whole population.

Mass parties are thus different, both by their organisations and structure and by the relationship between leaders and led, from parties of committees. All of these characteristics affect the extent to which parties can grow and, in turn, existing mass parties tend to develop mechanisms which enable them to reinforce these characteristics in ways best fitted to strengthen the party. But none of these characteristics is as central to the existence of the mass party as that of direct popular perception, even though, if access to the mass media is refused, for instance, a mass party may well not be able to develop. If we want to examine the relationship between mass parties and industrialised societies, it seems therefore natural to concentrate on the extent to which industrialised societies are more likely than other societies to enable parties to foster patterns of direct popular recognition.

16. MASS PARTIES
AND
TYPES OF MODERN SOCIETIES

J. BLONDEL

The examination of the relationship between mass parties and modern industrial societies raises three types of problems. First, we must examine if, and if so, why, modern industrial societies are likely to have political systems in which political organisations are of the mass party type. Second, we must consider under what circumstances modern industrial societies can have political systems which do not have mass parties. Third, we must consider the types of parties which exist in other societies and the conditions under which mass parties may develop in those societies as well. Only after the examination of the evidence in these three types of cases will it be possible to draw general conclusions about the relationship between mass parties and modern industrial societies. One must, however, note at the outset that dichotomies will be used in order to simplify the exposition. Both mass parties and parties of committees are somewhat idealised poles; there are gradations between the two poles and a more sophisticated analysis should be based on quantitative indices. Similarly, modern industrial societies and 'other' or developing types of societies are extremes, and countries should in fact be placed along a continuum.

1. MASS PARTIES IN INDUSTRIALISED SOCIETIES

Mass parties were defined earlier as political organisations which were perceived by the citizens and with which citizens identified. In comparison with parties of committees, mass parties require an effort of abstraction on the part of the citizens. It is not possible simply to recognise a name which is familiar and which has perhaps been important in a constituency for generations. There must be the recognition of a corporate entity which has no 'real' physical existence and whose destinies are merely held on trust by leaders and sub-leaders at any point in time. It is clear that such an effort of abstraction is a difficult one and that it requires some considerable sophistication on the part of the broad mass of citizens. Admittedly, citizens are helped in this effort of abstraction by the propaganda which is put over by the political parties: this is why it seems imperative, now that mass media exist, that mass parties should be able to make a relatively large use of them. This is also why the passage of time is very important indeed. Political regimes acquire legitimacy and authority with the passage of time, as more and more citizens become accustomed to their existence and indeed do not conceive of the feasibility of any other regime. The same applies to political parties: they become 'legitimate' through the passage of time, legitimacy meaning, in this case, that large sections of the population both perceive the existence of the parties and identify themselves with one of them. But propaganda and the passage have to be combined with a level of social and economic development which predisposes or at least enables citizens to receive the propaganda or become aware of the party through the passage of time. It is of course not possible to consider here in detail the process by which citizens become permeable to the abstract notion of party. But it may be sufficient to note that this process is closely associated with the general level of education, both formal and informal, and with the existence of other types of groups in society which are also abstract and require in the same way the allegiance of the citizens: this is why mass parties generally develop on the basis of other existing groups, such as Churches or trade unions, or even constitute a more abstract refinement of communal groups, such as ethnic minorities. Mass political parties are more abstract — in that they are concerned with the whole society more than with ethnic groups, Churches or even trade unions: the educative process by which citizens come to learn of corporate bodies through the development of Church associations or trade unions is essential to the development of a sense of perception of the political organisations of the 'mass party' type.

Modern industrial societies are societies in which both the level of general education is high and associational groups proliferate. They are therefore societies where the notion of an abstract party is more likely to take root. But modern industrial societies are also societies where the parties of the committee type are likely to be a hindrance to development for two main reasons: first, the national political system becomes simpler with the advent of mass parties and this simplification is crucial; second, only mass parties provide the community with a political system which is predictable, and predictability is highly important to the development of modern industrial societies.

Parties of the committee type are both concrete and simple to understand within the context of each individual constituency or small geographical area. But because the development of these parties is geared to the behaviour and aspirations of each political leader in his small domain, the whole political system becomes very complex at the national level. In a traditional society, this problem may have a relatively small importance, since the bulk of the economic and social activities of the population takes place within the confines of a small area. But modern industrial societies are characterised by a high percentage of activities taking place at national level or involving persons living at different points of the nation. More specifically even, the geographical mobility of persons is very much greater in modern industrial societies than in traditional societies and it becomes common for individuals to grow up in certain environments and to spend their adulthood in a different, or indeed several different environments. This is highly relevant to the problem of mass parties. Unless the political parties are of a national kind, it becomes almost impossible for newcomers to participate in the political life of the new community in which they arrive; indeed, traditional political organisations object to newcomers and try to prevent them from 'taking over' the political system. As some of these newcomers feel that participation would be to their advantage and the perpetuation on the old system is to their detriment, they fight for the opening of the traditional machines. Thus the newcomers very concretely contribute to the 'nationalisation' of the political system and, in particular, to the development of a 'national perception' of political parties. In doing so, they also contribute to a general simplification of the political system at the national level: if the system is to survive — and we shall see that the case of France is probably one in which political leaders have not adjusted to the process of simplification which modern industrial societies require —

the tensions against the political system will increase very markedly. Mass parties are thus a requirement of industrial societies in that mass parties, unlike parties of committees, can operate a simplification of the political system and thus be acceptable to the more mobile middle and working classes of these societies.

Mass parties are also preferable to parties of committees in industrial societies because they lead to the development of a political system which is much more predictable. Predictability is imperative in these societies because of the complexity of industrial societies and of the grave consequences for the whole economic system of even small errors in forecasts: the system tends therefore to maximise the impact of structures and processes which will make predictability easier and to minimise that of structures and processes whose effect cannot easily be forecast. A political system which has parties of the committee kind leads to less predictability than a political system which has mass parties, since in the first type of system decisions are the result of the actions of a large number of individual agents over whom one may or may not have control and whose individual aspirations may not always clearly be known. In particular, the interest groups and the bureaucracies have constantly to adjust to the possibility of shifting power structures and have to allow for a modicum of 'accidental' (i.e. 'unpredictable') success or failure. This means having to increase efforts to by-pass the system or accept considerable margins or uncertainty which may not be efficient and in any case are time-consuming and wasteful of political energies. Thus it is highly probable that a system of mass parties, based on an abstract identification with the political parties on the part of the citizens will be much more acceptable to modern industrial societies than a system which is based on other types of parties. It seems possible to state, at least at this stage, that other types of party are both less likely and more 'dysfunctional'.

2. PARTIES OF COMMITTEES IN INDUSTRIALISED SOCIETIES

Although mass parties appear to be more 'functional' than parties of committees in modern industrialised societies, it does not follow that modern industrial societies cannot operate without such parties. Modern industrial societies need a simple political system and one which is predictable: mass parties can meet these conditions. But if other types of political systems can meet these conditions, at least to some extent, the weight of tradition may prevent mass parties from developing or from developing fully. The analysis of modern industrial societies which do not have mass parties, or have limited mass parties should therefore concentrate on the substitutes for mass parties which can meet generally the two main conditions of modern industrial societies.

Broadly speaking, these substitutes must take the form of institutions and of processes which will either limit or totally suppress the consequences of parties of committees on the political system. In practical terms this means that either the political conditions will be such that no parties of any kind will be allowed to develop and the political organisation must throw up different types of structures which will replace parties, or that the effects of the parties of committees will be minimised by the superimposition of a national political system which will bring in simplicity and coherence at least at the national level. The first case, that of the total abolition of parties, is far from unrealistic. Such a political system may be difficult to operate in the long run, largely because the maintenance of the political order appears to be basically dependent on the loyalty of the citizens and of the administrative officials to the regime and to its leader. One can therefore predict that such regimes will survive only for limited periods and that problems of succession will always be acute. Spain is a good example of such a political system; although Spain may not be regarded generally as a 'modern industrialised society' it is surely in many ways more modern and more industrialised than societies which are deemed to be 'developing'. The political system of Spain ensures simplicity and predictability, as long as it lasts, to a considerable extent; it is probable that the political parties which would have developed in Spain would have remained nearer to parties of committees and to mass parties; it is possible that some of the parties which will emerge after the disappearance of Franco will still, for a period, remain parties of committees rather than mass parties; as popular identification with some of these parties is likely to be low, simply because time will have to pass before these parties acquire legitimacy, it is indeed very probable that the post-Franco political system will appear to be less 'efficient' or less 'functional' than that developed under Franco. What does seem to be the case, however, is that such non-party regimes as may exist in modern industrial societies have to be imposed and continually imposed: while Franco may have been in a position to impose such a regime in view of very special circumstances, the cost is clearly great.

The dictatorial or totalitarian one-party State has equally to be imposed: we shall indeed see that it has to be imposed in underdeveloped societies because of a totally different set of circumstances. If imposed on a modern industrial society, it may appear to be as 'functional' as a system of several mass parties. There is one important requirement, however: the single party must be a genuine mass party and develop profoundly its tentacles into the population. This is where most single party systems are probably unsuccessful: if a large section of the population becomes identified with the party, if it is really a mass party, it will lose some of its rigidity and come to be divided into factions at least at the local level; it is as if there were a number of parties of committees over which a form of national identification is superimposed. If on the other hand, the single party is to remain disciplined, large sections of the population will probably cease to remain identified with it. In fact, it seems that single parties have constantly to oscillate between one form and the other. Moreover, most single party systems started in developing societies; they have sometimes survived when the society became modern, but they are more often trying to solve the problems of the old society than the problems of the new.

Finally, parties of committees can survive in modern industrialised societies, but nowhere do they do so without some cost to the stability of the political system. Indeed, parties of committees may become so 'dysfunctional', in that they do not achieve the conditions of simplicity and predictability required by modern societies, that certain elements of the population may grow impatient with the political system and attempt to replace it by either a single party system or a non-party system. Where parties of committees survive, they have to be by-passed or some of their effects have to be neutralised. The only area where American parties seem to have the characteristics of parties of committees is the South. France is the other major modern country where parties of committees have remained in existence, but developments since the Second World War have clearly shown the inadequacy of the political system. French traditional parties benefited from the economic stagnation of the pre-war period; when the economy ceased to be Malthusian and society became modernised, the political system quickly appeared too complex and too unpredictable to be maintained without modifications. Two successive arrangements took place in practice. The first was the almost total by-passing of the political parties in many fields of economic and social life through the operation of a highly skilled and increasingly responsive bureaucracy; France became almost the ideal 'technocratic State' as civil servants attempted to understand and to meet the requirements of a modern society. The second modification of the system was due to De Gaulle, who superimposed his influence over the local influence of constituency leaders. The position of De Gaulle is in many ways different from that of other 'paternalistic' leaders such as Adenauer or Eisenhower: while the latter did not succeed in being 'irresponsible' and had to operate within the framework of a generally coherent structure of mass parties which imposed some myths to which they had to refer, De Gaulle is 'irresponsible' in that there are no myths which limit his initiative; in fact, the UNR (Union de la Nouvelle République) is generally responsible to him and UNR leaders and deputies are individually responsible to him. While, in a mass party, national leaders and legislators are elected within the framework of the myths of the party, with whom electors are identified, in the case of Gaullism, legislators and other national leaders are elected within the framework of De Gaulle, with whom electors identify themselves. What is very important, however, is that this system provides, if not predictability (except in that it is known that the regime will last as long as De Gaulle), at least simplicity. The French political system could not be maintained with only parties of committees. It seems therefore possible to conclude that mass parties are the most efficient way of achieving the simplicity and predictability which are required, and that modern industrial societies which do not have mass parties and experience substitutes for them, first cannot be maintained with parties of committees only and, second, find substitutes which are less functional in the short run and less stable and predictable in the long run.

3. MASS PARTIES AND 'OTHER TYPES' OF SOCIETY

It remains therefore to see whether mass parties are likely to develop in non-industrial societies. Here it is important to distinguish the 'natural' characteristics of political systems in pre-industrial societies from attempts which can be made by political leaders to foster certain types of developments, both political and social: the peculiar types of parties which often emerge in pre-industrial societies are largely the consequence of the tensions between the 'natural' political developments and the various forms of political engineering.

The natural development of political parties in pre-industrial societies is towards the party of committees. As we noted earlier, mass parties require popular identification with an abstract notion of party, which is unlikely to come naturally in pre-industrial society. The local notables are more present, more real, than the party; educational achievement is too limited and the impact of the mass media too weak to lead to the natural development of a party identification. The groups and associations from which mass parties tend to emerge in modern industrial societies are non-existent, or limited to rather isolated urban areas with which the bulk of the population has very few connections. The political functions of the political system are not perceived as sufficiently distinct from those of the social system for citizens to feel directly identified with a definite political group. Thus, where universal suffrage exists, it tends to produce an indirect system of elections which is, as we saw, the exact antithesis of the system of direct identification leading to mass parties.

Such a development is highly stable and highly 'functional'. Admittedly, with the gradual industrialisation which may be taking place, groups such as trade unions will come to have a greater impact on the population; political life in the large cities will come to have some of the characteristics of mass party politics; but this comes rather slowly and, in the large cities, modified parties of committees are likely to develop. Populist parties may be aiming at becoming mass parties and at generating in their favour a type of following which resembles that of mass parties, but, at the beginning of their development, their electoral basis bears many of the characteristics of the traditional parties: the support goes to the leader, rather than to an abstract party; indeed, few if any of the characteristics of mass parties can be seen to apply to populist parties. Their electorate is highly volatile. It is more volatile than that of either parties of committees or mass parties, in that, as one can see in Brazil, for instance, neither the party nor even the person can often command allegiance for a very long period of time: but it is clear that the party commands even less allegiance than the person. Voluntary help is limited, in comparison with the amount of expenditure which must be incurred by the leader if he wishes to retain electoral support. Local organisations are scarcely organised on a party basis: they are essentially manned by the supporters of the leader and depend almost exclusively on the leader's funds. Leaders are scarcely 'responsible' in the sense which was given for mass parties, because the framework within which they operate is not the image of the party, but the image which they have attempted to create for themselves. It is true that populist parties have to use the mass media, that they have to create some myths, and that they are in this sense 'modified' parties of committees; but these myths are closely associated with the leader himself and they are less stable than those of mass parties.

Populist movements thus constitute a modified version of parties of committees. They may even constitute an intermediary stage in certain circumstances; indeed, they only develop where the societies are already 'on the move'; but they are not mass parties. For all practical purposes, pre-industrial societies can survive and be maintained by one or the other form of party of committees. It is not really from within that the society needs a mass party, and unless an effort is made to change them, the 'natural' forces will not by themselves lead to mass parties. If certain political groups or certain political leaders however, are highly dissatisfied with the state of their society, in particular with the sectional, rather than uniform, tribal, rather than national, characteristics of the social system, they cannot hope to achieve their aims on the basis of a natural modification of the political and social system. The comparison with modern industrial societies also indicates that certain traits of the social structure of developing societies have to be modified or indeed eradicated if economic change is to take place at all. The aim of these political leaders and groups is therefore often to use certain political means in order to modify the social system, the economic structure and the traditional forms of political activity. The mass party is often chosen to be the means by which change is achieved, perhaps because it appears to be successful in modern industrial societies. But, in the case of developing countries, it is a tool. Instead of being 'functional' as in modern industrial societies, the mass party becomes an instrument of social development.

It has therefore to be imposed, if it is to take root in a pre-industrial society. It cannot be imposed everywhere in the same manner and with the same ease: certain conditions are more likely than others to permit a successful imposition of a mass party in a pre-industrial society. Circumstances of an accidental kind are likely to play a part: the process of de-colonisation in Africa has made it unquestionably much easier for mass parties to develop in African countries because de-colonisation led to the gradual development of certain national myths, to the annexation of these myths by the nationalist party and to the beginning of an identification of the mass of the citizens with the party. Mass parties are also helped by the emergence of 'charismatic' leaders; and the struggle for decolonisation, particularly where it was difficult, established more firmly the position of these leaders.

But these mass parties remain somewhat different from the mass parties of modern industrial societies because they are imposed on a social system which is not really suited for them. Identification with the party has constantly to be fostered — and one of the ways by which it is fostered is by relying either on the nationalistic past or on the identity between leader and party. The characteristics of mass parties in modern industrial societies are distorted to a varying degree. Ostensibly the system is the same, but certain traits are emphasised even more strongly than in the West because functions are reversed: it is the party which has to help to achieve the aims of simplifying and nationalising political systems, which, left on their own, would be sectional and complex. Nationalist parties have to put pressure on the political system and on the social system; if they do not, it reverts to a state of 'indirect' rule, as can be seen for instance, in the Congo.

Mass parties are therefore adapted to modern industrial societies, and only in modern industrial societies can they naturally develop. But they are — and appear to many to be — an instrument of modernisation of political structures and even of social structures. To that extent, the technique of the mass party is used, for specific aims, by leaders of political regimes of certain modernising States: it is not possible to predict accurately which developing States are likely to adopt the formula of the mass party, although it is possible to predict that States which have recently been subjected to a period of struggle for nationhood are more likely than others to try the experiment. Where it is used for purposes of modernisation, the mass party develops rather differently, however, in that it has to create the sense of identification with the party which is at the root of the mass party. In modern industrialised States, on the contrary, this sense of party identification is a very natural consequence of the processes of general education and of group formation which prevail in these societies. The formula of the mass party can sometimes be avoided as a result of certain historical traditions or the presence of certain leaders; but this is at a cost: the stability of the political system of modern industrial societies depends, in the long run, on the presence of the mass party. This is not to say that the political engineering of the modernising States is likely to fail, nor is it to say that leaders of modern industrial societies should all be prevailed upon to develop mass parties where they do not exist or where they do not occupy the whole of the political scene. But the disadvantages ought at least to be measured and the dangers for political stability adequately perceived.

17. ELECTORAL SYSTEMS AND PARTY SYSTEMS: THE DUVERGER DOCTRINE

C. LEYS

Duverger postulates (*a*) a 'natural dualism' of parties, and (*b*) a tendency to the proliferation of parties (through splits in old parties and the formation of new ones). The first of these is explicit (*Political Parties*, pp. 215–16). The second is implicit, an acknowledged actual phenomenon of all the countries which Duverger studies. The electoral system, according to Duverger, determines which of these forces shall dominate. Although he speaks of the problem as one of finding factors which 'thwart' the natural tendency (*a*) to dualism, he does not provide any reason for holding that, for example, PR 'thwarts' such a tendency; on the contrary, he tries to show how majoritarian systems 'thwart' the tendency (*b*) to greater fragmentation, or the continuation of an established multipartism. In fact, his exposition conforms in its details to the scheme of earlier ones, and his assumption (*a*) is superfluous.

His model is set up as follows. It is assumed (*c*) that third ('i.e. the weakest') parties are always 'under-represented' ('i.e. its percentage of seats [is] inferior to its percentage of the poll') and it is also assumed (*d*) that supporters of third parties transfer their *votes* to one of the two leading parties. For a system of PR, however, assumptions (*c*) and (*d*) are dropped.

Now it is obvious that assumption (*d*) is too strong. It simply cancels assumption (*b*); in fact it assumes the very thing that has to be explained. What is needed is an assumption from which the behaviour described in (*d*) — the transference of their supporters' votes away from third parties — may be derived as a conclusion; and for Duverger, as for other exponents of the doctrine, this is the assumption (*d'*) that un-

---

Reprinted from *Political Studies*, 1959, pp. 133–35, by permission of the author and the Clarendon Press, Oxford.

der the simple-majority vote system, in single-member constituencies, voters realize that a vote for a third candidate is wasted (and may be assumed to act rationally in accordance with this realization). To all protagonists of the doctrine known to me (and, apparently, to many of its critics) the assumption of (d') has seemed to fill the gap satisfactorily and create a working model of the kind required.

But, psychologically plausible though it may be, a brief consideration shows that it does nothing of the sort. So far from constituting the requisite dynamic element in the model, it totally immobilizes it, for it states, in effect, that supporters of parties which are third (or weaker) in their constituencies abandon them in favour of one or other of the two which are in first and second place, *no matter which two these are* (since the transfer of their votes is dictated solely by the consideration that they would be wasted on parties other than those in first or second place); and from this it follows that, other things being equal, all those parties will be established permanently in the field which are initially in first or second place in any constituency. If, to begin with, there are five parties represented in the legislature, *at least* five will always survive, since five come *first* in at least one constituency each: not to mention those which may also come second in one or more constituencies, although winning none.

The trouble is, in other words, that a vote for a party which is third or worse in terms of representation in the legislature is *not* wasted in those constituencies in which it holds first or second place: and the theory suggested by the model is not a theory of bipartism at all, but a theory of the *status quo;* a theory of *immobilisme*, perhaps, but one which states strictly nothing about the absolute number of parties in any political system.

At various points in his exposition Duverger, unlike some other exponents of the doctrine, shows an awareness of this fundamental difficulty; but because he draws no clear distinction between his model, his theory, and the evidence, the trouble is never isolated and cured, but leads to ambiguities and qualifications within the model, and variations and obscurities in its interpretation and application to the facts as theory. The 'true effect' of the simple-majority system, we are told, for instance, 'is limited to local bipartism'; this is undeniable on the assumptions which have been made, as we have seen. But instead of finding this conclusion inconsistent with the claim that this electoral system produces national bipartism, Duverger declares that none the less

> the increased centralisation of organisation within the parties and the consequent tendency to see political problems from the wider, national standpoint tend of themselves to project on to the entire country the localised two-party system brought about by the ballot procedure.

But of this evidently crucial assumption, vague as it is, no further explanation is offered. At other times Duverger speaks as if his 'psychological factor' (assumption [d'], called by Duverger the 'polarization effect') operates against parties which are third or weaker in terms of the total number of votes in the country at large; but as we have seen, this is too strong if it is simply assumed, and such behaviour cannot be deduced as the logical consequence of a rational response to the single-member constituency system.

The secondary weaknesses of Duverger's exposition of the doctrine, which flow more or less directly from this logical deficiency in the model, may be partially summarized as follows:

1. The logically necessary character of the model, and so the specific character of the predictions of the theory, are abandoned; the Friedman rule against 'maybe's and approximations' is broken. For example we are told that 'on the whole' PR only 'maintains *almost* intact the structure of parties at the time of its appearance' (my italics), although we learn also that it has a 'deep-seated tendency which always triumphs over the barriers set up against it' to produce a few more.

2. There are variations in the operational definitions of the variables; some facts are treated rather high-handedly. Britain, for example, is said to have a two-party system not on a 'restricted and fragmentary view' but on examination of the 'general tendencies of the system'; that is, if before the First World War the Irish Nationalists, and now the Liberals, are regarded as outside the general tendency. Elsewhere, however, the Liberals are included in the reckoning; what is meant is evidently that we have a two-party system in the sense that third parties are always either coming or going. But this depends, of course, on our accepting some theory which says that they must always be doing this, and it must be said at least that it took more than the electoral system to

get rid of the Irish. Here the definition of a 'two-party' system varies. Similar variations sometimes occur with respect to 'multipartism'; in one case a growth in the *size* of certain small parties is described as 'having much the same effect' as a growth in their number, in another a fourth party with only one seat is ignored with the words 'in practice therefore three parties alone were represented'. Sometimes such variations matter, sometimes they may be less cases of varying definitions than of legitimately varying interpretations of the facts: the point is that a logically sound model would in most cases render them unnecessary.

3. The 'explaining' of 'exceptions' is inconsistent; the consequences of the logical weakness of the model are here direct. Canada and pre-1920 Denmark are said not to be real exceptions because they have displayed bipartism at the constituency level, which is the system's 'true effect'. Why, then, does not Britain have multipartism in parliament and bipartism only locally? Duverger cannot legitimately appeal to other factors to account for this difference, for then it is a fair question whether factors strong enough to explain this (e.g. national sentiment) will not explain bipartism without any help from the electoral system. This comes out clearly in Duverger's appeal to the key evidence, the contrast between the elimination of the Liberal Party in Britain and elsewhere, and its survival in Belgium after introduction of PR. Since the doctrine provides no reason why the electoral system should have led Liberals to transfer their votes to other parties in Britain, this evidence is neither consistent nor inconsistent with it.

4. Assumption (c) — that third and weaker parties are always under-represented — is superfluous. In spite of some criticism this assumption remains in general highly realistic; the trouble is that no connexion is established by Duverger which would enable it to contribute to the desired behaviour of the model. It is a matter of indifference to a Liberal voter, for example, that the Liberals receive x per cent fewer seats than their percentage of votes in the country at large, if the electoral system will make him desert them only when they are not in first or second place in his constituency. None the less, this assumption can be made relevant to a reformulated version of the doctrine, by an adaptation which will by now probably seem obvious to the reader.

PART FOUR

CONSTITUTIONAL GOVERNMENT

18. THE 'LIVING' CONSTITUTION: SHADOW AND SUBSTANCE

K. LOEWENSTEIN

For an ontological evaluation of constitutions it is essential to recognize that the reality of a specific functional arrangement of powers depends to a large measure on the sociopolitical environment to which the pattern is applied. From its own experience the politically advanced Western world is apt to draw the conclusion that, once a constitutional order has been formally accepted by a nation, it is not only valid in the sense of being legal but also real in the sense of being fully activated and effective. If this is the case, a constitution is *normative*. To use a homely simile: the constitution is a suit made to measure and is actually worn. It is, however, an assumption that requires verification in every single case.

There are other cases where a constitution, though legally valid, is actually not lived up to. Its reality and activation are imperfect. This should not be confused with the universally recognized situation that the constitution as written differs from the constitution as applied. Constitutions change, not only by formal constitutional amendments, but even more so, imperceptibly, by constitutional usages. What is aimed at here is the factual state of affairs that a constitution, though legally valid, has no integrated reality. The American Constitution is the law of the land in all the United States, but the Fourteenth Amendment is not fully activated in, for example, Mississippi and Alabama. To continue the simile: it is a ready-made suit which is not worn; it hangs in the closet. In this case the constitution is merely *nominal*.

Finally, there are cases in which the constitution is fully applied and activated, but it is merely the formalization of the existing location and exercise of political power. The mo-

From *Constitutions and Constitutional Trends since World War II* (ed. A. J. Zurcher, New York U.P., 1951) pp. 203–20. We are grateful to the author for permission to reproduce this extract.

bility of power dynamics, to adjust which is the essential purpose of any constitution, is 'frozen' in the interest of the actual power holder. The suit is no suit at all but a fancy dress or a mere cloak. In this case the constitution is nothing but *'semantic'*.

The normative constitution prevails in the West where it serves as the procedural frame for the compromise of the power contest. Of the new constitutions, in addition to those of France, Germany, and Italy, those of Israel, India, and Ceylon come under this category, the first because it is manipulated by an intellectually Westernized people, the latter two because of the education the political elite had received in contacts with the British. Burma (constitution of 1947) can hardly be counted here, her experience with self-government being too scanty.

The nominal constitution, on the other hand, is merely a declaration of constitutional intent, a blueprint expected to become a reality in the future. Its habitat is in nations where Western constitutionalism is implanted into a colonial and/or agrarian-feudal social structure. Literacy, of course, is indispensable for the reality of a constitution. But even where literacy is extensive it may seem that the rationality of Western constitutionalism is alien, at least for the time being, to the Asiatic or African mind. This situation prevails definitely in states accustomed to authoritarianism like China (Chiang Kaishek's constitution of 1947), Southern Korea (1948) and Siam, and possibly also in the Philippines and most of the Arab states. But it is also not uncommon in Latin America where, however, Brazil, Argentina, Chile, Colombia, Uruguay, and Cuba must explicitly be exempted and ranked with Western normativism. The borderline may often be fluid. In the Latin American *ambiente,* constitutions are frequently abolished and rewritten, or suspended by the state of siege, according to shifts of the power cliques temporarily in control of the army. The existence or nonexistence of a constitution does, as a rule, not much affect the life of the business community or the common people.

The case of Japan (constitution of 1946) defies classification. Even the older (1889) constitution was not normative in the sense that it served as the frame for the orderly adjustment of the power conflict. In spite of its Westernized 'neutrality', it was wholly subservient to the ruling groups of industrial and agrarian feudalism and the army. The new constitution is S.C.A.P. inspired, S.C.A.P. dictated, and S.C.A.P. enforced, the democratically elected Diet operating as a mixed chorus. In the political vacuum of foreign occupation, under a foreign general as pseudo-Mikado and with party dynamics strictly controlled by him, there can hardly be a reality of the constitution even for a nation so adaptable as the Japanese.

Finally, where the written constitution is advisedly used for 'legalizing', stabilizing, and perpetuating an existing configuration of power, it cannot serve as the procedural frame for the competitive power elements. This is probably the generic characteristic of all or most authoritarian constitutions, with the instruments of the years VIII and X in France or the constitution of Napoleon III (1852) as historical and the Pilsudski Constitution of 1935 as more recent examples. The existence of the written constitution is merely the face-saving gesture demanded by the present-time universal belief in democratic legitimacy. If no constitution existed at all, the prevailing power monopoly of a person, group, class, or party would not be changed to a substantial degree. At the most, such constitutions regulate the assignment of high-level jurisdictions as the formal basis for the orderly conduct of the governmental business no state can do without. In the narrow sense of the term these instruments are positivist in that they 'freeze' the existing power situation. Actually their purpose is semantic camouflage.

Under this category come most of the Soviet satellite constitutions, but equally so those of other states of quasi-feudal structure (Egypt, Iran, Iraq). In underdeveloped countries the distinction between the semantic and the nominal constitution cannot always be applied with satisfactory precision.

COMPARATIVE OBSERVATIONS ON THE FUNCTIONAL STRUCTURE

1. The Legislative-Executive Relations

The legislative-executive relationship — whether in coordination or in subordination — is the essence of the 'form of government'. The solutions attempted reveal the differences between the normativism of the West and the semanticism of the East. In the fully developed 'people's democracy', exemplified by Hungary (1949), the problem offers no difficulty. In the place of co-ordination and cooperation there exists, by a curious inversion characteristic of assembly government, a strictly hierarchical system of subordination. The parliament, allegedly 'the highest state organ' (Art. 10), is completely dominated by its presidium (called 'Presidential Council of the People's Democracy', Arts. 20 and 21), which, in turn, completely controls the Council of Ministers, spoken of as the 'highest organ of state administration' (Art. 22) and controlling the local councils hierarchically. All levels are of course linked together by the Communist party (or, in other satellites, the National Front) concerning which the document is semantically silent. No simpler, less complex, and more direct technique for the exercise of political power ever has been put on paper.

In the Western climate, on the other hand, the executive-legislative relationship continues to remain the core of constitutional engineering. There is no longer the eighteenth-century illusion that government and parliament could be harmoniously equilibrized or mutually balanced. The alternatives are either a strong government superior to the parliament, at the expense of responsiveness to public opinion, or a government continually dependent on the whims of the parliamentary parties. The controlling viewpoint is the avoidance of cabinet crises occasioned by the lack of stability of the party coalition supporting the government.

The framers of the new constitutions were visibly impressed by the one hundred-odd cabinets that had occurred under the Third Republic in France within sixty-five years and the twenty-odd under Weimar within fourteen years. A sizable number thereof, being accidental and without deeper political implications, could have been avoided by rationalized parliamentary procedures. Consequently, technical efforts are now made to limit them by the injection of cooling-off periods between the motion for, and the vote of, nonconfidence, or the requirement of a minimum of signatures for the former (Italy, Art. 94) and of absolute majorities for the latter (France, Art. 45; Germany, Bonn, Arts. 67, 68). But the danger of recurrent cabinet crises seems somewhat overemphasized. The record will disclose that many, if not the majority, of the cabinet changes were occasioned by justified demands of the opposition for a change in legislative policies to which the new government conformed. This, after all, is the inherent function of parliamentary government. The exceptional situation under Weimar, to the effect that heterogeneous and basically antidemocratic opposition parties combine 'unconstructively' for the overthrow of the government without being able or willing to form an alternative government, may not easily present itself elsewhere. Moreover, breaks in governmental continuity are often mitigated by the 'replastering' technique in constituting the new cabinets. Outside France the record of governmental stability since 1945 leaves little to be desired, perhaps with the exception of Belgium while laboring under the singular pressure of the *question constitutionnelle* (the struggle for the removal of Leopold III). Moreover, it may seem doubtful whether cabinet crises are actually the congenital vice of parliamentarism, or whether it is the inability of any 'pattern of government' to reconcile political opposites refusing to agree on the socioeconomic fundamentals of the common existence. The common people, with their unstunted sense of realities, are much more aware of this basic dilemma than the politicians and party manipulators themselves.

At any rate, the search for the magic formula to establish a crisis-proof system continues, but the circle remains as unsquared as before. Where the distrust of the strong executive is nationally ingrained as in France, the recourse to unmitigated parliamentarism seems the lesser evil. The French rely largely on the skill of their parliamentarians. Where, as in Germany, the strong executive is an article of national faith, the legislature — and with it the democratic fundamentals — have to foot the bill. The Germans try to ward off spontaneous eruptions of the power conflict by making the Chancellor quasi-irremovable during the four-year term of the *Bundestag* and strengthening his hands, with the *dolus eventualis* of authoritarian government, by the ominous 'legislative emergency powers' (Art. 81), under which even if defeated he can operate without parliamentary support for at least six months. The historically less inhibited Italians trust the natural balance of the political forces and the fear of Communism holding together the artificial majority of the Christian Democrats. Evidently parliamentary crises are the price to pay for multiple parties, which Continental politics seemingly cannot be disabused of.

2. Dissolution

In the authentic form of parliamentary government, dissolution is the democratic fulcrum of the entire process of adjusting power conflicts by making the electorate the ultimate policy-determining factor. Compared with the period after 1919 dissolution takes a serious beating in the new constitutions even though the French have at long last cautiously revived it (Arts. 51, 52). The curbs to which it is subjected in France and Bonn, Germany, come under the same heading of the search for the crisis-proof constitution. Only in Italy (Art. 88) does the institution preserve its genuine plebiscitary function. Five years of experience in France have demonstrated that the party oligarchies, shifting power among themselves, are as afraid of the people as before, meaning the Communists to the left and the de Gaullists to the right. In Germany, likewise, where dissolution has been resorted to frequently under the empire and Weimar, it seems destined to wither on the vine. Moreover, as F. A. Hermens has emphasized, dissolution loses much of its plebiscitary effect if conducted under proportional representation, which tends to stabilize the existing party pattern. Dissolution, of course, is incompatible with assembly government except in the remote contingency of self-dissolution (Hungary, Arts. 18, 1).

3. Position of the President

Within the same context of legislative-executive relations the position of the President has been noticeably weakened in comparison with 1919 and after. Because of its greater democratic prestige, popular election is no longer favored except where, as in Latin America, the American pattern is followed. The President is generally confined to state integrating and ceremonial functions. He retains, however, the designation of the Prime Minister (France, Italy, Israel, India); in Western Germany this function has shifted to the *Bundestag* by election (Art. 63) and in Eastern Germany the strongest party automatically is charged to name the executive-designate (Art. 92). The discretionary powers of the President in dissolution are completely eliminated in France (Arts. 51, 52) and severely restricted by the mechanization of the entire procedure in Western Germany (Arts. 58, 63, 4). Assembly government as a rule dispenses with the office altogether, its functions being performed by the Presidium; for reasons of expediency, however, the office is retained without an actual share in power, in the U.S.S.R., Eastern Germany, Poland, Czechoslovakia, and Yugoslavia.

4. Second Chambers

Except in federal states the unicameral organization is now generally preferred. The final emasculation of the British House of Lords by the Labour government is paralleled by the powerless Council of the Republic in France and reflected, to some extent, in the position of the Federal Council (*Bundesrat*) under Bonn, which, while strengthening the position of the territorial subdivisions in matters affecting them, is confined to a suspensive veto in federal affairs and without influence on federal political dynamics. Italy has seen fit to restate full-fledged bicameralism with political equality of the Chamber and the Senate, the latter based on a spurious effort to achieve a different composition by 'Regions' and, at least in theory, capable of overthrowing the government.

If an 'upper' house were to serve as the brake on, or balance of, accidental party fluctuations within the lower house, it would require a different composition, based on corporate units, specific social strata, more mature age groups, or meritorious individual personalities. But this traditional function of the second chamber has become largely obsolete; an exception is the strictly consultative Senate in Bavaria (constitution of 1946, Arts. 34 ff.). While, thus, the decay of the second-chamber technique is a universal phenomenon, it may seem regrettable that corporativism, whose natural location would be the second chamber, though discredited by totalitarian abuse, has not been given the chance of a democratic trial; the Economic Council in France is weaker than other applications (in Czechoslovakia and Weimar Germany) after 1919. The professional stratification of socioeconomic life in organized power groups is one of the undeniable realities of countries professing a free economy; the powerful combines of labor, cooperatives, management, agriculture, civil servants, professional and other interest groups, deprived of legitimate participation in the formation of public policies, are forced to operate either through political parties or to exert power outside the constitution itself. On this score the postwar constitutions have not been able to face realities.

Under assembly government in nonfederal states the second chamber is at variance with the political doctrine and has been discarded everywhere.

5. *Federalism*

Federalism is on the decline, and this in spite of various institutionalizations in the West and the East. Experience in the oldest and best integrated federal states, the United States and Switzerland, demonstrates that, whatever strength of tradition and emotional values of political theory federalism is still imbued with, the economic imperatives of the technological state require unified if not uniform economic policies throughout the entire territory and do not brook that kind of economic fragmentation which goes with effective member-state sovereignties. To point it up sententiously: a state with a federal income tax is no longer a genuinely federal state. On the other hand, the realization is equally general that, even in relatively small areas, decentralization enhances administrative efficiency. Federalism as an organizational device cannot be divorced from the general political philosophy of the age. Federalism is a product of liberal thinking. It applied the (relative) freedom of the individual to the (relative) freedom of organization of territorial entities. It thrives as long as a free economy thrives. Speaking again sententiously: economic planning is the DDT of federalism. Constitutions, therefore, that take their federal premises too seriously can hardly escape becoming anachronistic.

However, federalism is essential and indispensable where strong tendencies of multinational or tribal diversity prevail. The Indian Constitution, trying to organize and govern a multinational subcontinent, could not operate without evolving a sort of superfederalism, being applied, in terms of the First Schedule to Article 1, to at least three different categories of states and territorial subdivisions with different legal status in regard to their relations to the Union. This kind of 'quantitative' federalism obviously is imperative for the growing together of literally hundreds of socially widely divergent separate communities. Federalism in India, and also in Burma, likewise a 'Union', seems a method of social integration rather than of perpetuated diversification.

Of the Iron Curtain constitutions, only that of Yugoslavia follows the Soviet federal pattern. But if the inclusive evidence permits an evaluation, the emphasis, as in the U.S.S.R., is on cultural autonomy rather than political self-government. How far the new collectivist way of life, emanating from planning, has succeeded in overcoming the age-old nationalism of the Croats, Montenegrins, and Macedonians, and their resentment of Serb ascendancy, remains to be seen. Whatever may be the degree of effectiveness of cultural autonomy, the social-planning mechanism extends uniformly to all subdivisions. With the older type of federalism in the West it has evidently nothing in common but the name. Federalism of the five *Länder* in Eastern Germany is wholly semantic, as can be easily seen from the unitarian constitution of the German Democratic Republic.

Nor is federalism in Western Germany any longer the genuine article, belying the endless labor of the military governments and the Germans in fashioning it. On the surface the constitution of Bonn is less unitarian than Weimar. But the facts of economic interdependence of the area militate against genuine federalism, except in certain cultural matters. Actually the elaborate and ambitious *Land* constitutions of the Western zones mean little for the people. The decisive socioeconomic issues, such as economic policies, social security, codetermination, and tax distribution, devolve on the federal government in Bonn. In Italy the new 'Regions' remain to date a dead letter (except, to a limited extent, in Sicily, Sardinia, and Alto Adige), and this for the same reasons as elsewhere; namely, that local autonomy cannot but be subservient to nation-wide economic and social policies. Federalism in Latin America (Argentina, Brazil, Venezuela, Mexico) finally never amounted to much in practice because of the constitutionally legalized and frequently used practice of federal intervention.

6. Suffrage, Electoral System, and Political Parties

Democratic equality for the formation of the will of the state is no longer problematic. Universal suffrage with, in some instances, a considerably lowered voting age is the general standard. All censitory vestiges have disappeared. But it is indicative of the existing cleavage between constitutional nominalism and political reality that, while proportional representation is universally favored, the operative technique of this (and any) electoral system, the political party, is almost universally ignored. Political parties are mentioned, it is true, in the Bonn (Art. 21) and the Italian (Art. 49) Constitutions as recognized instruments for the formation of the political will of the people. But the fact is carefully ignored that proportional representation, more than any other electoral sys-

tem, puts the actual exercise of political power into the hands
of the party oligarchies and their bureaucracies, which are
entirely beyond popular control. The ubiquitous result is the
political vacuum in which the party-manipulated parliaments
everywhere operate. The general lack of prestige of the political congeries called political parties cannot fail to be reflected in the waning respect the people have for the parliaments themselves.

It is readily admitted that the integration of the political
party into the mechanism of the frame of government — recognition of the party within the bill of rights as a phenomenon
of the individual right of political association is, of course,
merely declaratory — is one of the most difficult aspects of
constitutional renovation. The issue may, for the time being,
be inaccessible to legal formulas. But it is equally obvious
that silence of all constitutions on the emergence of new elites
— in the West the party bosses and their bureaucracies, the
parliamentary oligarchies, and, in the East, the powerful layer
of the officials of the state party and the managerial technicians of the state-owned industries — is a much more potent
reality than the ubiquitously proclaimed 'sovereignty of the
people' France, Arts. 3, 1; Italy, Arts. 1, 2; Germany, Bonn,
Arts. 20, 2). Sovereignty actually is located in the political
parties. The statement (Germany, Bonn, Art. 38, 1) that the
individual deputies in parliament represent the entire nation
is a piece of undiluted semantics.

The situation is aggravated by the visibly declining emphasis on participation of the people in the political process. It
is confined to elections of the parliament at regular intervals
or in the (rare) case of dissolution. Initiative and referendum
— the latter only in connection with the amending process
(France, Art. 90; Italy, Art. 138) — are conspicuous by their
absence in Western Europe, let alone elsewhere, probably because of the inconclusive result of direct democracy in the
constitutions after 1919. Monopolization of political power by
the party oligarchies makes the new constitutions less democratic than their predecessors.

In the monopolization of the popular will by the single or
state party, the people's democracies are more honest, and
probably can afford to be. The constitution is not a blueprint
to be activated in the future, but it closely reflects, and is syn-
chronized with, the actual power configuration reached in the
particular country. The paramount function of the single

party is admitted and exalted. No longer an abstraction, it is a stark reality, incorporated in the frame of government proper. In the Soviet Constitution of 1936 the Communist party as 'the vanguard of the toilers' is an official state organ (Arts. 126, 141). Since in the earlier elaborations of the Soviet system the transition to the single-party state was not completed, the Communist party (or its equivalent) could not yet be given the privileged position. But in the Hungarian Constitution (1949) the 'People's Democracy bases itself on the organization of the class conscious workers' and 'the leading force in [such] political and social activities is the working class' (Arts. 56, 2). Of the thirty-six times the 'workers', 'working class', or 'class conscious workers' are mentioned in this document, not a few refer to the workers as activators of political power rather than as its addressees. And the constitution of the German Democratic Republic could openly assign (Art. 92) the position of the Minister-President to the strongest party because the power apparatus could by now be trusted to identify this as the Socialist Unity party.

7. Constitutional Amendment

In this revolutionary age constitutions, however carefully projected into the future, cannot aspire to make permanent their political solutions. In this they differ from the optimism of the eighteenth century; the Directory Constitution of 1795 was practically unamendable. Consequently, the process of constitutional amendment everywhere is kept sensibly elastic, neither too rigid to invite, with changing conditions, revolutionary rupture, nor too flexible to allow basic modifications without the consent of qualified majorities. However, the amending procedure is rationalized in the sense that it can no longer be 'by-passed'. In France the Constitutional Committee (Arts. 91 ff.) determines whether a law passed by the National Assembly requires a revision of the constitution; this is a sort of substitute for judicial review of the constitutionality of statutes. In Western Germany the amendment requires the effective change of the text of the constitution (Arts. 79, 2). All the more surprising is the increasing illusion that certain fundamentals can be made 'unamendable' (republican form of government, Italy, Art. 139; France, Art. 95; federal structure and basic rights, Germany, Bonn, Arts. 79, 3). The Indian provision (Sec. 305), to the effect that certain minorities (Muslims, Scheduled Castes, etc.) shall not be deprived of their seats in the federal and state legislatures for a period of ten years, is one of functional utility rather than of governmental philosophy.

8. Judicial Power and the Judicialization of Political Power

Western constitutionalism believes traditionally in the clear-cut separation of the judicial function from the other two branches of government and, correspondingly, in the independence of the judiciary secured by tenure. The Soviet approach deliberately discards the separation of powers in whatever form and under whatever disguise. Assembly government, therefore, does not countenance any *capitis diminutio* either by an independent judiciary or by judicial review of legislation. In spite of some face-saving semantics the judicial function is strictly subordinated to the legislative by election and recall through the parliament, for example in the German Democratic Republic (Arts. 130, 131) or Hungary (Art. 39).

In the West serious efforts were undertaken to protect appointment and promotion of the judiciary from extraneous influence or political pressure. Neutralization of the patronage by the political parties is sought in France through the Supreme Council of the Magistrature (Arts. 83 ff.), and in Italy by the creation of the magistrature as an autonomous organization, charged with the exclusive responsibility for the composition and supervision of the judiciary (Arts. 104 ff.). Western Germany has gone furthest in setting up the judicial branch as co-equal with the other two. While the technical arrangements may seem impeccable, they do not go into the core of the problem. In Germany the judges are public officials and, therefore, not independent of the state. De-Nazification has not succeeded in breaking their class consciousness. Basically the independence of the judiciary resolves itself into the sociological dilemma of a judicial caste, a situation with which the American public in its own environment is thoroughly familiar.

Judicial review of the constitutionality of laws that previously had been recognized only for federal-state relations is now viewed with more favor. In Italy (Art. 134) and Germany, Bonn (Art. 93), it is assigned to a special Constitutional Court. It is generally implied in the judicial function in Japan (Arts. 76, 3, 8), while in France it is attenuated to the determination, by the Constitutional Committee acting only on a joint request by the President and the Council of the Republic, whether a law passed by the National Assembly would actually require a constitutional amendment (Arts. 91 ff.). Unavoidable differences of opinion in the interpretation of the new constitutions may well call for an objective judicial decision; but it may seem doubtful whether the institution will integrate itself into political life as the unique regulatory force it is in the United States.

But perhaps more important may become what may be called the judicialization of political power; namely, the efforts to tame the power conflict by subjecting political dynamics to judicial decisions. In Italy (Arts. 134 ff.) and Germany, Bonn (Art. 93), the constitutional tribunal is charged with deciding 'conflicts of jurisdiction between the powers of the state' or, in the German version, 'disputes concerning rights and duties of the supreme federal organs'. Insofar as such conflicts are determinable by positive constitutional norms — the rare exception — judicialization may lead to beneficial results. If, however, jurisdictional attributions of the constitution are being used by the various state organs — for example, by the President against the government or by the government against the parliament — in the competition for political power, the belief that power aspirations can be 'decontaminated' by legal formulas may seem to overtax the function of the judiciary. Seemingly the poor showing of the German Supreme Court in an analogous power conflict between the Prussian and the Reich Governments in 1932 was no deterrent. In older and wiser countries the courts exercise self-restraint by refusing to pass on 'political questions' or *actes de gouvernement*, which the Germans call *'justizlose Hocheitsakte'*. The basic issues of the power process are not justiciable. Reliance on normative legality may impede rather than promote the need for political compromise.

9. The Function of the Bill of Rights

Particularly pertinent for the inquiry into the ontological meaning of the constitutions are the principles contained in the bill of rights. In the earlier development of written constitutions the libertarian and equalitarian postulates of the bills of rights were as important as the functional arrangements of the frame of government. The French Declaration of 1789 has assumed the quality of a superconstitutional validity and reality even if the constitution, as, for example,

that of 1875, did not contain a restatement or failed to refer
to it *expressis verbis*. The (second) constitution of 1946, therefore, could confine itself to a global incorporation by confirm-
ing it in the preamble, with some additional socioeconomic
rights which the revolutionary fathers could not foresee. But
during the nineteenth century, when liberalism was taken for
granted, the accent shifted definitely to the functional organization, which, if properly arranged, could be expected to
accommodate any socioeconomic system the majority desired
to establish by constitutional means. That the Bismarckian
Constitution of 1871 failed to register a bill of rights was not
due to the authoritarian neglect of the framer but rather to
the belief generally adhered to in the period that a constitution should confine itself to functional arrangements and that
the main virtue of the declaration of rights consisted in sym-
bolizing the state under the rule of law.

The constitutions after World War I, in whose elaboration
the Socialist parties shared for the first time, appear more
alerted toward the need of implementing the classic catalogue
of libertarian and equalitarian freedoms from the state by a
new socioeconomic pattern of economic security and social
justice. But again the concept prevails that, beyond certain
programmatic aspirations, the decision should be left to the
social and political forces contending for power within the
framework of the constitution itself. The sociopolitical content
of the bills of rights became more important but still not important enough actually to determine and control the functional arrangements in the form of government.

Nothing is more indicative of the parting of the roads between West and East after World War II than the changed
position of the bill of rights. In most of the 'people's democracies' the relationship between the functional and the ideological parts of the constitution is reversed. What is variously
called socioeconomic structure or organization is not only
separated from the classical libertarian rights and freedoms —
whose actuality under the police state is obviously nominal
— but is moved forward into the body of the functional provisions and, thus, considered as binding as the latter. Nationali-
zation of natural resources, state ownership of the means of
production, economic planning, the foreign-trade monopoly
of the state, and the restrictions on private ownership and
property that go with them are no longer programmatic aspirations; they are now part and parcel of the structure of

government necessitating a new type of administrative organization. The functional organization is conditioned on the socioeconomic pattern.

In the West the program of the bills of rights has not materially advanced beyond what was reached after World War I. The bills are still large-scale and pretentious catechisms of socioeconomic, cultural, and educational postulates, nowhere raised to the rank of subjective rights the individual can enforce against the state or, what amounts to the same, implying duties of the state to carry out and implement the program by positive legislation. Moreover, without corresponding judicial protection even most of the libertarian freedoms are of paper value only. On the other hand, Bonn, Germany, is more advanced in converting the basic rights into positive rules of law immediately binding legislation, administration, and adjudication (Arts. 1, 3) and opening, by way of a general clause, access to the courts for redress against any violation of the constitutionally guaranteed private sphere by governmental or administrative action (Arts. 19, 4).

What may seem more important is the twilight zone in which the political philosophy moves. The bills of rights are as articulate and comprehensive as they are evasive on the decisive social issues of labor-management relations and the property complex as the key to the alternatives of private capitalism or socialization, *laissez faire* or planning. These temporizations are due, of course, to the structure of the party coalition, which was primarily responsible for them (in the three key states dominated by the Christian Democrats). That the elusiveness of the socioeconomic program deprives the most vital parts of the constitution of attraction for the masses can be easily realized by a comparison with Great Britain, where the unformalized character of the basic order permitted the general election of 1945 to become the plebiscite inaugurating a social revolution of the first magnitude.

19. STRUCTURES OF GOVERNMENT

D. V. VERNEY

Before some general conclusions are drawn about the three theories of government it may be useful to summarize them as follows:

- (i) parliamentary theory
- (ii) presidential theory
- (iii) convention theory.

1. THE ASSEMBLY

- (i) is transformed into a Parliament
- (ii) remains an Assembly only
- (iii) engrosses the executive as well as the legislative power.

2. THE EXECUTIVE

- (i) is divided into (a) Head of State (b) Government
- (ii) is not divided but is a President elected by the people for a definite term at the time of Assembly elections
- (iii) is abolished as a separate institution.

3. THE HEAD OF THE GOVERNMENT

- (i) is appointed by the Head of State
- (ii) is also Head of State (*Government* best avoided)
- (iii) does not exist, except possibly as chairman of a committee.

From *The Analysis of Political Systems*, 1959, pp. 75–77, 86–93. We are grateful to the Humanities Press, Inc. and to Routledge & Kegan Paul Ltd. for permission to reproduce this extract.

4. APPOINTMENT OF GOVERNMENT, ADMINISTRATION AND 'GOVERNMENT'

(i) The head of the Government (the Prime Minister) appoints the Ministry
(ii) The President appoints heads of Departments who are his subordinates
(iii) The whole 'Government' is appointed by the Assembly.

5. INDIVIDUAL AND COLLECTIVE RESPONSIBILITY

(i) The Government is a collective body
(ii) The President is sole Executive
(iii) The 'Government' is a collective body.

6. SEPARATION OF EXECUTIVE AND LEGISLATIVE PERSONNEL

(i) Ministers are usually members of Parliament
(ii) Members of the Assembly may not hold office in the Administration and vice versa
(iii) Members of the 'Government' are usually members of the Assembly.

7. LEGAL AND POLITICAL RESPONSIBILITY

(i) The Government is responsible politically to the Assembly
(ii) The Executive is responsible legally to the Constitution
(iii) The 'Government' is responsible politically to the Assembly.

8. DISSOLUTION OF THE ASSEMBLY BY THE EXECUTIVE

(i) The head of Government may advise the Head of State to dissolve Parliament
(ii) The President cannot dissolve or coerce the Assembly
(iii) The Assembly dissolves itself.

9. THE SUPREME BRANCH OF GOVERNMENT

    (i) Parliament as a whole is supreme over its constituent parts, Government and Assembly, neither of which may dominate the other

    (ii) The Assembly is ultimately supreme over the other branches of government, and there is no fusion of the executive and legislative branches in a Parliament

    (iii) The Assembly is supreme.

10. THE EXECUTIVE AND THE ELECTORATE

    (i) The Government as a whole is only indirectly responsible to the electorate

    (ii) The Executive is directly responsible to the electorate

    (iii) The 'Government' as a whole is only indirectly responsible to the electorate.

11. THE FOCUS OF POWER IN THE POLITICAL SYSTEM

    (i) Parliament is the focus of power

    (ii) There is no focus

    (iii) The Assembly is the focus.

Such, in outline, are the main characteristics of the three theories of government. But, it may be asked, how far do they explain the facts of political life in the world today? If this question means how far have states put into practice the theory of government outlined in their constitutions the answer must be that a large number of them, especially in Central and South America and Asia (to say nothing of Communist countries) appear to have the form but not the reality. There is not always a straightforward connexion between constitutional theory and political practice.

In short, the value of theories of government varies from country to country. The constitutions of Britain and the United States provide the framework in which political life is conducted. Elsewhere a constitution may only be the expression of an ideal. Yet even if the contrast between aspiration and reality is startling the very existence of a constitution at least shows that at some time the state has emerged from the pre-constitutional era of an *ancien régime*. . . .

The hallmark of parliamentary government is its ingenuity. The forms of the pre-parliamentary monarchies have been retained but the realities of political power have been transformed: the Assembly has become a Parliament and the Executive divided so that the main burden of Government has been taken from the shoulders of the Head of State. It is rather a subtle form of government and one hardly to be recommended to people who have just emerged from absolute rule. For the tradition is preserved whereby the Head of State continues to appoint his chief Minister, the latter selecting his own colleagues: the responsibility is not transferred to the people as in presidential systems, or even to the Assembly as in convention theory.

Nor is this all. In accordance with the principle that a group of men are better able to bear heavy responsibilities than one the notion of collective responsibility has been introduced into the Government, though Ministers remain individually responsible for their personal actions. Such a notion is alien to the American concept of good government. Moreover the line between the executive and legislative branches of government has been blurred (but not eliminated) by the custom whereby Ministers are members of Parliament.

As if this were not confusing enough, dissolution of the Assembly by a Head of State dissatisfied with the Legislature becomes dissolution of Parliament on the advice of the Prime Minister, a very different proposition. Above all there is the new notion of parliamentary supremacy, loyalty to Parliament transcending the individual's allegiance to the Government or the Legislature. The question of who is ultimately supreme, Crown, Parliament or people, remains as unsettled in Britain as it was when John Locke examined the implications of the Glorious Revolution of 1688. In a very real sense each can claim a degree of supremacy.

The fusion of powers implied by parliamentary government has helped to make the political system work efficiently and has provided a focus of power to which electors and administrators can look for decisions. Yet it is not without its weaknesses. So subtle is the interplay of forces that it is easy for the balance between Government and Assembly to be disturbed. The Government, thanks to its ambiguous position as part-Executive and part-Parliament can claim to be speaking for Parliament as a whole and to act on its behalf. As the dispenser of patronage it can sometimes curb members of the Assembly and even manipulate representatives. It may secure the election of sympathetic members by fancy franchises which do not reflect popular feeling. Only where the Assembly is well organized and where political parties have firm popular roots can the encroachment of the Government be resisted. There is often no constitutional safeguard in parliamentarism to prevent the Executive from engrossing power. In several countries in the Middle East, Governments have resorted to the expedient of dissolving Parliament (or, more accurately, the Assembly) without convoking another.

Alternatively the balance of forces in parliamentarism may be disturbed, as has occasionally happened in France, by an excess of power in an Assembly which is reluctant to grant the Government the support necessary for it to carry on its work. The Government is not, as in presidential theory, directly responsible to the electorate and therefore depends to a much greater extent on harmonious co-operation from the Assembly.

So delicate is the balance of forces that it is hardly surprising that it is so easily disturbed. Moreover, parliamentarism provides solutions to many problems of government but does not itself satisfy all the demands of those who want a popularly based political system. Many countries have copied merely the trappings of parliamentary government. Adolf Hitler compared in *Mein Kampf* the 'bogus Reichsrat' of the Austro-Hungarian Empire with the Houses of Parliament in Britain — 'the temple of the nation's glory'. The failure of parliamentary government to establish itself properly in much of western Europe before 1914 was followed by similar failures in eastern Europe during the inter-war period, as Professor Hugh Seton-Watson has demonstrated in his *Eastern Europe Between the Wars*. Today, when parliamentarism has spread to Asia and Africa there are signs in many of these countries that it is by no means firmly rooted in the people.

The presidential system, by contrast, appears at first sight to be a much simpler form of government and its presidential Executive readily comprehensible to those accustomed to Government in the hands of a King or Dictator. Indeed it seems to have much in common with the pre-parliamentary monarchy, as a glance at the first seven of the characteristics summarized indicates. The separation of the personnel of the executive and legislative branches is even more pronounced than in the *anciens régimes*.

These similarities need cause no surprise. The presidential experiment preceded the constitutional ferment of the French revolutionary period and was influenced by British experience and developments. Although we know today that the origins of parliamentary government can be traced back to the reign of George I the implications of the emergence of the Cabinet were not fully grasped even in the 1770s and 1780s when America was obtaining its independence. Montesquieu's admiration for the British Constitution in the mid-eighteenth century was based on its 'mixed' nature, monarchy, aristocracy and democracy being wondrously combined in the shape of King, Lords and Commons.

Against the background of the pre-parliamentary British monarchy, and still more the despotisms of continental Europe, the presidential system outlined in the American Constitution, nowadays taken for granted, is seen to be startlingly novel. The other attributes of presidential theory emphasize this. It is true that the removal of the President necessitates the cumbrous and old-fashioned legal remedy of impeachment in contrast to the simple vote of censure in parliamentary countries but this was a necessary consequence of the separation of the two branches of government. The very codification of the provision that the Head of State (and not only his Ministers) could be held legally responsible was a great constitutional innovation. For not all Englishmen, still less Scotsmen, had accepted the argument that James II had 'broken the fundamental laws of this kingdom' and therefore could be lawfully deposed.

Moreover, there was the explicit grant of ultimate supremacy of the Assembly over the President by the proviso that his veto could be overridden. This was only implied in Britain after the last use of the royal veto in 1707 and soon lost significance through the development of parliamentary supremacy instead. Most novel of all, occupation of the White House depended not on hereditary title or even the sufferance of the Assembly but on the vote of the electorate. So much has been said about the failure of the American Revolution to be a social revolution in the modern sense that we are in danger of forgetting that from the point of view of governmental theory the American Constitution, as contemporaries realized, challenged the very basis of the traditional social order in Europe.

The lessons of the constitutional struggles in seventeenth century England were truly learnt by the Americans. The King was removed and his place taken by a popularly-elected President, an Executive who had, incidentally, more to commend him than the Lord Protector. In contrast to England, where the upheavals of the 1650s were followed by the return of the monarchy in 1660 and a much slower pace of constitutional reform thereafter; and unlike France, where the execution of the King was the precursor of nearly a century of upheaval before parliamentary republicanism was finally accepted in 1875 (by one vote in the Legislature) the United States has moved serenely from colonial settlement to world supremacy proudly boasting of the oldest written Constitution in the world. Such longevity is in itself no mean tribute to the presidential system introduced about 170 years ago.

As we have seen, the criticism often made by superficial critics of the American presidential system is that the Constitution ossified at a particular point in its development a political system which was being transformed from a separation of powers into parliamentarism. The American Founding Fathers knew the disadvantages of hereditary monarchy but were naturally unaware of the severe constitutional limitations which were to be placed upon it in the future. However, the American system of government has been adapted to the needs of the nineteenth and twentieth centuries and is today hardly comparable to the eighteenth century theory of the separation of powers. The system in its constitutional outline and its subsequent evolution certainly merits no degree of condescension. It met the specific needs of the colonists and it continues to satisfy Americans today. Later copies of the United States system in South America were modified in the light of the development of parliamentary government—but were not noticeably more successful.

The weakness of the presidential system from the point of view of the political theorist lies in its apparent unsuitability for general application. Its operation in the United States owes much of its success to the historical setting, to the importance of British political ideas (to say nothing of a colonial system which could tolerate the public convention of the subversive Continental Congress), the calibre of American statesmen and the attachment to federal government. Many of the South American countries which have adopted the form seem very often to have missed the content, and for reasons not wholly explicable to enjoy few of the benefits this form of democratic government was intended to bring. It may be that presidential theory was adopted too soon by countries still unfitted for modern constitutional government. Of course it is also true that where parliamentary government has been adopted in backward, and some not so backward, countries the results have not been altogether happy. Be this as it may, presidential government is important as the system which governs American politics, and the outlook of Americans on the world.

The stability of presidential government in the United States may be compared with the many experiments in convention government by so many peoples who have felt oppressed by tyranny. Revolting peasants, English radicals, Rousseau, the Jacobins, and some of the early Russian Communists have all thought at one time or another that if only government could be placed in the hands of the people through their representatives true democracy would be achieved. They have hoped that instead of a hereditary monarchy and perhaps an Estate-type of Legislature founded on privilege a single popular Assembly would represent the 'will of the people'. Then the Executive would be swept away.

Supporters of the convention system of government have sought social justice but have tended to underestimate the importance of political institutions. Classical political theorists from Aristotle to Montesquieu have been aware of one important political principle which has been forgotten by reformers: the body which performs the functions of watchdog over Government is ill-fitted to act as Government itself. The theory of the separation of powers in its broadest sense implies that the political system shall consist not only of a Government but also of elected representatives whose duty is to watch over the Government. The function of watchdog is perhaps more important for an Assembly than that of lawmaker. In theory there may be no objection to an Assembly carrying on Government through committees, but in practice there appear to be many difficulties. Governments, uncontrolled, soon lose touch with public opinion however wellmeaning they may be; and an Assembly is unable satisfactorily to control committees which are part of itself. Assemblies given the responsibility of government neglect their other responsibility, that of representing the public. Men who are admirable representatives of the constituents so long as they are merely legislators are tempted to forget this responsibility when they are preoccupied with the tasks of Government.

Supporters of convention government also take a somewhat idealistic view of human nature by placing such a heavy burden on one body. It may seem a shade sinister for presidential and parliamentary theorists to argue that Government in their systems needs to be constantly watched over lest it cease to act in the public interest, but they are being realists. It is certainly desirable that government should be brought as close to the people as possible but it is naive to assume that an Assembly, unlike a Government, can do no wrong. It is distressing to observe the number of occasions when a convention has been formed in an idealistic reaction against absolutism only to disintegrate within a few years, often to be followed by a new form of despotism. With this in mind we can understand why modern convention-type countries have modified their political systems to avoid the pitfalls which Assembly government seems to involve. Communist states, however, seem to have gone too far in the opposite direction.

In his interesting book *The Price of Revolution* Professor Brogan has asked whether the price of the great revolutions in America, France and Russia, in each of which convention idealism played a large part, was not too high. Did these peoples gain more — or as much — as the British have achieved in the past two hundred years? It is perhaps natural for the British, whose own attempt long ago to revolutionize the social basis of their political system failed ignominiously, to be somewhat sceptical of these more recent attempts to create an ideal democratic society, and there is no doubt that in some important respects none of these revolutions was a success. But they by no means failed. The form of government, and still more of the society, which afterwards evolved was a great advance on the previous regime. With the abolition of entail, primogeniture, titles of nobility and established churches, people felt emancipated and free not only to form a new system of government but to create a new society. As the State Constitution of Massachusetts put it '. . . the whole people covenants with each citizen, and each citizen with the whole people, that all shall be governed by certain laws for the common good'.

This is the importance of convention theory — its inspira-

tion for revolutionaries who are destroying an old order and
are anxious to replace it with something new. Its monument
is less a particular system of government than its penetrating
influence on all modern political systems which claim in
some measure to be democratic.

The study of the forms of government, therefore, important though it is, clearly is only one aspect of political analysis.
It is not enough to examine the legal rules by which countries
are — or are supposed to be — governed, or even to pay tribute
to the things (or aspirations) contained in their constitutions.
One can hardly rest content with theories of government
which include the United States and Paraguay in one classification, the United Kingdom and Cambodia in another and
Switzerland together with the Soviet Union in a third.

Yet how do these political systems differ? Partly of course
they may be distinguished by the degree to which they implement their theories in practice. A country may have a
presidential, or parliamentary or convention-type constitution
which is little more than a scrap of paper designed to keep
the jurists happy. Often however there are other factors to be
taken into account. The political system is, after all, part of
a much wider social order. The class structure may make a
mockery of universal suffrage; a powerful leader may ride
roughshod over an Assembly; a dedicated political party may
dominate the whole apparatus of government.

No doubt it would be possible to take the social order
for granted and to concentrate on the formal political system,
but this is to be excessively legalistic. It is really impossible
to study modern government without considering its roots in
society. It is to the study of these roots, of the participation
by the people in the process of government, that we must now
turn.

20. THE DECLINE OF LEGISLATURES?

K. C. WHEARE

I

When Lord Bryce was putting together some general conclusions and observations about legislatures in his enormous
book *Modern Democracies,* he entitled one chapter 'The Decline of Legislatures'. And he followed it with a chapter
called 'The Pathology of Legislatures'. Both chapters really
deal with the same question: What are the ills to which legislatures are subject and which cause them to go into decline?
A careful study of what Bryce wrote shows that he did not
find it possible to give a straight or simple answer to this very
general question. It is sometimes assumed, however, by those
whose reading may perhaps have gone no further than the
chapter headings, that Bryce believed in a general decline of
legislatures.

The topic he dealt with many years ago is still of importance today. There are not wanting students of political institutions who speak of the decline of legislatures, of the
passing of parliament, of bureaucracy triumphant, and of
cabinet or executive dictatorship. Are they right? Is it necessary to apply to legislatures the tribute which that eloquent
Congressman, the Hon. Elijah Pogram, paid to the defaulting
postmaster in *Martin Chuzzlewit,* and say that their 'bright
home is in the setting sun'? It is a very difficult question to
answer, but it is necessary to make some attempt at it. If the
result is no more than a better understanding of the question itself and of the assumptions upon which it is based, the
effort may not have been in vain.

It is helpful in discussing whether or not legislatures have
declined to ask in what respect it is asserted that they have
or have not declined. Is it a decline in power? Or is it a decline

From *Legislatures,* Oxford U.P., 1963, pp. 219–23, 227–30. We are grateful to the publisher for permission to reproduce this extract.

in efficiency? The two do not necessarily go together. A legislature may be doing too much, it may be keeping control of too wide a range of functions and as a result may not have the time or the capacity to perform them effectively. If it declined in power, it might increase in efficiency. Again, is it a decline in public esteem that is alleged? It could be argued with some force that the French legislature did not decline in powers under the Third and Fourth Republics, but none the less it did decline in public esteem. Or it may be that a decline in public interest is suggested. Public esteem and public interest do not necessarily go together. The activities of a legislature may provide a great deal of news: legislators may often be in the public eye; their proceedings may be notorious. But they may stand low in public esteem. Or, finally, in some discussions of the decline of legislatures it would seem that it is a decline in manners, in standards of behaviour which is being asserted.

It is necessary, also, if a sound judgement on the subject is to be reached, to be clear by which standard the alleged decline is being measured. Is it being alleged that legislatures have declined in powers or in efficiency or in public esteem or in public interest in relation to their own former position, or is it that, in relation to other political or social institutions, particularly the executive or party organizations or the trade unions or employers' organizations or the radio and television, the decline has occurred. Legislatures may have retained their own powers or efficiency or prestige or indeed have increased them, but they may none the less have declined in these respects relatively to other institutions which have increased their powers and improved their position.

If a general survey is made of the position and working of legislatures in the present century, it is apparent that, with a few important and striking exceptions, legislatures have declined in certain important respects and particularly in powers in relation to the executive government. A feature of the development of political institutions in this period has been the great growth of executive power as a result largely of the demands made by two world wars, economic crises, the adoption of collective or socialist or welfare policies, and the persistence of international tension. Governments now do a great deal that they did not do formerly, but most of what they do was not done by anybody before. In particular it was not done by the legislature. The increase of powers by the executive has not been the result of taking away from the legislature things which it did before. Legislatures, indeed, do more than they did and legislators work longer hours and interest themselves in a wider range of subjects. Absolutely their powers have increased. Relatively to the executive government, however, they have in almost all cases, declined.

In one sphere, perhaps, it looks as if the executive has taken away a part of the legislature's functions, and that is in the matter of making the laws. The exercise by the executive of law-making powers, particularly by the growth of delegated legislation has meant that the legislature no longer makes all the laws or even all the important laws. Even if we put aside as exceptional and perhaps ephemeral the taking away from the legislature by the executive in France of a large part of the law-making power by the provisions of the Constitution of the Fifth Republic, there remains the fact that in most countries, though the legislature retains the power to make all the laws, it has in fact delegated to the executive the exercise of this power over a wide field. It is true that this delegation can be withdrawn and its exercise controlled, but none the less in practice it is clear that the executive makes part of the laws.

It can be argued, of course, that the legislature itself nowadays spends as much time on law making as ever it did or indeed more time than it did. It deals with important principles, and debates policies which are embodied in statutes. It could not find the time to deal effectively with the mass of rules which are made by the executive under delegated powers. This is true in many countries and to this extent it is permissible to say that the executive is not taking away from the legislature something which it has done or could do. In terms of time devoted to law making and the quantity of its legislative output the legislature may not have declined absolutely; it is only in relation to the executive that it can be said to have declined.

II

Against the background of a decline of legislatures in relation to the executives, there stand out one or two interesting exceptions. In the first place there are examples of legislatures whose position can hardly be said to have declined even relatively as against the executive. One example is the Con-

gress of the United States, whether it be considered as a bi-
cameral legislature or its two chambers be considered separately. It is true that the executive in the United States has
increased considerably in its powers in this century, particularly since the inauguration of President Franklin D. Roosevelt. But a strong case can be made for the view that Congress
has actually increased its power in the political system and
that its position in relation to the executive is at least as strong
as it was. There have been times when, as at the beginning
of President Franklin Roosevelt's first term, Congress was
willing to accept presidential leadership, but quite soon it
asserted its independence, and the task of managing Congress
has been as complex and difficult since that period as it was
before. It may be that the presidency has overshadowed Congress in public interest, and it is natural that the doings of
one man should be easier to visualize and to praise or con-
demn than the complicated workings of groups of representatives and Senators. But congressional committees of inquiry,
and individual Senators and Congressmen have rivalled and
at times overshadowed the doings of the President. It is, of
course, impossible to prove that Congress has or has not declined in relation to the executive. These judgements are
matters of impression and opinion. A careful study of the
American political system in operation, however, seems to
support the judgement that Congress still holds its own with
the executive. . . .

III

In discussing the relative decline of legislatures it is natural
to think first of the effect of the growth in power and importance of the executive. But there are other political and social
institutions whose existence and growth have affected the position of the legislature. One important function of a legislature
is to be 'a congress of opinions' (in John Stuart Mill's phrase),
a forum of debate and discussion on political and social questions. Walter Bagehot in his *English Constitution* described it,
in speaking of the British House of Commons, as the 'ex-
pressive' function and the 'teaching' function. These functions
legislatures have shared with the press for a long period. But
the invention of sound radio and television has produced a
formidable rival in this sphere. Citizens can now hear and see
speakers and debates and discussions on political and social

questions which may seem to them to be more interesting and persuasive, less concerned with the arid controversies of party warfare, than what is provided by the speeches of legislators, inside or outside their chambers. The legislature has to take its place as one only and that not always the most impressive of the forums in which public questions are discussed. Public opinion is influenced by these speeches and discussions on the air and legislators find themselves under pressure by their constituents who are less ready to accept the customary explanations. Some legislatures, indeed, have resented the discussion on the radio and television of issues which are being or are about to be discussed by the legislature itself, and have attempted to control this outside discussion. This attitude may be easy to understand, but it is difficult to justify. A wider and freer discussion of public questions may reduce the relative importance of the legislature as a forum of debate, but if it arouses a wider interest in such questions and produces a better informed electorate, it is a good thing.

Some legislatures — Australia and New Zealand are examples — have in fact seized the opportunity provided by radio to broadcast their proceedings or parts of their proceedings. In this way their debates have become better known; a greater number of citizens has an opportunity to hear and to see what goes on in the legislature. Such arrangements could produce an increase in the public interest in the legislature, if not inevitably in the public esteem. There is indeed some dispute about whether legislators behave better or worse when they know that they are being heard or seen by their fellow citizens. It can hardly be doubted that they would behave differently. It is clear, however, that although radio and television may have affected the position of the legislatures as a forum of debate by providing rival forums, they have also provided an instrument by which the work of the legislature may be made known to a far wider public than was ever possible when reliance was placed almost entirely on the press and the public meeting.

There is a further important function of a legislature which it has come to share with other institutions, and that is its function as a committee of grievances, as a body whose members individually and collectively have the task of bringing to the notice of the government and of the public the complaints of the citizens. Here again there is no question of an absolute decline. The amount of work which legislators do in attending to the complaints or requests of their constituents is greater, not less, than it was fifty years ago. These duties, more perhaps than any others, have converted the post of legislator from a part-time to a full-time job in Britain and in many other countries. At the same time, however, other institutions have taken up some part of the task and do much that would probably remain undone if legislators alone were expected to do it. The great extension of governmental power and services has brought the citizen into contact with the administration to a much greater extent than ever before, and the task of dealing with the complaints and difficulties which arise is more than members of the legislature alone can cope with. This is one reason why the institution of the Ombudsman, as developed in Scandinavia, has aroused interest in other countries. New Zealand appointed an Ombudsman in 1962.

Perhaps the principal development which has led to the redress of grievances becoming no longer the exclusive function of the legislature, however, is the growth of trade and professional associations, one of whose chief functions is the promotion and protection of the interests of their members. These organizations cover almost the whole economic and social field, and they are powerful enough and expert enough to be able to take up directly with the administration and at the appropriate level, any complaints or grievances which their members may have. They do not need to work through members of the legislature, though there may be occasions when they find it better to do so. In a wide range of matters, however, it will be more expeditious and more satisfactory both to them and to the executive, if they act direct with the department behind the scenes.

Departments on their side, too, have begun to develop a policy and a technique for dealing with the difficulties and complaints of citizens and to encourage them to come direct to the office with their grievances. The appointment of public relations officers is one example of the methods which the administration uses to deal with complaints and remove misunderstandings. These matters are no longer left exclusively to the minister's explanations in reply to criticisms and questions in the legislature.

21. CHIEF EXECUTIVES AND CABINET SYSTEMS

C. J. FRIEDRICH

INTRODUCTION

Of the American President, Harold Laski has said that he is 'both more and less than a king; both more and less than a prime minister'. The issue of executive leadership is dramatically projected in such a comparison. The American President was conceived by the makers of the American Constitution as a republican equivalent to the hereditary monarch of British constitutionalism. Hamilton, in the *Federalist,* went to great length comparing the two offices, insisting that 'there is no pretence for the parallel which has been attempted between him and the king of Great Britain'. He felt that anyone who thought that the President had anywhere near the power of the British king was absurd. Since that comparison was made, kings have vanished or become shadows of their former self, while the American President has assumed the central position in the American scheme. This was at least in part the result of his becoming the leader of the majority party. In the meantime, in Britain the Prime Minister has emerged as the keystone of the arch of what is today a cabinet rather than a parliamentary government. The same is true of the British Dominions and Eire. Countries with less sound political traditions have struggled in vain to produce a similar integration, and when they failed have reverted to authoritarian schemes of executive leadership.

Along with the chief executives, their cabinets, or councils, have undergone considerable change. Their relationship both to the chief executive and to the elected representative assemblies has changed in accordance with the increasing em-

Reprinted by permission of the publisher from Carl J. Friedrich, *Constitutional Government and Democracy* (Waltham, Massachusetts; Blaisdell Publishing Co., 1950), pp. 354–59, 363–64.

phasis upon executive leadership. Cabinets are older than parliaments. Princes surrounded themselves with councils or cabinets for the direction of their bureaucracies as soon as central administrative systems arose. In fact, these bodies, composed of leading administrative officials, are the very core of such centralized systems. It is therefore no wonder that the cabinet tends to occupy a somewhat independent position and is not ordinarily, as the phrase used to go, 'an executive committee of Parliament'. Cabinets today depend once again upon the chief executive, as they always have in the United States. What is more, the old formulas about policy-making and policy execution require extensive revision.

LEADERSHIP: MYSTIQUE AND REALITY

The crux of executive power is leadership. The doings of the Fascists have brought to the fore a conception which was dear to the hearts of romantic critics of constitutionalism and rationalism throughout the nineteenth century. Englishmen, Frenchmen, and Germans vied with each other in glorifying the hero, the Caesar, the superman. Carlyle, Maurras, Nietzsche, they all and many more vented their artistic spleen by contrasting the creative force of the leader with the equalitarian mediocrity of the majority and the mass. Nietzsche was inspired by Burckhardt, as Maurras was inspired by Taine, both great historians with a pessimistic bent of mind. Leopold von Ranke, greatest of German historians in the nineteenth century, while desirous of describing things 'as they had actually been' (*wie es eigentlich gewesen ist*), nevertheless saw history essentially as the product of the great state-builders, the Cromwells, Richelieus, and the rest. Looking at events primarily through the eyes of contemporary observers, like the Venetian ambassadors whose reports he so thoroughly explored, he too absorbed the Renaissance view of man and history.

Sociology and political science, psychology and economics, have more recently exploded a good part of these cherished historical premises. Indeed, economic determinism proceeded to interpret the leader as nothing but the product of favorable economic circumstance. 'He thinks he pushes while he's being pushed'; this snarl of Mephistopheles would best describe the 'leader' in a history preoccupied with price movements, inventions, discoveries, and trade. Meanwhile, Freudian hypotheses about sex as the ultimate propeller of human activity provided new hunches for an interpretation of history, not to mention the school of debunkers who delighted the reader by offering him the intimate view a butler takes of his hero, which proverbially destroys the illusion of greatness. Napoleon scolding Josephine for having mislaid his overcoat is a spectacle which suits the equalitarian impulse of democratic man. Increasing insight into the psychological processes associated with leadership, suggestions, egocentricity, and the whole range of propaganda, also contributed toward the eclipse of leadership as the decisive determinant of social development. But these mounting doubts of the intellectuals could not quell the psychic impulses which are generated in men by a feeling of insecurity: the demand for the leader increased as international and class conflicts undermined the confidence of the masses in the future.

Many attempts have been made to discover the traits of *the* leader, to discover an abstract, general pattern of qualities or characteristics which constitute 'leadership'. Indeed, many foundations, colleges, and other groups seeking to select the future 'leader' cheerfully take it for granted that these qualities are known. Yet, actually, the greatest diversity of opinion prevails as to what constitutes even 'executive ability', let alone leadership ability. A survey of the various inquiries, as well as our general knowledge, leads to the conclusion that these qualities depend very largely upon the conditions under which leadership operates. The nature of the group and of the task will make much difference. An American President needs different qualities from a British Prime Minister, and his qualities today need to be different from what they were a hundred years ago. Take only the single instance of radio appeal; we do not know for sure, but indications are that elections are being vitally affected by that intangible quality. No man can hope to be a success as Prime Minister in Britain who lacks the capacity of handling himself effectively in the give and take of parliamentary debate; the American President does not need that ability. This functional approach to the problem of leadership becomes even more essential when we go farther afield. A religious leader differs markedly from a business leader, and both contrast sharply with a military leader.

We are not at present in a position to 'explain' leadership, and we may never be. When we consider a great religious or spiritual leader, like Luther or Jean Jacques Rousseau, we are apt to admit that we are facing the ultimate creative force in human society working through such a leader. The same would be true of the scientific or artistic leader. When we come to political and social leaders, to the shapers of organizations and governments, we are obliged to be more skeptical. Many students of history would see a clear analogy between a work of art and a 'state'; indeed to Machiavelli the state appeared the greatest work of art of all. But recent history has shown or at least suggested that many, if not all, men can participate in the building and maintaining of a government; that a constitutional system is never the work of one great leader. Once law is placed in the center of attention, it is evident that many minds and many, many hands have gathered and are gathering the detailed insights, devising the particular solutions to particular problems, and that no one can know enough to devise a 'state'. The 'state' concept as such was an outgrowth of the opposite view — a view constructed to justify and rationalize the despotic powers of monarchical rulers in the seventeenth century.[1]

It is possible, however, to spell out, so to speak, certain functional aspects of a leader. One such functional aspect is the leader's representativeness. We all know that an Irishman is more likely to get Irish votes than a Yankee. Likewise a man wanting to reform a church would have to be a member of that church. Again, no one who was not a member of a given profession or craft would be apt to succeed in 'reforming' such a profession, no matter how sound his views might be. Representativeness is compounded of likeness of behavior, of outlook, and of general qualities of that sort. Another functional aspect of leadership is a capacity to find solutions to commonly recognized problems. Here the creative aspect is most apparent. The solution of problems presupposes in-

---

[1] More detailed analysis reveals that the 'great man' view is inappropriate in other fields, too. No one can go through the galleries in Holland without being struck with the many minor artists who preceded and surrounded Rembrandt; nor can anyone listen to the music of Bach's time and country without being struck with a similar 'environment'. It is clear that neither of these peaks of artistic achievement could have been achieved without the solid mass of less extraordinary, yet significant achievement. The 'great man' view is one of decadent times in which none but the greatest are recalled.

telligence; without intelligence there cannot be leadership—
that much is certain. But intelligence unrelated to problems
recognized by the group is unproductive of leadership. Intelligence is a matter of degree. Leadership, therefore, is likely
to be a matter of degree also. A governmental system always
presents many concrete problems; some are very small and
specific, others vast and comprehensive. The man who suggests a convincing solution acquires leadership as others follow his lead.

A third functional aspect, related to the preceding, but
distinct, is the capacity to foresee problems that are not yet
generally recognized, to bring them into clear view and to
dramatize their urgency. Again it is a matter of intelligence,
but of analytical insight rather than inventiveness, plus the
ability to generate and radiate emotion. All the progressive
movements, particularly of recent times, abound with leaders
of this type. They show, at the same time, how easily this
capacity is stultified by unexpected developments. Thus,
Marx's analysis, while a brilliant anticipation of the rising
labor-class problem, overlooked the importance of the managerial class in an expanding industrialism by indiscriminately
lumping it together with capital owners as the capitalist class.
His expectation of an inevitable labor majority has therefore
remained unfulfilled, and the policies of socialist parties built
upon that expectation have foundered. If the leader functions
well as an anticipator and solver of group problems, he will
naturally seem superior to his fellows.

Whether physical prowess distinguishes the leader, as it did
Achilles, or whether a keen wit enables him to succeed where
others fail, prestige will invariably be associated with his position. Prestige is not a separate result of leadership; it is part
and parcel of it. Napoleon, the winner of battles, can afford
to be a ruffian; a successful leader commands a margin of
freedom from communal restraints. This fact is universally
recognized. It is not limited to despotic regimes; everyone
knows that there is such a margin in the most democratic
constitutionalism, and when the British constitution to this
day maintains that 'the king can do no wrong', it gives symbolic
recognition to that fact. Here we can see once again the root
of constitutional restraints: they are designed to prevent the
erstwhile leader from becoming a despot which he might
otherwise do by utilizing this margin of freedom for the systematic destruction of his opponents.

NATIONAL EMERGENCIES AND PERSONAL INSECURITY

We have alluded, in the previous section, to the psychic impulse which a sense of insecurity generates in man, the impulse, namely, of either becoming or following a leader. There is nothing mysterious or novel about this; it is a most natural way to try to cope with pressing difficulties. Few are the people who, when seeing their house on fire, will calmly go their way, as if nothing had happened. Most men will either run in and get everybody to leave the house, form a bucket line, and send for help, in short *become* a leader; or they will call the fire department, that is, *seek* a leader. What an intelligent person will do depends a good deal upon whether the fire department is within easy, quick reach, whether the fire is far advanced, who is in the house — in short, upon all the conditions surrounding the concrete situation. This case, therefore, illustrates well the fact that the same person may elect to be a leader in one situation and a follower in another. The essential question always must be: what course of action offers the greatest probability of getting me out of the jam I am in. If I see no solution, I am likely to follow any man who asserts a reasonable claim to have a solution. Now it is an undeniable fact of our times that a great many people have a sense of personal insecurity, well-supported by incontrovertible evidence, such as the death of a close relative in war, bankruptcy, unemployment, etc. All these anxieties have lately been reinforced by the mysteries of the atomic and biologic weapons.

In the good old days of quick recovery, the standpat solution of turning the rascals out worked. Maybe the rascals you turned in did not bring about recovery, but the sense of insecurity was once more lessened. What if you have turned in and out all kinds of rascals, and the sense of insecurity remains? Then the broader question arises: what is wrong with the system? None but those bold enough to allege that they know the answers can satisfy the psychic impulse which demands leadership. Here the horrible abyss yawns: that you accept as leader a man who has no solutions, a wild man who just wants to be captain of the boat, regardless of the storm. Some writers have denied the quality of leadership to such persons. Only he who convinces reasonable men of right solutions is a true leader. The other is a seducer. But a seduced girl has a baby as much as a loved one; the Don Juan remains a lover, even if a false one.

Can constitutionalism, can democracy, guard against the demagogue? Within limits, yes. Like the thoughtful parent, it can provide for cooling-off periods. Institutional restraints can be provided. Even the constitutional emergency powers can be surrounded with safeguards. But when the sense of insecurity becomes too extreme, when people in their search for some remedy become frantic, all these institutional devices will prove of no avail. That is the reason why the capacity of self-control, of facing emergencies calmly, of enduring an abiding sense of insecurity without losing one's head, is an essential condition of a lasting constitutional order. Those qualities, in short, which make a man a leader himself, which make him seek solutions to his problems, must be widely dispersed amongst a people to enable it to govern itself. Potentially a large part of a democratic nation is possessed of the capacity for leadership. That is the crux of the matter.

CHIEF EXECUTIVES VS. CABINET

The relative strength and power of the single executive as contrasted with some collegial body, like the cabinet, is today at least as important as the relation of either to a body of elected representatives. There is need for a broad comparative analysis of executive leadership in such terms. Generally speaking, executive leadership may be vested largely in a single individual, as it is in the United States, where the Cabinet consists essentially of helpers of the chief executive. Or executive leadership may be exercised by a group of equals, as it is in Switzerland. Or it may fit somewhere in between — England, the Dominions, or France show intermediary patterns. Moreover, these national patterns have been changing gradually from the collegial toward monocratic control, owing to the development of large parties and the prime minister's increasing importance as party leader. The tendency toward the monocratic (presidential) pattern seems almost universal. Frequently it has been perverted into dictatorship; the slower evolution of the position of *Il Duce* merely foreshadowed the rapid rise of the *Führer*. The collegial pattern is more nearly compatible with parliamentary control, but it fails to produce the integration and symbolic representation of unity which the mass electorate seems to demand. In France, under the Third Republic, each of the several members of the cabinet figured as the leader of one of the groups which together constituted the parliamentary support of the cabinet. In Switzerland, the members of the cabinet (Federal Council) are not even necessarily leaders of groups or parties, but are merely representatives of such groups with high administrative qualifications. We find approximations to the collegial pattern in pre-Fascist Italy as well as in a number of the smaller countries of Europe. In many of these countries the pattern was subject to considerable variation, in response to different personalities — a fact which is of some importance even in more nearly monocratic systems. The instability of the pattern was particularly marked in Republican Germany. For a time, an effective leader such as Stresemann or Brüning would create a situation approximating the English arrangement. But the many parties would at other times, in the absence of such a leader, force a strictly collegial cabinet.

PART FIVE

POLITICAL RULE
OUTSIDE CONSTITUTIONAL GOVERNMENT

22. THE GENERAL CHARACTERISTICS OF TOTALITARIAN DICTATORSHIP

C. J. FRIEDRICH AND Z. BRZEZINSKI

Totalitarian regimes are autocracies. When they are said to be tyrannies, despotisms, or absolutisms, the basic general nature of such regimes is being denounced, for all these words have a strongly pejorative flavor. When they call themselves 'democracies', qualifying it by the adjective 'popular', they are not contradicting these indictments, except in trying to suggest that they are good or at least praiseworthy. An inspection of the meaning the totalitarians attach to the term 'popular democracy' reveals that they mean by it a species of autocracy. The leaders of the people, identified with the leaders of the ruling party, have the last word. Once they have decided and been acclaimed by a party gathering, their decision is final. Whether it be a rule, a judgment, or a measure or any other act of government, they are the *autokrator*, the ruler accountable only to himself. Totalitarian dictatorship, in a sense, is the adaptation of autocracy to twentieth-century industrial society.

Thus, as far as this characteristic absence of accountability is concerned, totalitarian dictatorship resembles earlier forms of autocracy. But it is our contention that totalitarian dictatorship is historically an innovation and *sui generis*. It is also our conclusion from all the facts available to us that fascist and communist totalitarian dictatorships are basically alike, or at any rate more nearly like each other than like any other system of government, including earlier forms of autocracy. These two theses are closely linked and must be examined together. They are also linked to a third, that totali-

Reprinted by permission of the publishers from *Totalitarian Dictatorship and Autocracy*, by C. J. Friedrich and Z. Brzezinski, Harvard U.P., pp. 3–13. Copyright 1965 by the President and Fellows of Harvard College.

tarian dictatorship as it actually developed was not intended
by those who created it — Mussolini talked of it, though he
meant something different — but resulted from the political
situations in which the anticonstitutionalist and antidemocratic revolutionary movements and their leaders found themselves. Before we explore these propositions, one very widespread theory of totalitarianism needs consideration.

It is a theory that centers on the regime's efforts to remold
and transform the human beings under its control in the image of its ideology. As such, it might be called an ideological
or anthropological theory of totalitarianism. The theory holds
that the 'essence' of totalitarianism is to be seen in such a
regime's total control of the everyday life of its citizens, of its
control, more particularly, of their thoughts and attitudes as
well as their activities. 'The particular criterion of totalitarian
rule is the creeping rape [sic] of man by the perversion of his
thoughts and his social life', a leading exponent of this view
has written. 'Totalitarian rule', he added, 'is the claim transformed into political action that the world and social life are
changeable without limit.' As compared with this 'essence', it
is asserted that organization and method are criteria of secondary importance. There are a number of serious objections
to this theory. The first is purely pragmatic. For while it may
be the intent of the totalitarians to achieve total control, it
is certainly doomed to disappointment; no such control is
actually achieved, even within the ranks of their party membership or cadres, let alone over the population at large. The
specific procedures generated by this desire for total control,
this 'passion for unanimity' as we call it later in our analysis,
are highly significant, have evolved over time, and have varied
greatly at different stages. They have perhaps been carried
farthest by the Chinese Communists in their methods of
thought control, but they were also different under Stalin and
under Lenin, under Hitler and under Mussolini. Apart from
this pragmatic objection, however, there also arises a comparative historical one. For such ideologically motivated concern
for the whole man, such intent upon total control, has been
characteristic of other regimes in the past, notably theocratic
ones such as the Puritans' or the Moslems'. It has also found
expression in some of the most elevated philosophical systems,
especially that of Plato who certainly in *The Republic, The
Statesman,* and *The Laws* advocates total control in the interest of good order in the political community. This in turn

has led to the profound and unfortunate misunderstanding of Plato as a totalitarian; he was an authoritarian, favoring the autocracy of the wise. The misunderstanding has further occasioned the misinterpretation of certain forms of tyrannical rule in classical antiquity as 'totalitarian', on the ground that in Sparta, for instance, 'the life and activity of the entire population are continuously subject to a close regimentation by the state'. Finally, it would be necessary to describe the order of the medieval monastery as totalitarian; for it was certainly characterized by such a scheme of total control. Indeed, much 'primitive' government also appears then to be totalitarian because of its close control of all participants. What is really the specific difference, the innovation of the totalitarian regimes, is the organization and methods developed and employed with the aid of modern technical devices in an effort to resuscitate such total control in the service of an ideologically motivated movement, dedicated to the total destruction and reconstruction of a mass society. It seems therefore highly desirable to use the term 'totalism' to distinguish the much more general phenomenon just sketched, as has recently been proposed by a careful analyst of the methods of Chinese thought control.

Totalitarian dictatorship then emerges as a system of rule for realizing totalist intentions under modern political and technical conditions, as a novel type of autocracy. The declared intention of creating a 'new man', according to numerous reports, has had significant results where the regime has lasted long enough, as in Russia. In the view of one leading authority, 'the most appealing traits of the Russians — their naturalness and candor — have suffered most'. He considers this a 'profound and apparently permanent transformation', and an 'astonishing' one. In short, the effort at total control, while not achieving such control, has highly significant human effects.

The fascist and communist systems evolved in response to a series of grave crises — they are forms of crisis government. Even so, there is no reason to conclude that the existing totalitarian systems will disappear as a result of internal evolution, though there can be no doubt that they are undergoing continuous changes. The two totalitarian governments that have perished thus far have done so as the result of wars with outside powers, but this does not mean that the Soviet Union, Communist China, or any of the others necessarily will become involved in war. We do not presuppose that totalitarian societies are fixed and static entities but, on the contrary, that they have undergone and continue to undergo a steady evolution, presumably involving both growth and deterioration.

But what about the origins? If it is evident that the regimes came into being because a totalitarian movement achieved dominance over a society and its government, where did the movement come from? The answer to this question remains highly controversial. A great many explanations have been attempted in terms of the various ingredients of these ideologies. Not only Marx and Engels, where the case seems obvious, but Hegel, Luther, and a great many others have come in for their share of blame. Yet none of these thinkers was, of course, a totalitarian at all, and each would have rejected these regimes, if any presumption like that were to be tested in terms of his thought. They were humanists and religious men of intense spirituality of the kind the totalitarians explicitly reject. In short, all such 'explanations', while interesting in illuminating particular elements of the totalitarian ideologies, are based on serious invalidating distortions of historical facts. If we leave aside such ideological explanations (and they are linked of course to the 'ideological' theory of totalitarian dictatorship as criticized above), we find several other unsatisfactory genetic theories.

The debate about the causes or origins of totalitarianism has run all the way from a primitive bad-man theory to the 'moral crisis of our time' kind of argument. A detailed inspection of the available evidence suggests that virtually every one of the factors which has been offered by itself as an explanation of the origin of totalitarian dictatorship has played its role. For example, in the case of Germany, Hitler's moral and personal defects, weaknesses in the German constitutional tradition, certain traits involved in the German 'national character', the Versailles Treaty and its aftermath, the economic crisis and the 'contradictions' of an aging capitalism, the 'threat' of communism, the decline of Christianity and of such other spiritual moorings as the belief in the reason and the reasonableness of man — all have played a role in the total configuration of factors contributing to the over-all result. As in the case of other broad developments in history, only a multiple-factor analysis will yield an adequate account. But at the present time, we cannot fully explain the rise of totalitarian dictatorship. All we can do is to explain it partially by identifying some of the antecedent and concomitant conditions. To repeat: totalitarian dictatorship is a new phenomenon; there has never been anything quite like it before.

The discarding of ideological explanations — highly objectionable to all totalitarians, to be sure — opens up an understanding of and insight into the basic similarity of totalitarian regimes, whether communist or fascist. They are, in terms of organization and procedures — that is to say, in terms of structure, institutions, and processes of rule — *basically alike*. What does this mean? In the first place, it means that they are *not wholly alike*. Popular and journalistic interpretation has oscillated between two extremes; some have said that the communist and fascist dictatorships are wholly alike, others that they are not at all alike. The latter view was the prevailing one during the popular-front days in Europe as well as in liberal circles in the United States. It was even more popular during the Second World War, especially among Allied propagandists. Besides, it was and is the official communist and fascist party line. It is only natural that these regimes, conceiving of themselves as bitter enemies, dedicated to the task of liquidating each other, should take the view that they have nothing in common. This has happened before in history. When the Protestants and Catholics were fighting during the religious wars of the sixteenth and seventeenth centuries, they very commonly denied to one another the name of 'Christians', and each argued about the other that it was not a 'true church'. Actually, and in the perspective of time, both were indeed Christian churches.

The other view, that communist and fascist dictatorships are wholly alike, was during the cold war demonstrably favored in the United States and in Western Europe to an increasing extent. Yet they are demonstrably not wholly alike. For example, they differ in their acknowledged purposes and intentions. Everyone knows that the communists say they seek the world revolution of the proletariat, while the fascists proclaimed their determination to establish the imperial predominance of a particular nation or race, either over the world or over a region. The communist and fascist dictatorships differ also in their historical antecedents: the fascist movements arose in reaction to the communist challenge and offered themselves to a frightened middle class as saviors from the communist danger. The communist movements, on the other hand, presented themselves as the liberators of an oppressed people from an existing autocratic regime, at least in Russia and China. Both claims are not without foundation, and one could perhaps coordinate them by treating the totalitarian movements as consequences of the First World War. 'The rise [of totalitarianism] has occurred in the sequel to the first world war and those catastrophes, political and economic, which accompanied it and the feeling of crisis linked thereto.' As we shall have occasion to show in the chapters to follow, there are many other differences which do not allow us to speak of the communist and fascist totalitarian dictatorships as wholly alike, but which suggest that they are sufficiently alike to class them together and to contrast them not only with constitutional systems, but also with former types of autocracy.

Before we turn to these common features, however, there is another difference that used to be emphasized by many who wanted 'to do business with Hitler' or who admired Mussolini and therefore argued that, far from being wholly like the communist dictatorship, the fascist regimes really had to be seen as merely authoritarian forms of constitutional systems. It is indeed true that more of the institutions of the antecedent liberal and constitutional society survived in the Italian Fascist than in the Russian or Chinese Communist society. But this is due in part to the fact that no liberal constitutional society preceded Soviet or Chinese Communism. The promising period of the Duma came to naught as a result of the war and the disintegration of tsarism, while the Kerensky interlude was far too brief and too superficial to become meaningful for the future. Similarly in China, the Kuomingtang failed to develop a working constitutional order, though various councils were set up; they merely provided a facade for a military dictatorship disrupted by a great deal of anarchical localism, epitomized in the rule of associated warlords. In the Soviet satellites, on the other hand, numerous survivals of a nontotalitarian past continue to function. In Poland, Czechoslovakia, Hungary, and Yugoslavia we find such institutions as universities, churches, and schools. It is likely that, were a communist dictatorship to be established in Great Britain or France, the situation would be similar, and here even more such institutions of the liberal era would continue to operate, for a considerable initial period at least. Precisely this argument has been advanced by such British radicals as Sidney and Beatrice Webb. The tendency of isolated fragments of the preceding state of society to survive has been a significant source of misinterpretation of the fascist totalitarian society, especially in the case of Italy. In the twenties, Italian totalitarianism was very commonly misinterpreted as being 'merely' an authoritarian form of middle-class rule, with the trains running on time and the beggars off the streets. In the case of Germany, this sort of misinterpretation took a slightly different form. In the thirties, various writers tried to interpret German totalitarianism either as 'the end phase of capitalism' or as 'militarist imperialism'. These interpretations stress the continuance of a 'capitalist' economy whose leaders are represented as dominating the regime. The facts as we know them do not correspond to this view. For one who sympathized with socialism or communism, it was very tempting to depict the totalitarian dictatorship of Hitler as nothing but a capitalist society and therefore totally at variance with the 'new civilization' that was arising in the Soviet Union. These few remarks have suggested, it is hoped, why it may be wrong to consider the totalitarian dictatorships under discussion as either wholly alike or basically different. Why they are basically alike remains to be shown, and to this key argument we now turn.

The basic features or traits that we suggest as generally recognized to be common to totalitarian dictatorships are six in number. The 'syndrome', or pattern of interrelated traits, of the totalitarian dictatorship consists of an ideology, a single party typically led by one man, a terroristic police, a communications monopoly, a weapons monopoly, and a centrally directed economy. Of these, the last two are also found in constitutional systems: Socialist Britain had a centrally directed economy, and all modern states possess a weapons monopoly. Whether these latter suggest a 'trend' toward totalitarianism is a question that will be discussed in our last chapter. These six basic features, which we think constitute the distinctive pattern or model of totalitarian dictatorship, form a cluster of traits, intertwined and mutually supporting each other, as is usual in 'organic' systems. They should therefore not be considered in isolation or be made the focal point of comparisons, such as 'Caesar developed a terroristic secret police, therefore he was the first totalitarian dictator', or 'the Catholic Church has practiced ideological thought control, therefore . . .'.

The totalitarian dictatorships all possess the following:

1. An elaborate ideology, consisting of an official body of doctrine covering all vital aspects of man's existence to which everyone living in that society is supposed to adhere, at least passively; this ideology is characteristically focused and projected toward a perfect final state of mankind — that is to say, it contains a chiliastic claim, based upon a radical rejection of the existing society with conquest of the world for the new one.

2. A single mass party typically led by one man, the 'dictator', and consisting of a relatively small percentage of the total population (up to 10 percent) of men and women, a hard core of them passionately and unquestioningly dedicated to the ideology and prepared to assist in every way in promoting its general acceptance, such a party being hierarchically, oligarchically organized and typically either superior to, or completely intertwined with, the governmental bureaucracy.

3. A system of terror, whether physical or psychic, effected through party and secret-police control, supporting but also supervising the party for its leaders, and characteristically directed not only against demonstrable 'enemies' of the regime, but against more or less arbitrarily selected classes of the population; the terror whether of the secret police or of party-directed social pressure systematically exploits modern science, and more especially scientific psychology.

4. A technologically conditioned, near-complete monopoly of control, in the hands of the party and of the government, of all means of effective mass communication, such as the press, radio, and motion pictures.

5. A similarly technologically conditioned, near-complete monopoly of the effective use of all weapons of armed combat.

6. A central control and direction of the entire economy through the bureaucratic coordination of formerly independent corporate entities, typically including most other associations and group activities.

The enumeration of these six traits or trait clusters is not meant to suggest that there might not be others, now insufficiently recognized. It has more particularly been suggested that the administrative control of justice and the courts is a distinctive trait, but actually the evolution of totalitarianism in recent years suggests that such administrative direction of judicial work may be greatly limited. We shall also discuss the problem of expansionism, which has been urged as a characteristic trait of totalitarianism. The traits here outlined have been generally acknowledged as the features of totalitarian dictatorship, to which the writings of students of the most varied backgrounds, including totalitarian writers, bear witness.

Within this broad pattern of similarities, there are many significant variations. To offer a few random illustrations: at present the party plays a much greater role in the Soviet Union than it did under Stalin; the ideology of the Soviet Union is more specifically committed to certain assumptions, because of its Marx–Engels bible, than that of Italian or German fascism, where ideology was formulated by the leader of the party himself; the corporate entities of the fascist economy remained in private hands, as far as property claims are concerned, whereas they become public property in the Soviet Union.

Let us now turn to our first point, namely, that totalitarian regimes are historically novel; that is to say, that no government like totalitarian dictatorship has ever before existed, even though it bears a resemblance to autocracies of the past. It may be interesting to consider briefly some data which show that the six traits we have just identified are to a large extent lacking in historically known autocratic regimes. Neither the oriental despotisms of the more remote past nor the absolute monarchies of modern Europe, neither the tyrannies of the ancient Greek cities nor the Roman empire, neither yet the tyrannies of the city-states of the Italian Renaissance and the Bonapartist military dictatorship nor the other functional dictatorships of this or the last century exhibit this design, this combination of features, though they may possess one or another of its characteristic traits. For example, efforts have often been made to organize some kind of secret police, but they have not even been horse-and-buggy affairs compared with the terror of the Gestapo or the OGPU (afterwards MVD, then KGB). Similarly, though there have been both military and propagandistic concentrations of power and control, the limits of technology have prevented the achievement of effective monopoly. Again, certainly neither the Roman emperor nor the absolute monarch of the eighteenth century sought or needed a party to support him or an ideology in the modern party sense, and the same is true of oriental despots. The tyrants of Greece and Italy may have had a party — that of the Medicis in Florence was called *lo stato* — but they had no ideology to speak of. And, of course, all of these autocratic regimes were far removed from the distinctive features that are rooted in modern technology.

In much of the foregoing, modern technology is mentioned as a significant condition for the invention of the totalitarian model. This aspect of totalitarianism is particularly striking in the field of weapons and communications, but it is involved also in secret-police terror, depending as it does upon technically advanced possibilities of supervision and control of the movement of persons. In addition, the centrally directed economy presupposes the reporting, cataloging, and calculating devices provided by modern technology. In short, four of the six traits are technologically conditioned. To envisage what this technological advance means in terms of political control, one has only to think of the weapons field. The Constitution of the United States guarantees to every citizen the right to bear arms (fourth amendment). In the days of the Minutemen, this was a very important right, and the freedom of the citizen was indeed symbolized by the gun over the hearth, as it is in Switzerland to this day. But who can 'bear' such arms as a tank, a bomber, or a flamethrower, let alone an atom bomb? The citizen as an individual, and indeed in larger groups, is simply defenseless against the overwhelming technological superiority of those who can centralize in their hands the means with which to wield modern weapons and thereby physically to coerce the mass of the citizenry. Similar observations apply to the telephone and telegraph, the press, radio and television, and so forth. 'Freedom' does not have the same potential it had a hundred and fifty years ago, resting as it then did upon individual effort. With few exceptions, the trend of technological advance implies the trend toward greater and greater size of organization. In the perspective of these four traits, therefore, totalitarian societies appear to be merely exaggerations, but nonetheless logical exaggerations, of the technological state of modern society.

Neither ideology nor party has as significant a relation to the state of technology. There is, of course, some connection, since the mass conversion continually attempted by totalitarian propaganda through effective use of the communication monopoly could not be carried through without it. It may here be observed that the Chinese Communists, lacking the means for mass communication, fell back upon the small group effort of word-of-mouth indoctrination, which incidentally offered a chance for substituting such groups for the family and transferring the filial tradition to them. Indeed, this process is seen by them as a key feature of their people's democracy.

Ideology and party are conditioned by modern democracy. Totalitarianism's own leaders see it as democracy's fulfillment, as the true democracy, replacing the plutocratic democracy of the bourgeoisie. From a more detached viewpoint, it appears to be an absolute, and hence autocratic, kind of democracy as contrasted with constitutional democracy. It can therefore grow out of the latter by perverting it. Not only did Hitler, Mussolini, and Lenin[1] build typical parties within a constitutional, if not a democratic, context, but the connection is plain between the stress on ideology and the role that platforms and other types of ideological goal-formation play in democratic parties. To be sure, totalitarian parties developed a pronounced authoritarian pattern while organizing themselves into effective revolutionary instruments of action; but, at the same time, the leaders, beginning with Marx and Engels, saw themselves as constituting the vanguard of the democratic movement of their day, and Stalin always talked of the Soviet totalitarian society as the 'perfect democracy'; Hitler and Mussolini made similar statements. Both the world brotherhood of the proletariat and the folk community were conceived of as supplanting the class divisions of past societies by a complete harmony — the classless society of socialist tradition.

Not only the party but also its ideology harken back to the democratic context within which the totalitarian movements arose. Ideology generally, but more especially totalitarian ideology, involves a high degree of convictional certainty. As has been indicated, totalitarian ideology consists of an official doctrine that radically rejects the existing society in terms of a chiliastic proposal for a new one. It contains strongly utopian elements, some kind of notion of a paradise on earth. This utopian and chiliastic outlook of totalitarian ideologies gives them a pseudo-religious quality. In fact, they often elicit in their less critical followers a depth of conviction and a fervor of devotion usually found only among persons inspired by a transcendent faith. Whether these aspects of totalitarian ideologies bear some sort of relationship to the religions that they

---

[1] Lenin's Bolshevik Party was quite different in actuality from the monolithic autocratic pattern that he outlined in *What Is To Be Done?*

seek to replace is arguable. Marx denounced religion as the opium of the people. It would seem that this is rather an appropriate way of describing totalitarian ideologies. In place of the more or less sane platforms of regular political parties, critical of the existing state of affairs in a limited way, totalitarian ideologies are perversions of such programs. They substitute faith for reason, magic exhortation for knowledge and criticism. And yet it must be recognized that there are enough of these same elements in the operations of democratic parties to attest to the relation between them and their perverted descendants, the totalitarian movements. That is why these movements must be seen and analyzed in their relationship to the democracy they seek to supplant.

At this point, the problem of consensus deserves brief discussion. There has been a good deal of argument over the growth of consensus, especially in the Soviet Union, and in this connection psychoanalytic notions have been put forward. The ideology is said to have been 'internalized', for example — that is to say, many people inside the party and out have become so accustomed to think, speak, and act in terms of the prevailing ideology that they are no longer aware of it. Whether one accepts such notions or not, there can be little doubt that a substantial measure of consensus has developed. Such consensus provides a basis for different procedures from what must be applied to a largely hostile population. These procedures were the core of Khrushchev's popularism, as it has been called, by which the lower cadres and members at large of the party were activated and the people's (mass) participation solicited. By such procedures, also employed on a large scale in Communist China, these communist regimes have come to resemble the fascist ones more closely; both in Italy and Germany the broad national consensus enabled the leadership to envisage the party cadres in a 'capillary' function. As was pointed out in the last chapter, such consensus and the procedures it makes possible ought not to be confused with those of representative government. When Khrushchev and Mao talk about cooperation, one is reminded of the old definition aptly applied to a rather autocratic dean at a leading Eastern university: I operate and you coo. There is a good deal of consensual cooing in Soviet Russia and Communist China, there can be no doubt. That such cooing at times begins to resemble a growl, one suspects from some of the comments in Russian and Chinese sources. There is here, as in other totalitarian spheres, a certain amount of oscillation, of ups and downs that they themselves like to minimize in terms of 'contradictions' that are becoming 'nonantagonistic' and that are superseded in 'dialectical reversals'.

23. TOTALITARIAN POLICIES TO RESIST DISINTEGRATION

K. W. DEUTSCH

If the trends and conflicts making for the loosening or dissolution of totalitarian regimes are not counteracted effectively
by technological developments, we may well ask how any
totalitarian governments have managed to maintain themselves for longer periods of time. Perhaps the persistence of
totalitarian governments or movements, and of social institutions having at least some totalitarian features, over several
decades or even several generations, may be due in part to
their development of a whole series of resources for the
maintenance of the unity of command. Such unity of command, or consistency of decisions, depends to a large extent
upon the unity of consistency of the memories, both of factual
data and of operating preferences, in terms of which all such
decisions must be made. The problem of maintaining unity of
command is thus essentially that of maintaining a sufficient
unity of memories, and it is by providing for a larger share
of relatively uniform memories, and of relatively uniform
processes for adding new but uniform, or at least compatible
experiences, that totalitarian governments or movements have
attempted to persist over larger expanses of space and over
longer periods of time.

The first and most obvious method of totalitarian regimes
to maintain unity among their subjects and subordinate organizations consist, of course, in setting them a common goal.
It is such a goal in terms of which totalitarianism carries out
its attempts to bring about the mobilization of all material and
human resources which is so characteristic for its workings.
Since the totalitarian goal is by definition overriding, its im-

Reprinted by permission of the publishers from *Totalitarianism*, ed.
by C. J. Friedrich, Harvard U.P., pp. 326–33. Copyright 1954 by the
President and Fellows of Harvard College.

position resolves many, though not all, possible conflicts with established habits of procedure, or even with lesser policies of the regime.

Such unification through an overriding goal which is then to be sought spontaneously by all loyal subjects of the government is based on the hidden assumption that the government knows, and that its subjects can know easily, just which actions will in fact bring the country nearer to the goal, or will in fact promote the best interests of the regime, nation, or ideology. This totalitarian assumption often proves unwarranted. As the inhabitants of the ruined cities of Germany have had occasion to find out, the usefulness of Nazi policies to the German people had been greatly overrated. Yet without certain and easily available knowledge of how to promote in fact the proclaimed goal, the united striving for a common purpose is likely to degenerate into endless wrangling over means and methods, made only more bitter by the total devotion and intolerant zeal which totalitarianism enjoins upon all its followers.

Another method of promoting unity might consist in standardizing common rules of procedure for the finding of facts and the making of decisions, either in addition to the stating of goals, or even in place of them. The Koran of Mohammed, the Corpus Juris of Justinian, the Corpus of Canon Law and the Code Napoleon are all examples of pre-totalitarian or in some cases perhaps proto-totalitarian, attempts to insure the unity of far-flung or long-lasting organizations or regimes. All of the codes listed have been successful in some measure, although their success has at times been greater, and their life span longer, than that of the regimes which gave them birth. No such codes were lastingly established by the totalitarian regimes of Italy and Germany. Whether the growing body of Soviet law shows any signs of playing a similar unifying role in the eventual development of Russian society might well be an interesting question for research.

A more far-reaching attempt to insure effective unity of memories consists in the imposition of a common ideology. Such an ideology may be couched in secular or in religious terms. In either case it includes not only common statements of value, common assertions of supposed fact and some common rules of procedure in decision-making, but it also contains often a common epistemology, at least by implication. Its inherents are told which kinds of knowledge, which sources, and which methods of gaining it, are to be trusted and which ones are to be shunned. With common goals, common procedural values, common memories, and common methods for screening and acquiring new information, the probability of maintaining consistency among future decisions and commands is greatly enhanced, even if these decisions have to be made by individuals cut off from communication with each other.

Despite the potential effectiveness of ideologies, most people are more likely to respond to personal experiences and personal contacts than to abstract thoughts or even to colorful symbols. Totalitarian regimes, like other governments, may attempt to maintain their unity by creating a common pool of leading or decision-making personnel — perhaps in the form of a common political party — or of particular institutions, formal or informal, for the training and rotation of leaders. They may make a point of drawing to the capital leading personnel from potentially doubtful outlying districts, somewhat as the Nazis brought wittingly or unwittingly an unusual number of Catholics and Bavarians to Berlin, or as the Soviets put some Georgians, Armenians, and Jews on their central decision-making bodies. They may send their officials from one district to another, so as to maintain the unity of a service corps among them even at the expense of making more casual and distant their relations to the population among whom these officials reside during any particular tour of duty; or they may even command their officials to do two potentially contradictory things at one and the same time: to retain absolute loyalty to the common center and yet to develop numerous deep and intimate contacts with the people among whom they work as in the case of model Communist Party workers extolled in Soviet literature.

Perhaps the most effective way of insuring a community of memories is one over which totalitarian regimes have only very limited control. It is the community of memories that derives from the possession of a common universe of experiences as they are produced by a new way of life, a new fundamental pattern of culture, a new economic system, or a new religion. To the extent that a totalitarian regime becomes established in the course of such a fundamental rearrangement of society, and to the extent that it draws its personnel from those who share in the common ensemble of continuing new experiences resulting from that fundamental change, it can count on at least some significant degree of similarity or uniformity in the outlook both of its decision-making personnel and of its underlying populations, not only in the central regions of its territory but throughout the areas over which the full effects of the fundamental social changes have become extended.

What is perhaps even more important, a totalitarian regime that has arisen in the course of such a fundamental change can count on the unifying effect of the antagonism of the populations and groups of personnel among whom these changes have become accepted against the outside world which has remained skeptical or hostile to the new dispensation. Foreign threats to the totalitarian regime appeal then readily as threats to the new way of life, the new gospel of salvation, or the new institutions of society, and even the remaining domestic opponents of the regime appear in the eyes of the converted population as aliens or infidels.

The contrast between the two types of totalitarianism becomes reinforced by the differences between the psychological and educational techniques employed by each regime. The main emphasis of Nazism was on hardness, will and action; on obedience and command; and on the subordination or annihilation of inferior races. Nazi theories of learning were rudimentary; inventiveness and creativity were considered biological rather than psychological categories. Little if anything in the Nazi education encouraged listening to other people. The circular flow of information from the led to the leaders and from the leaders to the led was to be replaced by a one-way arrangement of commands coming from the top down. In the Nazi world the loudspeaker thus outgrew the microphone and the mouth the ear; and the result seems to have been a gradually increasing bias throughout the system against discovery and against learning.

The Soviet rulers, too, like all dictators, have been eyeing rather warily the human capacity for new discoveries and new social learning, but instead of ignoring it, or trying to stifle most of it outright as the Nazis did, the Soviets have tried to control this capacity and use it for their purposes. Soviet literature in education, psychology, science, and the arts constantly urges individuals to display resourcefulness, initiative, and creativity, while at the same time insisting that they should keep closer to permitted patterns. This double insistence cannot but burden the individuals concerned with a good deal of constant strain and tension; and, to the extent that genuine learning capacity and initiative can survive and grow under such strained circumstances, they may well in the long run contribute their share toward the undermining of the conformity that is essential for the continuation of the totalitarian regime. The strains and stresses inherent in these aspects of Soviet life, terrible as they are for many of the individuals concerned, are occurring on a higher level of complexity and are leaving a wider range of resources available to the regime than did the comparable educational and psychological practices in fascist countries. These differences do not make the Soviet dictatorship less of an opponent of democracy and of the Western world; rather they make it a more formidable one.

SOME TENTATIVE PROSPECTS

Considerations of this kind bring us back to the problem of assessing the capabilities and performance characteristics of different governments and types of government. In many cases, the communicating of information and the reaching of decisions may be as vital to the survival of governments as the functioning of the nervous system would be to the survival of some complex organism. Governments, of course, are not organisms, and the metaphor should not be pushed too far. Even so, different political systems may be profitably compared in terms of the performance of their 'nerves of government', and particularly in terms of their ability to maintain political cohesion and unity of decision-making under conditions of social, political or economic strain. Applied to existing governments, an analysis of this kind reveals major differences between totalitarian and democratic governments in general, as well as between different types of totalitarian regimes, and perhaps between different kinds of democratic policies and institutions.[1]

---

[1] A brief survey of some of the unifying or unity-maintaining techniques and policies of the totalitarian regimes of Soviet Russia and Nazi Germany was presented to the Conference on Totalitarianism of the American Academy of Arts and Sciences as part of the present paper. The length of this survey precluded its inclusion here without disturbing the balance; and it may be published in due time elsewhere. Some of its findings, however, have been used in the section which follows here;

At this stage, any inference from our survey of the patterns of disintegration of totalitarian systems must be tentative and provisional. Thus qualified, they will be indicated here, at the risk that readers will call obvious those findings which fit in with their views, while calling unsound those which do not. Both strictures may turn out to be correct; yet perhaps it may be hoped that they will be imposed only after some careful testing. If treated thus as inferences to be tested, rather than as conclusions to be believed, the following suggestions may yet fulfill some useful function.

1. Totalitarianism is by no means immune from processes of disintegration; on the contrary, many of the dictatorial techniques which are intended to combat schism or disintegration may in fact tend to accelerate and intensify these very processes.

2. The basic processes of political integration and disintegration occur on a more fundamental level than that of mere political, military, or police techniques, or of government-run propaganda. This is even more true in the occurrence of schisms and secessions of supra-national philosophies or ideologies. Research on the probability of a future split — for instance, between the Communist regimes of Russia and China — might most profitably be aimed at these more fundamental levels.

3. Although there are significant analogies in the behavior of different totalitarian systems, the aims of particular totalitarian regimes may make a considerable difference to their ability to maintain cohesion for a longer period of time. The same seems true of the nature of the underlying social changes in the course of which a totalitarian regime may become established; and further considerable differences may be due to the specific practices and institutions by which particular totalitarian regimes may attempt to combat their own automatic drift toward pluralization and disintegration.

4. For all these reasons, no schematic predictions can be made concerning a general probability of all totalitarian regimes to split up or disintegrate within a short period of time. In particular, a number of important performance characteristics of Russian Soviet totalitarianism, on the one hand, and of German Nazi totalitarianism on the other, differ radically

---

and the indulgence of the reader is asked for omitting references to specific policies and cases, which were presented to the Conference.

from each other. What imperfect data we have surveyed seem to suggest that the Soviet dictatorship in Russia still disposes of substantial resources to stave off its own disintegration or pluralization for a considerable time.

5. These considerations apply, however, only to time scales of about twenty to fifty years. Most of the major economic and social changes in history which were violent enough to give rise to regimes with some totalitarian features were substantially completed within a period of the order of fifty years, and with the slowing down of the rate of major changes there has usually followed a period of pluralization and a dwindling of totalitarian expansiveness. If similar considerations should apply to the totalitarian regimes of Russia and China, which established themselves in consequence of revolutions which disrupted the *status quo* in these countries as early as 1911 and 1917, respectively, then we might well expect the 1970s or 1980s to bring a slowing of the expansive pressure from these two regimes, or a growing divergence of policies between them, or among some of their constituent regions, or some combination of all these changes, leading in either case to a diminution in 'classic' patterns of totalitarian behavior.

6. In the meantime, the free countries of the world cannot rely on the disintegration of Soviet-type regimes to rid them of their present opponents; nor does there seem to be much evidence that any propaganda or underground activities short of all-out war could influence the course of events behind the Iron Curtain decisively in favor of freedom. Even the political results of an all-out war against totalitarianism might be hazardous to predict, quite apart from its probable atomic devastation, so long as even the final results of our 'reëducation' of the German and Japanese peoples are by no means clear. The prospects seem to indicate, therefore, a period of prolonged tension until at least the 1980s, followed perhaps then, with luck, by a slackening of pressure.

7. Throughout this period it will be essential to maintain the political, economic and moral strength of the free world. This involves the maintenance of adequate military strength for defense, and the protection of the territories of the democratic countries. In the long run, such Western power will be not very much aided by centering our whole attention on the task of confining the Communist regimes to a particular line or perimeter drawn somewhere on the map of Asia, nor by

borrowing doubtful strength for the cause of the democracies from a motley crew of minor totalitarian regimes who detest our ideals but offer us support for pay. Rather the essential strength of the free world in all likelihood will have to come from the genuinely free countries within it, and our best defense during the next thirty years may well consist in the strengthening of the free world from the ground up and from the inside out, through the growth and strengthening of centers and core areas of genuine freedom.

In geographic terms, this might mean particularly the strengthening of the English-speaking countries, the democracies of Western Europe, and on the Asiatic continent perhaps India and Pakistan. Within these areas, and in terms of politics and economics, as well as of our whole cultural, moral and spiritual climate, it might mean the insistence on the continuing growth of freedom and democracy in all their dimensions.

24. THE MILITARY IN THE POLITICS
OF TODAY

S. E. FINER

The year 1962 opened with brisk outbursts of military revolt.
Four risings — those in the Lebanon, Portugal, Turkey and
Venezuela — were unsuccessful, but the month of March witnessed three victorious revolts in quick succession. In Burma,
General Ne Win deposed the government and established
direct military rule. In Argentina the armed forces removed
President Frondizi and set up a Provisional President in his
place. In Syria, exactly six months after the 1961 coup, military factions first swept away the civilian régime and then,
quarrelling among themselves, restored it.

The date of the unsuccessful Lebanon rising, between the
last day of the old year and the first day of the new, was sym-
bolical: in all this military activity, 1962 was but continuing
where 1961 had left off. For 1961 was also a busy one for the
armed forces. They overthrew the provisional government in
El Salvador in January. In April the 'Four Generals' staged
their unsuccessful coup in Algeria. In May it was the turn of
the South Korean army; it overthrew its government and established a thorough-going military dictatorship. In August,
the Brazilian armed forces strove to prevent Vice-President
Senhor Goulart's accession to the Presidency (which had been
vacated by the resignation of President Quadros). In September the army of the Syrian province of the U.A.R. revolted,
drove the Egyptian officials out, and established a government
for an independent Syria. In November Ecuador's army and
air forces clashed as to who was to succeed the President —
who had himself resigned as the result of a military revolt.

Nor was 1961 very different from 1960. That year had seen

From *The Man on Horseback*, Pall Mall Press and Frederick A.
Praeger, Inc., pp. 1–5, 86–89. We are grateful to both publishers for
permission to reproduce this extract.

the Turkish army revolt of May, and the establishment of General Gürsel's dictatorship; the mutiny of the Congolese Force Publique in July and the subsequent rapine and carnage throughout the new-born Republic; the Laotian coup of Captain Kong Lee in August — the move that sparked off the civil war; the bloodless coup by which Colonel Osorio ousted President Lemus of El Salvador in October; and finally, the revolt of the Palace Guard against the Emperor of Ethiopia in December.

In every case the armed forces had defied or indeed used violence against the government of the state. In May 1960 on the occasion of General Gürsel's revolt, *The Times* commented: 'It has been a good year for Generals'; but this was not only belated but quite misleading. For 1959 had witnessed an unsuccessful rising in Iraq, an unsuccessful military plot in Cambodia and a successful coup in the Sudan, while 1958 was — for the military — an *annus mirabilis*. That was the year when Marshal Sarit abrogated the constitution of Thailand and made himself dictator; in which Generals Ayub Khan, Kassim and Abboud seized power in Pakistan, Iraq and the Sudan respectively; in which, also, General Ne Win was raised to power in Burma and General de Gaulle in France.

Yet perhaps this period 1958–61 is exceptional? Hardly so. Consider the sovereign states that are at least seven years old, i.e. those created in or before 1955. Leaving aside small states of nominal sovereign status such as Liechtenstein, San Marino or the Trucial States, 79[1] sovereign states existed in or before 1955: 15 came into being between 1945 and 1955, and of these 9 have suffered from military coups (including the Lebanon). Another 13 states came into being between 1918 and 1944 (including the 3 Baltic States, now absorbed into the Soviet Union). Of these 6 experienced military coups, and one of them (Jordan) may fairly be said to be a royal military dictatorship. The three states created between 1900 and 1917, i.e. Albania, Cuba and Panama, have all witnessed military revolt and dictatorship since 1918; and so likewise have the two — Bulgaria and Serbia — which became fully independent between 1861 and 1899. 46 states have been independent for more than a century. Since 1918 no less than 26 of these have

---

[1] Properly, 76. The figure of 79 includes Esthonia, Lithuania and Latvia, now absorbed into the U.S.S.R., but independent from 1918 to 1940.

suffered from some form or other of military intervention in their politics, usually of a violent kind.[2]

Thus the military coups of 1958–61 were certainly not exceptional. Of the 51 states existing in or before 1917, all but 19 have experienced such coups since 1917; while of the 28 created between 1917 and 1955, all but 15 have done so. Independent political activity by the armed forces is therefore frequent, widespread, and of long standing.

Nor are its effects transitory. On the contrary. At the moment of writing some 11 states are military dictatorships: Thailand, Pakistan, Egypt, the Sudan, Iraq, Spain, Portugal, South Korea, El Salvador, Paraguay and Nicaragua. In addition, in a large number of countries the army alone guarantees the régime: e.g. in Jordan, the Congo, Persia, Honduras. In many other countries, e.g. Indonesia, Argentina, Brazil, Venezuela, Peru, Ecuador and Guatemala, the régimes must needs court the armed forces' goodwill – a favour which may be suddenly withdrawn, as in the past.

Finally, this political activity of the military is *persistent*. In certain areas of South America, earthquakes are so frequent that the people date great events from the years when by rare chance no earthquake has occurred. Likewise with the political activity of the military; there are areas where it can fairly be described – by virtue of its recurrent and its widespread nature – as endemic. Such an area is Latin America, where the phenomenon has persisted for a century and a half; the Middle East; and likewise South East Asia. A fourth such area lay in Europe (up to the communization of most of its countries) in the strip connecting the Baltic, the Balkans and Turkey.

From what has been said so far we may draw two conclusions. In the first place there is a distinct class of countries where governments have been repeatedly subjected to the interference of their armed forces. They are certainly not liberal democracies of the British or American kind wherein the military are strictly subordinated to the civilians. Nor are they despotisms or autocracies of a totalitarian type, where, we must emphasize, the military are subordinated to the civilians as much as or even more than in the liberal-democratic régimes. These régimes of military provenance or military rule

---

[2] China falls outside this classification. It was a prey to incessant civil war and military turbulence until 1949.

are *sui generis*. They constitute a large proportion of those sovereign states which are neither communist nor liberal-democratic, and will soon comprise most of them; for the two other main types of government in the world, the colonial oligarchies (like Angola or Kenya) are disappearing, and so likewise are the proto-dynastic régimes like those of Nepal or Arabia or the Yemen. The régimes where the military are the decisive political factor form a distinct class which we may call the *empirical autocracies and oligarchies*. 'Empirical' distinguishes them from the ideological autocracies and oligarchies of the Soviet type; 'autocracies and oligarchies' distinguishes them from the democracies.

Secondly, the military as an independent political force, constitutes a distinct and peculiar political phenomenon. Consider that the armed forces have intervened in the politics of many and widely diverse countries; that they have done so continually in the past, and are doing so today; that their intervention is usually politically decisive; and that, above all, they tend to intervene persistently, over and over again, in the same countries. None of this suggests that we are observing a mere set of ephemeral, exceptional and isolated adventures. On the contrary, it does emphatically suggest that we are in the presence of a peculiar political phenomenon: one that is abiding, deep seated, and distinctive.

The régime of military provenance or direct military rule is, in short, a distinctive kind of régime; and the military as an independent political force is a distinctive political phenomenon.

Little attention has been given to either. For one thing, few have tried to distinguish between the forms that military intervention takes; or the depth to which it is pressed. At first glance the characteristic mode of military intervention is the violent overturn of a government and the characteristic 'level' is the establishment of overt military rule. Yet the military often work on governments from behind the scenes; and even when they do establish a military dictatorship they usually fabricate some quasi-civilian façade of government behind which they retire as fast as possible. Overt military rule is therefore comparatively rare, and, apparently, short-lived. It is this that gives the appearance of transience to military régimes. But the modes of military intervention are as often latent or indirect as they are overt or direct. Likewise the 'level' to which the military press their intervention varies;

they do not always supplant the civilian régime. Often they merely substitute one cabinet for another, or again simply subject a cabinet to blackmail. When all these varied modes of military intervention in politics are examined and the 'levels' to which the military press such intervention are recognized, the phenomenon appears in its true light — distinctive, persistent and widespread.

Secondly, there is a common assumption, an unreflecting belief, that it is somehow 'natural' for the armed forces to obey the civil power. Therefore instances which show civilian control to have broken down are regarded, if at all, as isolated disturbances, after which matters will again return to 'normal'. But no reason is adduced for showing that civilian control of the armed forces is, in fact, 'natural'. Is it? Instead of asking why the military engage in politics, we ought surely ask why they ever do otherwise. For at first sight the political advantages of the military *vis-à-vis* other and civilian groupings are overwhelming. The military possess vastly superior organization. And they possess *arms*.

THE LEVELS OF INTERVENTION
(1) COUNTRIES OF DEVELOPED POLITICAL CULTURE

'Levels' of intervention

Intervention can be pushed to various levels of completeness. The activities of a Von Seeckt are not different in kind from the activities of, say, a Kassim or Nasser, but differ in degree.

We can recognize four levels of military intervention. First we have the level of *influence* upon the civil authorities. By this is meant the effort to convince the civil authorities by appealing to their reason or their emotions. This level is the constitutional and legitimate one, entirely consistent with the supremacy of the civil power. The military authorities act in precisely the same way and with the same authority as any elements in the bureaucracy, though their influence may well be weightier and on occasion over-riding, in view of the greater risks involved by the rejection of their advice.

The second level is the level of *pressures*, or *'blackmail'*. Here the military seek to convince the civil power by the threat of some sanction. The span of such pressures is wide. It can range from hints or actions that are just barely constitutional at one end to intimidation and threats that are clearly unconstitutional at the other. It would be difficult to say that the Curragh 'mutiny' was downright unconstitutional, and it can even be argued that in strict legal terms it was not unconstitutional at all. Nevertheless, it constituted an effective exercise of pressure on the British government. In his *Memoirs,* Lord Montgomery says that he assembled the military members of the Army Council and got them to agree to resign in a body if the cabinet decided on anything less than 18 months' National Service, and that he notified the Secretary of State of this decision.[3] Mr. Shinwell (the Secretary of State in question) has denied this. However, supposing it happened as described, again, it is doubtful whether the action was unconstitutional. It is on the margin. At the other extreme, threats to stage a coup, for example, are plainly unconstitutional.

At both the first and second levels, the military is working upon and through the civil authorities. Even in a complete form, its power is always exercised behind the scenes. The military is, at most, a puppet-master. The third level, however, is that of *displacement,* i.e. the removal of one cabinet or ruler for another cabinet or ruler. This is achieved by violence or the threat of violence. The object is to replace one set of civilian politicians by another and more compliant set. However, the civilian régime as such is not overthrown — only one particular set of civilians.

The fourth level sweeps away the civilian régime and establishes the military in its place. This is the fourth and most complete level of intervention, the level of *supplantment.*

The parameters of the levels of intervention

The levels to which the military press their intervention are related to the *level of political culture* of their society. We must therefore look at this concept more closely.

The level of political culture is high, when

(1) the *'political formula'*, i.e. the belief or emotion by virtue of which the rulers claim the moral right to govern and be obeyed, is generally accepted. Or, to say this in another way, where

---

[3] *The Memoirs of Field-Marshal Montgomery.* (Fontana edn., 1960), pp. 486–87.

(2) the complex of civil procedures and organs which jointly constitute the political system are recognized as authoritative, i.e. as duty-worthy, by a wide consensus. Or, again in other words, where

(3) public involvement in and attachment to these civil institutions is strong and widespread.

The criteria by which we can assess this attachment to and involvement in the institutions of the régime are three. We must ask:

(1) Does there exist a wide public approval of the procedures for transferring power, and a corresponding belief that no exercise of power in breach of these procedures is legitimate?

(2) Does there exist a wide public recognition as to who or what constitutes the sovereign authority, and a corresponding belief that no other persons or centre of power is legitimate or duty-worthy?

(3) Is the public proportionately large and well-mobilized into private associations? i.e. do we find cohesive churches, industrial associations and firms, labour unions, and political parties?

Where all these conditions are satisfied the level of political culture may be said to be high; to the extent that they are not, it is correspondingly low.

These conditions are obviously better satisfied in Britain than in Iraq. It is more difficult, however, to say whether they are better satisfied in Britain than in Sweden. Furthermore, this notion of 'political culture' is not unitary. It is a complex of the three conditions, and these can be ranked in different ways. Thus we might find one country in which the public was weak and ill-organized but reasonably united, while in another it was disunited but very strongly organized. For these reasons it would be difficult to arrange societies in a continuous rank-order, and even more difficult to find one that satisfied everybody.

It is not so hard, however, to group societies in a number of broad categories of descending orders of political culture (though borderline cases still offer difficulties). And, for purposes of relating the level of intervention to the order of political culture, it is much clearer.

In the first group, where the order of political culture is highest, all three of the conditions are fulfilled. In such countries, the intervention of the military would be regarded as a wholly unwarrantable intrusion. Public sanction for such action would be unobtainable. Britain, the United States, the Scandinavian countries, Switzerland, Canada, Australia and New Zealand, Eire, and Holland are examples. We shall call these, countries of a *mature political culture*.

In the second group, civil institutions are highly developed. The public is a proportionately wide one, well organized into powerful associations. Civil procedures and public authorities are well rooted. But, unlike the first group, the legitimacy of the procedures for transferring political power and the question of who or what should constitute the sovereign authority are both in dispute. Germany from the Empire to the accession of Hitler, Japan between the two wars, and France from the Third Republic onwards, fall into this group. So too, as we shall see, does the U.S.S.R. In such countries, the military would have to reckon on a strong public resistance to their interventions. We shall call these, countries of a *developed political culture*.

In the third group are those countries where the public is relatively narrow and is weakly organized, and where the institutions and procedures of the régime are in dispute also. Here opinion would not be strongly resistive to military intervention; this opinion, being weak and self-divided, is in a fluid state. At the top of this category we can place countries like Turkey, Argentina and Spain; at the bottom countries like Egypt and Syria, Pakistan, Iraq and the Sudan, or South Korea. We shall call these countries of a *low political culture*.

Fourth come the countries where for practical purposes any government can ignore public opinion – the politically articulate are so few and weakly organized. Mexico and Argentina in the first half century of their existence, Haiti or Paraguay or the Congo today, are of this kind. We shall call these countries of *minimal political culture*.[4]

---

[4] There is also a fifth class, with which we shall not be concerned. This might be styled the antediluvian class (the deluge in question being the French Revolution). These are the traditional monarchies where the ideals of nationality, liberty, equality and popular sovereignty have

As long as the listed characteristics persist in such societies, the legitimation of military rule would be *unobtainable* in the first group, *resisted* in the second, *fluid* in the third, *unimportant* in the fourth.

The levels to which intervention is pushed vary according to the group into which a society falls. These four orders of political culture form, as it were, the parameters of the levels of military intervention.

---

not yet penetrated. Another and better description is perhaps the proto-dynastic societies, societies where allegiance is owed to the dynasty. In these societies the public, as an active and organized force, does not exist. It is a passive body, still in its traditional moulds of kinship and village communities. This traditionally structured opinion exhibits a passive consensus on the mode of transferring power (i.e. through the dynastic line) and on the sovereign authority, the monarch. These proto-dynastic states are fast passing: but the Yemen, Saudi Arabia and Ethiopia still remain. Any military intervention in such states as these would be exercised in the name of the dynasty — as it was in the revolt of the Ethiopian Imperial Guard in 1960.

25. THE BUREAUCRATIC MIND

E. STRAUSS

The bureaucratic defects of large organizations may arise
either from the effects of administrative duties on the behaviour of the individual official or from the structure and
processes of the administrative system. They are naturally
most prominent in the government service; the public official,
civil servant, *fonctionnaire* or *Beamter,* for this reason looms
overwhelmingly large in the popular picture of the bureaucrat, but many of his characteristic traits can also be dis-
covered amongst the professional administrators of other large
bodies.

A useful summary of the everyday criticisms of the bureaucratic official was given towards the end of the second World
War by a British parliamentary committee on the training of
civil servants, and it undoubtedly forms an impressive catalogue: 'The faults most frequently enumerated are overdevotion to precedent; remoteness from the rest of the community, inaccessibility and faulty handling of the general
public; lack of initiative and imagination; ineffective organization and waste of manpower; procrastination and unwillingness to take responsibility or to give decisions'.[1]

With the exception of ineffective organization and waste of
manpower, which are defects of the administrative system, all
the faults mentioned relate to the individual official and his
behaviour. They are not all due to the same circumstances,
nor are they equally important in all types of organization or
in all countries. 'Remoteness from the rest of the community'
is more characteristic of the public official than of the em-
ployee of a trade union or corporation, and perhaps more

From *The Ruling Servants,* Allen & Unwin, Ltd. and Frederick H.
Praeger, Inc., pp. 43–47, 56–61. We are grateful to both publishers for
permission to reproduce this extract.
[1] *Report of the Committee on the Training of Civil Servants* (May
1944), Cmd 6525.

typical of the English civil servant and the German *Beamter* than of their American counterpart. Nevertheless it is comparatively easy to see the extent to which these faults reflect the position of administrative officials and are, therefore, to some extent inherent in their work, but the logical sequence is somewhat different from the order in which the public, and the parliamentary committee of inquiry, tends to look at them.

The typical administrative official is a professional who devotes most of his time and energy to his employment, and public administration in particular is normally a lifetime 'career'. The difference between success in a profession and in a career is the existence of a definite organizational framework for the latter. In the professions, success may at least to some extent be measured by technical achievement. Professional eminence may be associated with outward rank, but this is not invariably the case, and the two are by no means necessarily identical. It is, to say the least, possible to be a great lawyer without being a Lord Chancellor, or a great divine without being an Archbishop, and *vice versa*. Even in the armed forces, acknowledged greatness is not necessarily identical with highest rank — the greatest genius produced by the British navy died as a Vice Admiral. In an administrative career, on the other hand, success is identical with promotion: there is no 'great' junior clerk. It is a career in the sense of an obstacle race, where success is measured entirely by the official position attained within the hierarchy, with promotion the key to higher rank, greater power and bigger income. The chances and effects of promotion are, therefore, of overriding importance for the individual official and influence his outlook to an extent which can hardly be exaggerated.

The individual official may only be a small cog, but he forms part of a very large wheel, and his modest share in the power wielded by the organization as a whole tends to colour his attitude towards all outsiders who have no part in his great mystery. If he is in the service of the government, the consciousness of belonging to the paramount organization of the country naturally intensifies this attitude, but every large organization has its full-time staff, with its scale of ranks, its promotion system and its material rewards. This setting is the primary and decisive fact which conditions the daily life and outlook of the individual official. He is, therefore, inevitably somewhat removed from the rough-and-tumble of the outside world and primarily concerned with the official world to which he belongs, with its rules of procedure and conduct, its chances of promotion and its gossip, which is of absorbing interest to the initiate, however fatuous it may appear to the outsider.

Although inherent in the position of the administrative official, and therefore to some extent inevitable, this aloofness is a definite drawback to the proper functioning of the organization. There are many routine jobs within a large organization whose holders have little or no contact with the outside world, but the body as a whole is not a self-contained and self-regulating mechanism but an instrument for the furtherance of specific social interests, and therefore intimately concerned with the world at large and its problems. Its officials, therefore, have to maintain contact with the outside world, and the ability to respond quickly and correctly to changes in the social environment is vital for the success, or even for the survival, of the whole organization.

The administrative official thus belongs to two worlds, and has to perform the difficult task of balancing their requirements in his daily work. One of the symptoms of failure consists in 'faulty handling of the general public'. This defect is most acute at the base of the administrative pyramid, where routine officials are in daily contact with the public. In the higher ranks of the administration different problems arise, and the 'remoteness from the rest of the community' with which many higher officials are charged is largely due to the insulating effect of a number of administrative layers between themselves and the outside world. Although the senior official usually has his own outside contacts and deals directly with important problems or personalities, the bulk of his duties normally consists of official matters reaching him at the second or third remove through the administrative chain.

'Overdevotion to precedent', combined with 'lack of initiative and imagination . . . procrastination and unwillingness to take responsibility or to give decisions' are closely related bureaucratic defects, due in the last resort to the hierarchic structure of large-scale administration. The ordinary official is far below the policy-making level, where the primary purposes of the organization are transformed into a scheme of administrative action. For him, policy consists of definite, though not unalterable, instructions governing his behaviour in typical circumstances and supplemented by rulings on special cases which he obtains in case of need from his superiors.

While he is dealing only with matters adequately covered by his instructions, the routine work will run smoothly, but social life is essentially a changeable and unruly element, and sooner or later the official will be confronted by an unexpected combination of circumstances, because the policy of the organization and the instructions given from the top are based on past experience and have not caught up with the march of time. When this happens, the subordinate official may have to choose between different courses: either to apply his rules to a case which they do not properly fit, or to deviate from his orders and make an independent decision, or to do nothing and ask for new instructions.

The attempt to force changing facts to fit the established policy of the organization, though always made by routine officials, cannot be indefinitely kept up, because sooner or later it is bound to end in failure. The disregarding of official rules by junior officials is for very good reasons discouraged in every large organization, for it is incompatible with orderly administration. More important from the point of view of the individual, it may have serious repercussions for the culprit, and 'disobeying orders' is, therefore, one of the gravest steps a subordinate official can take.[2] Barring acute emergencies, a display of independence is neither expected from a junior official, nor would it be countenanced by authority.

The decision of administrative cases by precedent is, therefore, deeply routed in the structure of the whole system, and where precedent is lacking, or where its application is resisted by powerful outside interests, the official will not feel entitled to give a decision on the spot and thereby accept a responsibility which the rules of the administration withhold from him. He will instead refer the matter to his superior, and if the case is unusually difficult it may slowly travel along the 'return line of responsibility', until a decision is made at top level, whence it will return to the starting point in the form of an instruction, after an exasperating time lag. . . .

---

[2] A characteristically illogical recognition of the inherent dilemma was to be found in the Order of Maria Theresa in the Imperial Austrian army (cr. 1757), which could be obtained by successful action by an officer in disregard of orders — with the court martial as penalty for failure.

DEPARTMENTALISM

Departmentalism is the most serious bureaucratic defect and invariably indicates a serious deterioration in the efficiency of the administrative system as a whole. The symptom of this disease is a decay in the consciousness of an overriding common purpose between different departments and a corresponding decline in the authority of the central leadership. Its result is the replacement of co-operation between different departments in the service of common aims by chronic friction which may flare up into acute inter-departmental warfare.

A common and comparatively harmless form of this disease follows the sudden expansion of existing organizations. Where new purposes have to be carried out with insufficient preparation, the administrative centre of gravity moves away from its traditional place, and new men may dispute the authority of the established leaders. The sudden growth of the administrative machine may affect its balance and overtax the technical abilities of the administrators, and a few important departments may attempt to supplant the aims of the whole organization by their own interests.

In great emergencies the dividing line between legitimate ruthlessness and departmental megalomania is difficult to lay down and still more difficult to observe; admirers of the methods used by Lord Beaverbrook as British Minister of Aircraft Production during the Second World War will probably never be able to agree with his critics on this point. However, healthy organizations may survive even gross excesses without permanent damage, provided the emergency does not last so long as to destroy the existing balance between the primary purpose of the organization and its institutions.

In *politics,* the classical modern illustration of rampant departmentalism in a comparatively healthy environment is, curiously enough, the United States Government of the New Deal and the Second World War and its aftermath. The number of new federal organs, departments and agencies, among them the notorious 'alphabetical' agencies, created between 1933 and 1943 reached the fantastic total of 195, including not only the special New Deal departments but also the massive block of war-time emergency organizations.[3] Thus it is not surprising and hardly even shocking that the great inquest carried out by the Hoover Commission on the structure of American Government after fifteen years of almost uninterrupted expansion brought in a general verdict of departmental anarchy: 'Instead of being unified organizations, many departments and agencies are but loose federations of bureaus and sub-divisions, each jealously defending its own jurisdiction'.[4]

In this 'chaos of bureaus and sub-divisions', the National Security Organization held, perhaps, pride of place, because its growth had been particularly precipitate, and the Commission found 'continuous disharmony and lack of unified planning, extravagance in military budgets and waste in military expenditure'.[5] The Veterans' Administration was taken to task for the excessive number of its staff officers and the complexity of its structure, with its 88 different manuals, 665 varieties of technical bulletins and over 400 circulars of various kinds, adding up to a wealth of 'instructions on internal methods and procedures which defy intelligent execution'.[6]

The co-existence of the manifold departments of the American Government, whether old or new, was and is by no means always peaceful. The outstanding example of interdepartmental rivalry in the civilian field is an administrative heirloom going back well before the origin of the New Deal. It concerns the soil conservation services of the Departments of the Interior and of Agriculture, and particularly the Forestry Service. Their vendetta warfare went well beyond official levels, and at times the Forestry Service was lobbying against a Bill put before Congress by the Department of the Interior,[7] while the latter submitted programmes to Congress without even informing the Secretary of Agriculture.[8] More recently, such breaches of decorum have been completely eclipsed by the notorious wrangling between different

---

[3] L. Sullivan, *Bureaucracy Runs Amuck* (New York, 1944), pp. 304–10, gives a complete list.

[4] *Hoover Commission Report*, p. 6.

[5] Ibid. p. 17.

[6] Ibid. p. 361.

[7] *The Secret Diary of Harold L. Ickes: The First Thousand Days, 1933–1936* (New York, 1953), pp. 598 ff.

[8] *Hoover Commission Report*, p. 249.

branches of the armed forces which show a remarkable latitude in their interpretation of military discipline and the constitutional proprieties.

Not even the severest critics of the American system of government would describe it as a full-fledged bureaucracy, however alarming some of these recent manifestations. The growth of departmentalism, though spectacular like all things American, has so far not gone unchecked, but if it is allowed to proceed without the self-assertion of the top leadership which is the guardian of the conscience of the organization as a whole, such processes may reach the point of non-return.

Soviet Russia provides unsurpassed illustrations of these tendencies, particularly in the *economic* field. The economic bureaucracies of capitalist countries function in the discreet seclusion of private enterprise, but in the Soviet Union glimpses at the way in which things are done, or remain undone, may be obtained as a by-product of official 'self-criticism' on the occasion of changes in policy. Thus it was at least one of the purposes of the Great Massacre of the Ministries carried out in the summer of 1957 under Khrushchev's leadership to break the stranglehold of central departments on the operation of industry.

In his speech in May 1957, Khrushchev complained: 'It is very difficult indeed to carry through specialization and co-operation in production where there are so many ministries and departments, because the departmental interests of the numerous ministries and central boards raise obstacles in the way'.[9] The meaning of this general statement was made clear with the help of everyday illustrations, of which there was obviously no shortage: 'Often enterprises that are closely linked with one another and situated side by side operate as independent units, because they are managed by different central boards of one and the same ministry. . . . The directors of those enterprises copy the methods of the central boards in seeking to shut themselves off from each other as best they can. Comrade Maximov, who heads the Zhdanov coke and by-products plant, being intent on upholding his "sovereignty", had a slag stone of 915 metres (3,000 feet) long and 2½

---

[9] N. S. Khrushchev, *Improvement of Industrial Management in the U.S.S.R.* (London, 1957), p. 28.

metres (over 8 feet) high built to shut off the Azovstal works, spending about 200,000 roubles on this useless idea'.[10]

The next example is less naïve and much more serious, because it emphasizes the threat of departmentalism to administrative efficiency. It concerns a cement works and an asbestos and slate plant occupying the same premises and processing the cement produced by the former: 'The two enterprises are virtually one. But see how the bureaucratic practices prevailing in some departments deform industry. The Ministry of the Building Materials Industry has artificially divided that single production unit into two independent ones under two different central boards — the Glavzapadsement and the Glavaboshifer respectively. The result is two directors, two chief engineers, two independent accounts departments and other departments that are duplicating each other's work . . . and in Moscow there are two central departments in charge of the twin enterprises, and hence if there are any differences between the two departments, the matter can only be settled by the top level executives of the ministry'.[11]

With an acute sense for the intrinsic logic of this process Khrushchev finally quotes the following result of the division of responsibility for the Moscow electrical works between three ministries: 'What used to be factory shops have been turned into three different plants with three independent managements and the corresponding staffs'.[12]

Large departmentalized organizations tend to reproduce bureaucratic defects on a much bigger scale; whole departments behave like individual officials, and departmental inertia, refusal to make decisions and other forms of procrastination are added to, and intensify, parallel tendencies among individuals. The acknowledged impotence of the private person faced by the lack of sympathy of a bureaucratic machine may then be matched by the helplessness of one department in obtaining the necessary co-operation of other departments.

This state of affairs is, perhaps, more characteristic of old-established administrations whose efficiency has been allowed to run down than of new mushroom organizations like the 'alphabetical' agencies of the New Deal in America. There is more than a suspicion that something of this kind occurred

[10] Ibid.
[11] Ibid. p. 29.
[12] Ibid.

in the British government service during the 1930s. This was at least the experience of a somewhat unorthodox British diplomat of the period, Sir Walford Selby, who attributed a good deal of the responsibility for the unsatisfactory diplomatic policy of the British Government to the 'seeming inability of the Foreign Office to obtain decisions of any kind from other departments of Government'.[13] This agrees well enough with the impressions of an experienced politician like Dr. Dalton who reflected on the vagaries of the 'Whitehall obstacle race — of trying to push or pull some piece of policy over, or through a long series of obstacles. This included in this case [an amendment to the Statute of the International Court of Justice] first, some of our own officials in the Foreign Office; second, some other Departments, particularly the Service Departments; third, some members of the Cabinet; fourth, some of the Dominion Governments'.[14]

Unchecked departmentalism does not exhaust itself in protestations of one's good intentions and protests against unsympathetic and, therefore, ignorant critics. Every department easily convinces itself that it cannot carry out its functions (which are invariably interpreted in the most liberal manner and may include a growing amount of duplication) without bigger and better staff, and is thus firmly set on the way towards carving out its own empire. In this virulent stage of the disease of departmentalism, self-aggrandizement becomes the main principle of every department, either on its own or in temporary coalition with others. At this point the original purposes of the organization are in imminent danger of losing their creative and guiding function, although they may still be evoked as formulae. It will depend on the vitality of the primary organization whether such dangerous tendencies can be curbed by a reform regime, or whether the whole administrative system degenerates into a jungle of jarring and warring departmental factions.

This is the watershed between bureaucratic defects, which arise in the common soil of technical difficulties, and the great social evil of bureaucratic degeneration.

---

[13] Sir Walford Selby, *Diplomatic Twilight* (1953), p. 98.
[14] Hugh Dalton, *Call Back Yesterday* (1953), p. 238.

PART SIX

CONCLUSION
FUTURE OF DEMOCRACY

26. POLITICAL OPPOSITION
IN WESTERN DEMOCRACIES

R. A. DAHL

To one who believes in the essential worth of a democratic polity, how much opposition is desirable, and what kinds? What is the best balance between consensus and dissent? Even among democrats there is not much agreement on the answers to these questions.

It is easy to see why. These questions seem to demand nothing less than a complicated assessment of democracy itself. Or to put the matter more precisely, one can judge the desirability of different patterns of political opposition only by employing a number of different criteria that would be used if one were appraising the extent to which a political system as a whole achieves what are usually considered democratic goals or values.

Eight of these standards seem directly relevant in judging different patterns of opposition. In comparison with other possible arrangements, one might ask, to what extent does a particular pattern maximize:

1. Liberty of thought and expression, including opportunities for dissenting minorities to make their views known to other citizens and policy-makers?
2. Opportunities for citizens to participate in political life?
3. When political conflicts occur, control over the decisions of government by majorities (rather than minorities) of citizens, voters, and elected officials?
4. Rationality in political discussion and decision-making, in the sense of increasing understanding by citizens and

From *Political Opposition in Western Democracies*, by R. A. Dahl, Yale U.P., 1965, pp. 387–91. We are grateful to the publisher for permission to reproduce this extract.

leaders of the goals involved and the appropriate means?[1]

5. Consensus in political discussion and decision-making, in the sense that solutions are sought that will minimize the size, resentments, and coercion of defeated minorities, and will maximize the numbers of citizens who conclude that their goals have been adequately met by the solution adopted?

6. The peaceful management of conflicts and the minimization of political violence?

7. Resolution of urgent policy questions, in the sense that the government directs its attention to any question regarded as urgent and important by a substantial proportion of citizens or leaders, and adopts solutions satisfactory to the largest number of citizens?

8. Widespread confidence in and loyalty to a constitutional and democratic polity?

A number of other criteria might be advanced, but these are enough to give an idea of the magnitude of the problem of evaluation. What is most obvious and most important about these criteria is that, like most standards of performance for complex achievements, they conflict with one another; if a political system were to maximize one of these ends it would probably do so only at considerable cost to some of the others. Moreover, because different individuals disagree about the relative importance of different goals, they disagree as to what is the best solution in general, and even for a specific situation. How then can one prescribe an optimal balance among competing goals, when the goals are nonquantitative and imprecise, and when one man's optimum may be another man's prison? Nor are these the only sources of disagreement. The eight criteria conflict with one another; there is a certain tension among them; we cannot maximize one goal beyond some range without sacrificing another goal.

In spite of all these obstacles to finding an 'optimal solution', it is possible to clarify some of the costs and gains of different solutions, actual or proposed. Let me start by ex-

---

[1] Cf. Bagehot, who refers to 'one of the mental conditions of Parliamentary Government, by which I do not mean reasoning power, but rather the power of hearing the reasons of others, of comparing them quietly with one's own reasons, and then being guided by the result'. *The English Constitution*, p. 44. See also p. 280.

amining the tension created by wanting — as most good democrats do — freedom, dissent, and consensus.

FREEDOM, DISSENT, AND CONSENSUS

The first criterion listed above emphasizes opportunities for dissent; and it is no doubt their concern for this goal that explains, in the main, why liberals and radicals have usually been keenly sensitive to problems of political opposition. For to look at any political system from the point of view of an opposition inclines one to stress the virtues of dissent, of *opposing*. Yet the last criterion in our list emphasizes the virtues of stability; and the penultimate criterion, the importance of resolution and dispatch, avoiding deadlock, paralysis, impotence in government. Sensitivity to these criteria leads one to be concerned with the high costs of unlimited dissent and to stress the importance of consensus, particularly if governments willing to protect dissent are to survive.

There are, we all know, many varieties of freedom. One variety of freedom exists to the extent that every citizen has opportunities to engage in political activities without severe social and governmental constraints. In all political systems this freedom — let me call it Freedom of Political Action — is, like other freedoms, limited by government and society; yet it is the differences in these limits that distinguish libertarian from authoritarian systems. In libertarian systems, the right to dissent from the views of government — to oppose the government — is a vital form of Freedom of Political Action. And political oppositions are a crucial expression of this Freedom.

Yet the very existence of dissent and political opposition is a sure sign that someone is constrained by government to do or to forbear from doing something that he would like to do and very likely feels he has a moral right, or even an obligation, to do. To feel politically free because one obeys laws one believes in, to obey a government one approves of, to obey governmental policies one wants or agrees with — here is a second variety of freedom. Since this variety, like the other, bears no accepted name, let me call it Freedom in Political Obligations.

Now if the existence of political opposition is evidence of Freedom of Political Action, it is also a symbol of the Unfreedom in Political Obligations[2] of those opposed to the government. I expect that some readers will now move a well-known objection. Even citizens who are opposed to the laws enforced by their government may nonetheless yield their implicit consent, provided these laws are adopted by procedures they regard as legitimate; in this sense, their Freedom in Political Obligations is not diminished by their need to obey specific laws to which they object. Let me recognize the force of this familiar argument and put it to one side as irrelevant here. I do so in order to distinguish (1) a polity in which a large and permanent minority accepts the constitutional procedures and arrangements, yet detests the policies of government, which seems to it tyrannical in what it does if not in the way it acts; from (2) a polity in which agreement is so extensive that minorities are microscopic and evanescent, and no one ever feels much injured by the laws he is obliged to obey. In the first case, members of the outvoted minority might accept the obligation to obey the laws because these were adopted according to legitimate constitutional processes, and yet feel constrained to obey laws they hold wrong. In the second case, they would feel no such constraint.

If you will allow me this distinction, it follows, I think, that in a democratic system where Freedom of Political Action is widely enjoyed, the less the dissent, the greater the Freedom in Political Obligations. In fact the only system in which every citizen would be completely free in his Political Obligations would be one in which political consensus was perfect; for no citizen would then feel constrained by government to do something he believed he should not do. The more extreme the dissent permitted, the greater the range of Freedom in Political Action; yet the more numerous the extreme dissenters, the greater the number who are (at least temporarily and perhaps indefinitely) Unfree in their Political Obligations.

Let me try to make these abstractions more concrete by comparing a high-consensus system like Sweden with a low-consensus system like Italy. In a high-consensus system most citizens are only moderately opposed, if at all, to the character and conduct of government; by comparison, in a low-consensus system a great many more people are strongly op-

---

[2] The notion of 'unfreedom' is defined in Felix E. Oppenheim, *Dimensions of Freedom* (New York, St Martin's Press, 1961), chap. 4, 'Unfreedom'.

posed to the conduct and even the form of the government. The proportion of citizens who feel themselves coerced or constrained by government, and thus Unfree in Political Obligations is, naturally, much larger in the low-consensus systems than in the high-consensus ones.

Yet an extreme dissenter may enjoy more freedom to express his dissent in a low-consensus system like Italy than in a system with considerably more consensus like the United States. For (aside from any other reasons) the very magnitude of extreme dissent in Italy and France limits the extent to which dissent is coerced by social and governmental actions; in the United States, however, where extreme dissent is so small that it can be coerced at less cost, social and governmental constraints are rather powerful. Thus in the United States opportunities for discussing one's views with others, attending meetings, reading newspapers sympathetic to one's cause, joining in a like-minded party, and voting for like-minded candidates are extensive for most citizens — but not, often, for the extreme dissenter.

Thus a low-consensus country like Italy may actually provide more Freedom of Political Action (to Communists, Monarchists, and Fascists, for example) than a country like the United States where there is considerably higher consensus. Is low consensus a better guarantee of political freedom, then, than high consensus? Hardly, for a low-consensus system greatly increases the amount of Unfreedom in Political Obligations among its citizens. What is more, widespread Unfreedom in Political Obligations is inescapable as long as consensus remains low; for even if the Outs were to displace the Ins, their positions would only be reversed. The Freedom in Political Obligations of the one-time Outs would now be greater; but so would the Unfreedom in Political Obligations of the one-time Ins. Then, too, a low-consensus system is much more likely to impose other costs such as deadlock, political violence, constitutional instability, and destruction of democracy itself.

If, then, the most desirable long-run solution for a low-consensus country would be to increase consensus, surely the most desirable long-run solution for a high-consensus country would not be deliberately to foster extreme dissent! An obvious alternative solution would be to reduce the legal obstacles that limit the Freedom of Political Action among dissenters until they are legally on a par with all other citizens.

This is, in fact, the solution adopted in a number of high-consensus countries. In this respect, the United States is a somewhat deviant case: most other stable democracies have not imposed as severe a set of legal and social obstacles to political dissent as exist in the United States.

27. THE FUTURE OF DEMOCRATIC SOCIETY

D. E. APTER

In the evolution of democracy, constitutionalism is dependent on the assertion of individuality in the modern world.
This in turn is dependent on a refinement of human sensibili-
ties by means of which the worth of individuals will be established on grounds other than economics or politics. Creativity, social commitment, individual expression — these are
the needs of the times rather than the intense and frenetic
urge to confound society while accepting its standards.

THE TRANSITION TO POLITICAL DEMOCRACY

What other conditions are necessary to ensure the formation of a democratic polity? Clearly the primary emphasis
has been on information, with coercion treated as a negative
and residual factor. This is logical because of the nature of
the relationship between the two. All systems employ coercion.
If coercion occurs throughout a network of roles in a system
as a natural result of the integration of those roles, it will not
necessarily reduce information. The best illustration of this is
the modernizing autocracy, where coercion is exercised by
traditional means and does not necessarily reduce information
because it has not been initiated by deliberate government
policy.

The two most useful general indicators of coercion (when
we wish to evaluate it in connection with government) are
as follows: (1) the amount of privacy in the system; and
(2) the amount of centralized governmental application of
coercive measures. The second indicator can be examined

Reprinted from the *Politics of Modernization,* by D. E. Apter, pp.
453–56, 458–63, by permission of the University of Chicago Press. Copyright © 1965, by the University of Chicago. All rights reserved.

empirically through the contingent structures of government. The question of privacy requires further comment.[1]

Where much of social life is politicized, as in most modernizing nations, privacy is regarded as virtually subversive. As an idea, it runs counter to the view of politics in which the collectivity takes precedence over the individual and the individual's personality is regarded as dependent upon the state. Privacy could be said to begin when a man shields his views, feelings, or activities from his fellow man. This shielding process occurs as the result of many developments. Growing urbanization is a stimulus. The anonymity of the city makes possible a kind of privacy impossible in the close rural and kinship environments of earlier times. Bureaucratization, which is often seen as a depersonalizing force in the West, may in fact provide an opportunity for privacy in the modernizing countries. Men may use their professional roles for social discourse and draw on their inner resources to build a private world, as they learn how to avoid trouble. In the process they will convey to their children something of their attitudes. Industrialization helps to create conditions under which privacy becomes possible even in highly politicized states. When the desire for privacy is reinforced by the practical needs of political leaders for accurate information, the opportunity for constitutional government may present itself.

In order to protect privacy, there must be a check on the arbitrary use of state power against the individual. That is, there must be private rights that the state is not empowered to modify. The only way to guarantee private rights is to place checks on the executive. These checks may take many forms, but whatever the form, one cannot speak of liberty without a regularized and legitimate form of opposition, a parliament or its equivalent, a multiparty system, and so on. It is no longer Western provincialism to say that a democratic society, as distinct from a reconciliation system, requires freedom, elections, representative institutions, and all the rest.[2]

---

[1] I have discussed the conditions of a democratic society in 'Some Reflections on the Role of a Political Opposition', *Journal of Comparative History and Society*, January 1961.

[2] The basis of representation may vary, however. In the West representation is determined largely on the basis of roughly equal geographical areas. It is by no means out of the question, however, that functional roles – that is, students, farmers, workers, engineers, and so on – be

What are the conditions under which the transition to democracy is possible, and what are the criteria for a functioning democratic society? In terms of the present analysis the following general conditions need to prevail for a democratic society to emerge.

1. Privacy must be a consummatory value. 'Privacy' is not merely a new name for individualism, although individualism is the consequence of the desire for privacy. This precondition requires that individuals see their identity in private rather than public terms, that they preserve some sense of wholeness and unity. The desire for privacy in modernizing and industrializing societies may be understood as a reaction to the growing visibility of life in the schools, factories, and public places in general; individuals begin to feel the need to be able to withdraw from certain aspects of the modernizing process. Privacy as a consummatory value implies a protected area of life, free from political intervention.

2. Authority problems must be transformed into equity problems. In a modernizing polity, where the paramount emphasis is potentiality, democratic institutions cannot be expected to work very well. When modernization and industrialization have proceeded to the point where inequality and other problems of distributive justice are threats to continued authority, a mechanism for establishing equity, as well as equity itself, should become the new basis for solidarity in the society. Equity as a basis for solidarity implies that (*a*) a well-defined sense of equity is shared by the public, and (*b*) regularized political procedures exist for periodically revising the definition of equity.

3. Information must be available from a variety of sources including free public communication media, opposition parties, and the like. This precondition of democracy rests on the faith that coercion will be limited, bounded, and therefore constitutional. In terms of ideology, a climate of practical realism must prevail, with a high degree of accountability registered through parliamentary and legislative bodies.

4. The means of maintaining equity, accountability, and practical realism (and therefore, identity and solidarity) are (*a*) the constant translation of value conflict into interest conflict, (*b*) conciliar control over the executive, (*c*) legal and

---

the basis of representation instead (as was once suggested in the ill-fated proposals of the guild socialists in England).

formalized opposition secured by a representative principle, and (d) a meaningful definition of public sovereignty expressed in universal suffrage and periodic elections.

These are well-worn universals in democratic theory. Modern expressions of them are common enough.

CONCLUSION

When decision-making in a mobilization system becomes complex enough to require reform of the basic structure of government, several choices are possible. One is to create a more narrow and more centralized system of authoritative decision-making, less accountable and more remote from day-to-day concerns. This choice leads in the direction of totalitarianism, increasing coercion, and inefficiency. An alternative is to decentralize decision-making, thereby increasing accountability. Decentralization may take the form of a proliferation of decision-making subunits, so that the central pattern of government is extended through a number of local governments and becomes more effective on a regional or territorial level. Decisional subunits based on region make it possible for the public to participate in problems that are central to their interests and to develop a tradition of civic responsibility.

Even though it does not seem likely that most of the modernizing countries can move directly in a democratic direction, important subgroups already exist within these societies that are the long-run carriers of democratic values and that will be important in the future for democratic society. I have discussed these subgroups in terms of their need for information and have referred, of course, to those that appear to be non-political, that is, the scientists and social scientists, engineers and technologists.

These are the roles whose functional significance increases as modernization moves into industrialization, and as industrialization intensifies. In order to deal with increasingly complex technical matters, the occupants of these roles require greater and greater amounts of information. Government, too, requires increasing amounts of information in order to operate efficiently and carry out the recommendations of the scientists and technicians. These needs result, as I have said before, in a decline in coercion, a sharing of decision-making, and a widening of accountability. Hence, the scientific elites are fundamentally revolutionary.[3]

They are revolutionary because of their economic importance. Clearly, scientists and technicians are unlikely, in the long run, to become effective participants in the political sphere, if only because technical expertise generally inheres in functionally subordinate roles. But in the economic sphere, their activities have great importance for basic productivity, the organization of resources, and the utilization of the new technology in the employment of human and physical resources. This, of course, would not in itself make them revolutionary, except for the fact that *in industrializing societies it is the economic variable that is independent.* The political system is the dependent variable — dependent, that is, on the needs of the economic system and the changes in the industrial sphere. The new scientific elite — as a result of the economic changes it can bring about and as a result of its need for information with which to make these changes successfully — must therefore be viewed as a revolutionary force. If this analysis of the role of the scientific elite is correct, it follows that the long-term tendency of industrializing countries is toward reconciliation systems.

How can the reconciliation system be transformed into a democracy, the conditions of which have been outlined above? Obviously, something more is needed than the distribution of information among functionally significant elites. At this point, we must return to the moral sphere. The ideals of liberty and privacy can move a reconciliation system toward democracy in an industrial setting. The scientists and the social scientists, the writers and the intellectuals, the teachers and the students — all will have to fight for these ideals. They cannot be won all at once.

How important, then, are the world-wide associations of scientists and technicians, the links between universities, and the free exchanges of information and knowledge! Modern

---

[3] Indeed, Michael Polanyi has hailed this new development as the basis of what he calls a 'Republic of Science', which, in his view, is dynamic, a 'society of explorers', and which, because it is based on self-improvement and excellence, will create a free society. See his fascinating discussion, in 'The Republic of Science, Its Political and Economic Theory', *Minerva*, I (Autumn 1962). Somewhat the same point of view is expressed in the *Robbins Report* in England.

societies need freedom to continue to evolve even if some of
them cannot yet afford it. The ultimate aim of the West ought
to be clear from the foregoing analysis. Not only must we
more fully realize freedom in our own society, but must not
deny the eventual possibility of freedom to modernizing and
industrializing nations. If democratic institutions, as we know
them, suffer under hammer blows during the period of modernization, it should come as no surprise. The total modernization process will take a very long time. The fantastic changes
required will often run contrary to political convenience.
Our objective should be fixed and unchanging, to keep the
libertarian option open, since, as we have seen, systems
change according to the political needs of modernization and
the economic needs of industrialization. We should expect
false starts, backward steps, new fashions in political systems,
and the explicit downgrading of libertarian values. If we can
take a long (and this means a realistic) view of the total
process of development from modernization to industrialization, we will find ourselves supporting countries whose policies, in the short run, go counter to everything that we consider important to a democratic way of life. We need to
accept countries like Ghana and Mali as changing polities
and not mistake stability in form for an incapacity to change.
We must consider Yugoslavia and Poland, and perhaps China
as well, as prototypes of an early stage of industrialization.
Nor should we be surprised if the conversion from late modernization to early industrialization in Latin America is accompanied by the spread of mobilization systems. This is precisely why Cuba is so attractive to many of the more romantic
young socialists in these countries.

Clearly, we are going to need to learn to live in a world in
which the ethic of science has become the ethic of man. Indeed, the scientific Philistines may already have become a
greater danger to democracy than the ideologues. How urgent
it becomes to civilize the civilizers, that is, to give those who
know something about science and the public welfare a sensitivity to human rights and values. Without such sensitivity,
the new technocrats will have little attachment to democracy.

For us in the West, the task is to know what we are about
— to know what is important. Questions of property and ownership, for example, are less and less significant. Managerial
control (whether the proprietor is the state, a public board, a
body of citizens who are joint owners and managers, or an

individual) is not an issue any more. Indeed, practical distinctions between private and public enterprise are disappearing almost as quickly as distinctions between private and public university educations. What is important is the problem of inequality, the relationship between equity and freedom. Will this relationship be determined by natural talent rather than particularistic ties, traditional impediments to mobility, or wealth? And will talent produce its own hierarchy? Can democracy come to grips with problems such as these? The answer is important for our own society, as well as for all the others.

Is an information-creating and knowledge-using elite the critical instrumentality for producing the conditions of a reconciliation system? Can the scientific elite be brought into a democratic pattern? These are critical questions.

How well we answer these questions, and others similar to them, will effect our ability to make sensible choices about the future. Nor are such matters purely academic. The continued existence of our way of life hangs in the balance. Political forms do change. If it is true that there is a perpetual dialogue between the two main forms we have discussed, the mobilization system and the reconciliation system, it is also true that they are perpetually vulnerable to each other. By means of empirical comparative studies, we should be able to discover the ways in which this mutual vulnerability is made manifest. Specific queries are in order. For example, if political change in the context of modernization is not an inevitable progressive evolution from predemocratic forms of government, what conditions do favor such a long-term development? What conditions are prerequisite to a successful transition from a modernizing to an industrial society in the direction of democracy? When conditions in a society point to the economic system rather than the political as the independent variable, how are we to evaluate the forms of industrialization and their impact upon the polity? Is it correct to say that, under the conditions of modern industrialization, the need for information is so great that decentralization, the emergence of pyramidal instead of hierarchical authority, and the preoccupation with instrumental rather than consummatory ends are greatly facilitated? Is it meaningful to speak of a political system with a long-term tendency toward a reconciliation system as the form most appropriate for highly industrialized societies? Will our Western definition of democracy continue to be appropriate?

These questions cannot be answered here. I think that in the long run the most revolutionary force in political affairs will be a new form of the secular-libertarian ideal and, more specifically, a democratic system of government. Modernization is a critical step by means of which this ideal will be universalized. A fresh appraisal of our own institutions, however, is required. Democracy cannot be meaningful unless it realizes its libertarian beliefs more completely. It needs to blend its instrumental and consummatory values more effectively. How can the West serve as the model for a highly industrialized society if it fails to utilize the information it so freely creates and ignores many of its obligations in the fields of civil rights, poverty, education, and foreign affairs? If reconciliation systems fail, it will be because of the blindness or inability of the people to comprehend the knowledge they have at their disposal. This is why the need for new methods and theories for organizing and comprehending facts is so urgent. The ability to find wider meanings in information already available and to create new forms of knowledge is the greatest strength our society has. But only if we use it well can choice and freedom give added strength to our democracy. The future of democratic society will depend on its ability to find new and effective ways to secure personal identity through liberty and solidarity through knowledge. This has always been the basis of the democratic ideal. These are the ultimate standards by which we evaluate both ourselves and others.

SELECT BIBLIOGRAPHY

The number of works on comparative government is so vast that the present bibliography has of necessity to be very selective. Its main aim is to direct the attention of the reader to some of the most important works of a comparative character, although we also include a short final section devoted to individual country studies. This bibliography follows the plan adopted in the course of this volume: works are therefore discussed under the headings of General, Bases of Politics, Political Parties, Constitutional Government, Political Rule outside Constitutional Government, and Country Studies. Classification under one of these rubrics is difficult in some cases, however; where a study overlaps two sections, it is discussed in relation to the section of politics with which it is most concerned.

GENERAL

A number of general introductory texts appeared in the last decade — this in itself being perhaps a sign of the growing concern for the comparative study of government. The most informative of these texts are perhaps those of G. M. Carter and J. H. Herz, *Government and Politics in the Twentieth Century* (Praeger, 1961), and of D. W. Brogan and D. V. Verney, *Political Patterns in Today's World* (Hamish Hamilton, 1963). An even shorter, but also even more systematic treatment of the subject (a uniform pattern of analysis of the various structures of government is attempted), can be found in *Comparative Political Institutions*, by R. C. Fried (Collier-Macmillan, 1966). H. Eckstein and D. E. Apter published a massive Reader entitled *Comparative Politics* (Free Press, 1963), which covers all aspects of comparative government, though, despite its size, the text treats these aspects somewhat unevenly; a section on comparative politics can also be found in N. W. Polsby, R. A. Dentler and P. A. Smith, *Politics and Social Life* (Houghton Mifflin, 1963).

Problems of method are examined at some length in the relevant sections of these two readers. But this question has come to be, as was noted in the Introduction, such an important preoccupation of writers engaged in comparative government that it requires a careful study at least of some of the original proponents of the new approach. The general principles of systems analysis as applied to the study of comparative politics are discussed at length in D. Easton, *A Systems Analysis of Political Life* (Wiley, 1965); an abridged version can be found in Easton's previous book, *A Framework for Political Analysis* (Prentice-Hall, 1965), or even in Easton's article of 1957, 'An Approach to the Analysis of Political Systems', *World Politics*, (April 1957, pp. 383–408), in which the author discussed his model for the first time. H. D. Lasswell's study of *The Decision Process* (Bureau of Governmental Process, University of Maryland, 1956) constitutes an important background to modern comparative government, as well as, of course, the works of T. Parsons and E. Shils, *Toward a General Theory of Action* (Harvard U.P., 1951) and of T. Parsons, *The Social System* (Free Press, 1951).

These books describe the basic sociological and political concepts which lay behind the development of modern comparative government. They need to be studied in order to measure both the considerable changes and the limitations of the present revolution in the field. As was noted in the Introduction, R. C. Macridis discussed, in his short book entitled *The Study of Comparative Government* (Random House, 1955), both the limitations of the traditional method and the ways in which a systematic study could develop. But, as we noted, the concrete turning-point was due to G. A. Almond and J. S. Coleman with their work on the *Politics of Developing Areas* (Princeton U.P., 1960), followed in 1966 by *Comparative Politics* (Little, Brown & Co.), by G. A. Almond and G. B. Powell. Enough has been said about both these works in the Introduction to make it unnecessary to emphasise again the importance of their contributions to the discipline. Reference should also be made to D. E. Apter's *The Politics of Modernization* (Chicago U.P., 1965), which is in large part devoted to substantive findings about the politics of developing areas, but includes a substantial methodological section, which could be read in conjunction with Apter's article on 'A Comparative Method for the Study of Politics' published in the

American Journal of Sociology (November 1958, pp. 221–37). A penetrating critical analysis of both Almond's and Apter's model can be found in the opening chapters of R. T. Holt and J. E. Turner, *The Political Basis of Economic Development* (Van Nostrand, 1966). Finally, a 'communications' approach to the study can be found in K. Deutsch's pioneering work, *The Nerves of Government* (Free Press, 1963).

BASES OF POLITICAL SYSTEMS

Most of the studies discussed in the previous paragraph consider at some length the bases of political systems, the conditions leading to stability and the patterns which can be found in the world today. A number of studies are more specifically devoted to the description of precise indicators and to the testing of the relationship between socio-economic and political variables. The two most comprehensive works listing raw data about political systems are those of A. S. Banks and R. B. Textor, *A Cross-polity Survey* (Massachusetts Institute of Technology Press, 1963), which presents in the form of statistical tables a wide variety of data extending indeed from the bases of political systems to party and governmental structures. B. Russett *et al.*, *World Handbook of Political and Social Indicators* (Yale U.P., 1964), confines itself to more 'objective' socio-economic data and does therefore to some extent run the risk of not covering sufficient ground in the field of politics itself; but the information provided in both these works is of immense value for those who are engaged in empirical work on the basis of political systems.

The analysis of the influence of social forces on political systems was pioneered by W. Kornhauser, whose *Politics of Mass Society* (Free Press, 1959) constituted a general framework for the analysis of the influence of mass participation in both Western and Eastern polities, and by S. M. Lipset, whose *Political Man* (Doubleday, 1960) starts with a general discussion of the social bases of a stable democracy; P. Cutright's study of 'National Political Development' (*American Sociological Review*, April 1963) begins indeed with a critique of Lipset's findings and should be seen as a refinement on the analysis presented in *Political Man;* a similar type of analysis was conducted by R. H. Fitzgibbon and K. F. Johnson, under the title of 'Measurement of Latin American Political Change' (*American Political Science Review*, September 1961, pp. 515–26). All studies on modernisation include sections on the comparative bases of politics in developed and developing societies: it is clearly impossible to discuss them in any detail within the compass of this bibliography, but two works should perhaps be mentioned: L. W. Pye's short study of *Aspects of Political Development* (Little, Brown & Co., 1966) constitutes an excellent introduction to the problems of the relationship between politics and society in countries of various levels of development, while J. L. Finkle and R. W. Gable's Reader on *Political Development and Social Change* (Wiley, 1966) constitutes a detailed contribution to the whole subject and D. Lerner's *Passing of Traditional Society* (Free Press, 1958) examines the consequences of social change in the particular context of the Middle East. Finally, as we noted in the Introduction, G. A. Almond and S. Verba's *Civic Culture* (Princeton U.P., 1963) is the most comprehensive cross-national study of the phenomenon of culture and of its influence on political systems: as the five countries covered include both the United States and Mexico, the work does unquestionably attempt to present a cross-section, though not a wholly representative one, of cultural experiments and political systems.

The study of groups and of the articulation of interests progressed very rapidly in the 1950s and 1960s, but most of the work took place in the context of individual countries: perhaps surprisingly, few studies of *types* of groups on a cross-national basis have been undertaken. The one truly comprehensive study, which was sponsored by the International Political Science Association, was published by H. Ehrmann under the title of *Interest Groups in Five Continents* (University of Pittsburgh Press, 1958). A model for the comparative study of groups can be found in several studies, however, and in particular in D. Truman's *Governmental Process* (Knopf, 1951), which attempted to apply and develop an approach which had been initiated by A. F. Bentley in *The Process of Government* (Unwin, 1908), in J. Meynaud's *Les Groupes de Pression* (A. Colin, 1958) and in H. Eckstein's *Pressure Group Politics* (Allen & Unwin, 1960): though these works are concerned with individual countries (the United States, France and Britain respectively), a general framework with considerable potential for a comprehensive study of groups can be found in each of them. But, overall, genuinely cross-national studies of groups and articulation processes need to be undertaken before the considerable mass of data acquired on labour unions, employers' organisations, peasant and students' associations, as well as churches or kinship groups, can be introduced fully in a model of comparative government and help to advance the theory of modes of articulation.

POLITICAL PARTIES

The literature on individual political parties or on political parties in individual countries is large, though, perhaps surprisingly, still far from comprehensive even for some of the most important countries of Europe. Cross-national studies have also been undertaken, though there is still considerable scope for development. But the study of political parties attracted very early the attention of some of the most prominent political scientists: the two 'classics' in the field, those of Ostrogorski, *Democracy and the Organisation of Political Parties* (Macmillan) and of Michels, *Political Parties*, were published respectively in 1902 and 1914. Duverger's work, *Political Parties* (Methuen, 2nd ed., 1959), which was discussed at length in the Introduction, probably also deserves to be described as a classic. An interesting study of political parties in a number of countries, followed by a general model, can also be found in S. Neumann, *Modern Political Parties* (Chicago U.P., 1956).

These works concentrate almost exclusively on European and American parties, however. Since the late 1950s, numerous books have been devoted to non-Western political parties, sometimes on a cross-national basis, though none of them has as yet covered parties truly generally. The most systematic of these works is perhaps that of T. Hodgkin, *African Political Parties* (Penguin Books, 1961), which presents a general model of the structure and characteristics of party systems in modern Africa, though change has taken place so rapidly in that continent in the 1960s that many of the detailed points have become invalid. No such study of the same depth has as yet been conducted for any other continent or subcontinent of the developing world. Nor have cross-national studies of parties of the same type been undertaken: one must go back to Ostrogorski and Michels to examine Socialist parties cross-nationally and the only comparative study of Christian Democratic parties, that of F. Goguel and M. Einaudi, *Christian Democracy in Italy and France* (University of Notre Dame Press, 1952), covers only these two countries.

Party systems and the functions of parties in the whole polity have been examined in a number of texts: R. A. Dahl's *Political Oppositions in Western Democracies* (Yale U.P., 1966) considers types of oppositions both on a country-by-country and on a systematic basis. E. Allardt and Y. Littunen's *Cleavages, Ideologies and Party Systems* (Helsinki, The Academic Bookstore, 1964) includes monographs on a number of parties as well as various cross-national studies which throw considerable light on party systems. Finally, the one-party system prevailing in Eastern societies has not received as yet the attention which it deserves, though, as will be seen later, comparative studies of whole polities of the Eastern world have begun to appear.

The literature on electoral systems and on the relationship between electoral systems and the number of parties is large, though the argument cannot be said to have been settled. W. J. M. Mackenzie's *Free Elections* (Allen & Unwin, 1958) is a straightforward and dispassionate description of electoral systems. E. Lakeman and J. D. Lambert's *Voting in Democracies* (Faber, 1955) constitutes probably the most comprehensive account: but the book also argues the case for proportional representation against those who, both before and since Duverger, had stated that only majority systems could lead to stable governments. Among Duverger's predecessors, the strongest case against proportional representation had been made by F. A. Hermens, in *Democracy or Anarchy* (University of Notre Dame Press, 1941) on the basis of Weimar experience. Duverger's own thesis was developed at length in *L'Influence des Systèmes Electoraux sur la Vie Politique* (A. Colin, 1950) and was criticised by G. Lavau in *Partis Politiques et Réalités Sociales* (A. Colin, 1953). A systematic critique of the 'Duverger law' can also be found in A. B. Wildavsky's 'Methodological Critique of Duverger's Political Parties' (*Journal of Politics*, 1959, pp. 303–18). Clearly, the matter of the relationship between electoral systems and party systems still requires further systematic investigation before the controversy comes to an end.

CONSTITUTIONAL GOVERNMENT

Constitutional government has given rise to a large number of works of a formal and institutional character, both on general aspects of constitutions and on their general working. The clearest presentation of the traditional 'institutional theory' can be found in D. V. Verney, *The Analysis of Political Systems* (Free Press, 1959). But the two most comprehensive texts remain, despite having been first published a generation ago, C. Friedrich's *Constitutional Government and Democracy* (Ginn & Co., rev. ed., 1950) and H. Finer's *The Theory and Practice of Modern Government* (Methuen, rev. ed., 1961). Both books extend beyond constitutional government proper, but their main emphasis is on the study of structures and practices of Western countries. K. C. Wheare's *Modern Constitutions* (Oxford U.P., rev. ed., 1966), *Federal Government* (Oxford U.P., rev. ed., 1963) and *Legislatures* (Oxford U.P., 1963) constitute very concise but full studies of various aspects of constitutions, which, taken together, cover most aspects of constitutional government. Finally, A. J. Zurcher's *Constitutions and Constitutional Trends since World War II* (New York U.P., 1955) includes a series of monographs aiming especially at looking at the *real* life of constitutions in the contemporary world.

As was noted in the Introduction, little has been done to analyse in detail on a cross-national basis the behavioural patterns of the most typical institutional structures created by constitutions, such as legislatures, executives or courts. M. Ameller's *Parliaments, a Comparative Study* (Cassell, 1966) is a useful study of the characteristics and procedures of Parliaments throughout the world, but it does not attempt to examine the real power of Parliaments. Almost all of the behavioural studies are American and deal with either American federal or American State institutions. The work which comes closest to a comprehensive comparative analysis and which does include monographs on a number of European countries, is that of J. C. Wahlke and H. Eulau, *Legislative Behaviour* (Free Press, 1959).

The comparative study of executives is perhaps even less advanced. An important study of power in both the United States and the Soviet Union was published by Z. Brzezinski and S. P. Huntington, under the title *Political Power, U.S.A./ U.S.S.R.* (Chatto & Windus, 1964): it develops a model which could be applicable to a large number of countries, both Western and Eastern. Two other studies, both in French, cover a number of European countries in succession, but give important material for the study of executives (as well as legislatures) in Western countries: they are those of R. Fusilier, *Les Monarchies parlementaires européennes* (Les Éditions Ouvrières, 1960) and of P. Lalumière and A. Demichel, *Les Régimes parlementaires européens* (Presses Universitaires de France, 1966).

Federal government and supreme courts are perhaps the aspects of constitutional government which have been treated most satisfactorily on a comparative behavioural basis, though most of the studies are confined to the four major federal countries, namely the United States, Canada, Australia and Switzerland. Wheare's work, which has been already mentioned, does attempt, however, to consider the problem more generally, though Western German federalism would deserve a more exhaustive study which has to be found in texts devoted to that country. Both W. S. Livingston in *Federalism and Constitutional Change* (Oxford, Clarendon Press, 1956) and A. H. Birch in *Federalism, Finance and Social Legislation in Canada, Australia and the United States* (Oxford, Clarendon Press, 1955) consider, as the title of their works indicate, some important 'behavioural' patterns in the contemporary development of federalism and attempt to examine the effect of increased federal interference in social and economic matters on the nature of federalism.

POLITICAL RULE OUTSIDE CONSTITUTIONAL GOVERNMENT

Totalitarian government first attracted the attention of political theorists, but its empirical study has also made considerable progress since the 1950s. Perhaps the three basic works in the field are those of J. L. Talmon, *The Origins of Totalitarian Democracy* (Praeger, 1960), which is indispensable to trace back the line of thought linking some earlier thinkers to modern totalitarianism, of C. J. Friedrich, *Totalitarianism* (Harvard U.P., 1954) and of C. J. Friedrich and Z. Brzezinski, *Totalitarian Dictatorship and Autocracy* (Praeger, 1961): these last two works attempt to cover most of the ideological and empirical characteristics of totalitarian régimes. A concise but illuminating presentation of the socio-economic bases of dictatorships was given by M. Duverger in *De la Dictature* (Plon, 1961). Works on the Soviet Union (and on Nazism and Fascism) also naturally usually consider in a general fashion the characteristics of modern totalitarian rule, but studies of other Communist systems have become more numerous recently: a collection of important papers on various Communist governments can be found in *Communist Political Systems,* edited by A. Z. Rubinstein (Prentice-Hall, 1966), while the systematic study of recent trends in Eastern European governments is the subject of G. Ionescu's *The Politics of the European Communist States* (Weidenfeld & Nicolson, 1967).

The appearance of studies of patterns of military rule throughout the world constitutes one of the major developments of the 1960s in the field of comparative government. Among the most important of these works one should probably cite those of S. E. Finer, *The Man on Horseback* (Pall Mall, 1962), which is wholly systematic but also considers carefully a number of important cases, of S. P. Huntington, *The Soldier and the State* (Harvard U.P., 1957), whose first part only is devoted to the role of the military in general, two by M. Janowitz, *The Professional Soldier* (Free Press, 1960), which considers the position of the military from 'inside', and *The Military in the Political Development of New Nations* (Chicago U.P., 1964), which is a short but careful attempt at describing the various types of roles played by soldiers in the politics of new nations.

The field of bureaucracy is of course an independent branch of study linked with organisation theory. A background in this field can be provided by H. Simon's *Administrative Behaviour* (Collier-Macmillan, 1957): although the book draws its examples from the United States only, it constitutes a necessary prerequisite to the study of administration in general. Indeed truly comparative empirical studies of administrations are still relatively limited in number as the case-study method has had considerable success in this field, although J. LaPalombara's *Bureaucracy and Political Development* (Princeton U.P., 1964) indicates a new concern for a truly cross-national approach and E. Strauss's *Ruling Servants* (Praeger, 1961), though considering especially the behaviour of civil servants in three countries, does attempt to generalise on bureaucracies and their impact on societies. Moreover, the theoretical content of some individual country studies is sufficiently large to warrant their being included in a comparative study of government; this is true, in particular, of M. Crozier's *The Bureaucratic Phenomenon* (Tavistock, 1964), which considers general characteristics of bureaucracies through the empirical study of behavioural trends in two French state organisations. Finally, reference should be made to P. Blau's *Bureaucracy in Modern Society* (Random House, 1956), in which a model of the relationships between officials and society is being presented and discussed.

COUNTRY STUDIES

As was suggested at the beginning of this bibliography, only a small number of major studies of various governments can be mentioned, as even a preliminary list of texts and monographs would require almost a volume: indeed studies on various aspects of American government alone might extend into a volume of their own. There will therefore be no substitute for the usually exhaustive bibliographies which can be found in many of the country studies which are mentioned here. Work on comparative government does still require and will require for a long time the examination of individual country studies as in many instances only these consider institutions and processes at a sufficiently detailed level to make further progress possible.

Fortunately, studies on individual countries have been published in the form of series discussing these governments from a broadly similar standpoint. This is particularly true of the Little, Brown series edited by G. A. Almond in which a structural-functional approach is adopted. Volumes have appeared in England, the U.S.S.R., Germany, France and the Philippines. Both the Crowell series (Methuen or University paperbacks in Britain), under the editorship of A. A. Rogow, and the Harper series, edited by M. Curtis, cover a larger number of countries, most of which are European but which also include some non-Western polities. Several texts, mainly American, are devoted to 'major foreign governments' (and therefore normally do not include the United States). Perhaps the two most illuminating are those of S. Beer *et al.*, *Patterns of Government: The Major Political Systems of*

Europe (Random House, 1958) and of R. C. Macridis and R. E. Ward, *Modern Political Systems* (2 vols, Prentice-Hall, 1963).

The selection of a limited number of texts on American government is an almost impossible task. Perhaps the best are those which have been published in Britain in that they provide a general introduction. Those of D. W. Brogan, *An Introduction to American Politics* (Hamish Hamilton, 1953), of M. Beloff, *The American Federal Government* (Oxford U.P., 1959) and of A. M. Potter, *American Government and Politics* (Faber, 1955) should be suggested in this context. However, it is difficult not to mention also at least a small number of American works which cover individual parts of the Federal structure of American government. Among these works, those of V. O. Key, *Politics, Parties and Pressure Groups* (Crowell, rev. ed., 1964), of R. Neustadt, *Presidential Power* (Wiley, 1960), of R. McCloskey, *The American Supreme Court* (Chicago U.P., 1960), of R. L. Warner, *The American Federal Executive* (Yale U.P., 1963) and of E. S. Griffith, *Congress: its Contemporary Role* (New York U.P., 1956) deserve to be suggested because of their intrinsic merit and, in some cases, because they have constituted landmarks in their particular fields.

European States and countries of the old Commonwealth have also been studied in detail, though many aspects of these governments are still little known. Apart from the texts coming within the general framework of the 'series' which have been previously mentioned, a special note should be made, for Britain, of R. Rose's *Studies in British Politics* (Macmillan, 1966), a reader which includes a number of hitherto unpublished and illuminating studies of certain aspects of British politics, of J. Blondel's *Voters, Parties and Leaders* (Penguin Books, rev. ed., 1967), which concentrates on general sociological characteristics of modern British political life, of R. T. McKenzie's classic on *British Political Parties* (Heinemann, rev. ed., 1963), of I. Jennings' five-volume comprehensive, but perhaps over-historical, study of British government *Parliament* (1957), *Cabinet Government* (1959) and the three volumes of *Party Politics* (1960–2) (Cambridge U.P.) and of W. J. M. Mackenzie and J. W. Grove's standard text on *Central Administration in Britain* (Longmans, 1957). The study of French politics is dominated by P. M. Williams's massive study on the Fourth Republic, *Crisis and Compromise,*

(Longmans, 1964), for which there is no substitute either in French or in English and which is of great value even for those who are essentially concerned with the Fifth Republic. U. W. Kitzinger's *German Electoral Politics* (Oxford U.P., 1960) does give a general insight into the German political process in general, although it is based specifically on the politics of the 1957 election, while J. F. Golay's work, *The Founding of the Federal Republic of Germany* (Chicago U.P., 1958), is one of the best studies of the reasons why 'political engineering' can and of the extent to which it does take place in a constitutional régime. Of the other European countries, Sweden (D. Rustow, *The Politics of Compromise,* Princeton U.P., 1955) and, of the older Commonwealth countries, Australia (J. D. B. Miller, *Australian Government and Politics,* Duckworth, 1959) have probably been best covered.

The study of the Soviet Union is dominated by M. Fainsod's classic, *How Russia is Ruled* (Harvard U.P., 1953) and L. Schapiro's comprehensive historical study of *The Communist Party of the Soviet Union* (Methuen, 1963). The number of case-studies on individual structures of the Soviet Union has increased in recent years, partly on the basis of documents found during the Second World War, partly because of the gradual opening-up of Soviet society: J. Erickson's *Soviet High Command* (Macmillan, 1962) and J. A. Armstrong's *Soviet Bureaucratic Élite* (Praeger, 1959) are among the most successful of these detailed case-studies and reveal the structures within which and the processes by which groups function in the Soviet Union.

Studies of developing countries often cover more than one country: studies of Latin American politics and, to a lesser extent, of African politics are often undertaken on the basis of cross-national, if not necessarily cross-cultural, assumptions. Perhaps the most comprehensive account of Latin American politics is that of R. D. Tomasek, whose Reader entitled precisely *Latin American Politics* (Doubleday, Anchor Books, 1966) covers politics in all its aspects, from the social bases of the polity to the role of parties, armies and élite groups, while C. Veliz's *Obstacles to Change in Latin America* (Oxford U.P., 1965) describes a number of standpoints relating to political development. Individual country studies are gradually covering an increasing number of the new countries, and not more than a small selection can be mentioned here. Perhaps the two most important, both for the theoretical analysis and for the empirical findings which they contain, are those of D. E. Apter, *Ghana in Transition* (Atheneum Press, 1963) and of L. W. Pye, *Politics, Personality and Nation-Building* (Yale U.P., 1962), on the politics of Malaya. Of the several studies on Mexico, that of R. E. Scott, *Mexican Government in Transition* (Indiana U.P., 1959) is perhaps the most informative and illuminating; Brazil, Argentina and Chile have not been, as yet, surprisingly enough, extensively covered in English. Finally, three countries need to be singled out as being the subject of extensive studies. Japanese politics have been analysed in detail: the study of R. A. Scalapino and J. Masumi, *Parties and Politics in Contemporary Japan* (University of California Press, 1962) is only one of a large number of works which those interested in the politics of that country (also covered in some of the 'series' mentioned earlier) could profitably consider. India has attracted the attention of numerous political scientists; M. Weiner's *Party Politics in India* (Princeton U.P., 1957) should perhaps be mentioned as one important general study. Finally, South Africa has been the object of a penetrating work by G. M. Carter, *The Politics of Inequality* (Thames & Hudson, 1958), which considers in detail the implications of South Africa's current racial policies for the whole of the political system.

Except occasionally, this bibliography has not mentioned articles (though many can be found in the various Readers to which reference has been made). Clearly, even an attempt at covering some of the major articles published in the last decade would have been beyond the scope of this survey. Yet it must be remembered that many of the most important theoretical and empirical analyses are to be found in articles, especially in the several American political science journals and among them in the *American Political Science Review,* the *Journal of Politics* and *World Politics.* Comparative government requires an extensive general bibliography which has not appeared as yet. It is only hoped that this short selection, however brief, will give readers a first impression of the scope of recent work and will help all those interested in the subject to begin constituting for themselves a more extensive bibliography of those aspects of the discipline in which they happen to specialise.

LIST OF CONTRIBUTORS

G. A. ALMOND is Professor of Political Science at Stanford University, and co-author (with J. S. Coleman) of *The Politics of the Developing Areas*, (with S. Verba) of *The Civic Culture*, and (with G. B. Powell) of *Comparative Politics*.

D. E. APTER is Professor of Political Science and Director of the Institute of International Studies at the University of California at Berkeley, author of *Ghana in Transition, The Political Kingdom of Uganda, The Politics of Modernization* and co-editor (with H. Eckstein) of *A Reader in Comparative Politics*.

Z. K. BRZEZINSKI is Professor of Public Law and Government at Columbia University and co-author (with C. J. Friedrich) of *Totalitarian Dictatorship and Autocracy* and (with S. Huntington) of *Political Power: USA–USSR*.

P. CUTRIGHT is Professor of Sociology at Vanderbilt University.

R. A. DAHL is Sterling Professor of Political Science at Yale University, co-author (with D. Lindblom) of *Politics, Economics and Welfare*, author of *A Preface to Democratic Theory, Who Governs?, Modern Political Analysis, Pluralist Democracy in the United States*, and editor of *Political Oppositions in Western Democracies*.

K. W. DEUTSCH is Professor of Political Science at Harvard University, author of *Nationalism and Social Communication*, and *The Nerves of Government*. He launched and directed the Yale University Political Data Program.

M. DUVERGER is Professor of Law and Political Science at the University of Paris and author of *Political Parties, De la Dictature, Methods of the Social Sciences* and of numerous works on the Fourth and Fifth French Republics.

S. E. FINER is Professor of Government at the University of Manchester, author of *A Primer of Public Administration, The Life and Times of Ernest Chadwick, Anonymous Empire*,

A Study of the Lobby, The Man on Horseback, and co-author (with H. B. Berrington and D. Bartholomew) of *Backbench Opinion in the House of Commons.*

C. J. Friedrich, formerly Professor of Government at Harvard University, is Professor of Political Science at University of Heidelberg and author of *Constitutional Government and Democracy* and *Man and His government,* co-author (with Z. Brzezinski) of *Totalitarian Dictatorship and Autocracy,* and editor of *Totalitarianism.*

C. Leys is Professor of Political Science at the University of Sussex and author of *European Politics in Southern Rhodesia.*

S. M. Lipset is Professor of Sociology and Director of the Center for International Affairs, Harvard University, co-author (with M. Trow and J. S. Coleman) of *Union Democracy* and author of *Agrarian Socialism, Political Man* and *The First New Nation.*

K. Loewenstein is Professor of Political Science at Amherst College and author of *Political Power and the Governmental Process.*

R. C. Macridis is Professor of Political Science at Brandeis University, author of *The Study of Comparative Government* and editor (with R. E. Ward) of a two-volume work on modern political systems.

S. Neumann is Professor of Political Science at Cologne University and author of *Modern Political Parties.*

G. B. Powell is Research Associate at Stanford University and co-author (with G. A. Almond) of *Comparative Politics.*

E. Strauss is author of *The Ruling Servants.*

D. Verney is Professor of Political Science at York University, author of *Parliamentary Reform in Sweden* and *The Analysis of Political Systems* and co-author (with D. W. Brogan) of *Political Patterns in the World To-day.*

K. C. Wheare is Rector of Exeter College, Oxford, formerly Professor of Government and Public Administration, Oxford University, and author of *Modern Constitutions, Federal Government, Legislatures, Government by Committee,* and *Constitutional Structure of the Commonwealth.*

INDEX